All Things Mary

All Things Mary

Honoring the Mother of God—
An Anthology of Marian Reflections

MARK G. BOYER

WIPF & STOCK · Eugene, Oregon

ALL THINGS MARY
Honoring the Mother of God—An Anthology of Marian Reflections

Copyright © 2018 Mark G. Boyer. All rights reserved. Except for brief quotations in critical publications or reviews, no part of this book may be reproduced in any manner without prior written permission from the publisher. Write: Permissions, Wipf and Stock Publishers, 199 W. 8th Ave., Suite 3, Eugene, OR 97401.

Wipf & Stock
An Imprint of Wipf and Stock Publishers
199 W. 8th Ave., Suite 3
Eugene, OR 97401

www.wipfandstock.com

PAPERBACK ISBN: 978-1-5326-6483-0
HARDCOVER ISBN: 978-1-5326-6484-7
EBOOK ISBN: 978-1-5326-6485-4

Manufactured in the U.S.A.   OCTOBER 29, 2018

The Scripture quotations contained herein are from the New Revised Standard Version Bible, copyright © 1989 by the Division of Christian Education of the National Council of the Churches of Christ in the U.S.A., and are used by permission. All rights reserved.

Dedicated to

St. Meinrad Seminary School of Theology Class 1976

Ronald Ashmore, Richard McCracken-Bennett, David Bergs,

Kenneth Bohlinger, Gilles Brault, Kevin Bryan, Conrad Cambron,

Noah Casey,+ Henry Cecil, Stephen Churchwell,+ Robert Cushing,

Richard Daunhauer,+ Roger Dorcy,+ James Dvorscak,

Richard Faulk, G. Patrick Garrity, Mark Gottemoeller,+

William Haegelin, Christian Hearing, H. Michael Hilderbrand,

David Hillier,+ James Holmer, Robert Hull, C. David LeSieur,

John McCaffrey, Ramon Marrufo, David Martin, Jerome Martinez,

Thomas Morrison, Francis Murd, Joseph Scheib, Ernst Schuler,+

Benedict Swiderek, Stephen Trippy, Walter Verbish

+ = deceased

"What the Catholic faith believes about Mary is based on what it believes about Christ, and what it teaches about Mary illumines in turn its faith in Christ."

—Catechism of the Catholic Church, par. 487.

"... [T[he ultimate purpose of devotion to the Blessed Virgin is to glorify God and to lead Christians to commit themselves to a life which is in absolute conformity with his will."

—Paul VI, *Marialis Cultus*, par. 39.

"Masses of the Blessed Virgin Mary have their meaning and purpose from her close participation in the history of salvation. Therefore when the Church commemorates the role of the Mother of the Lord in the work of redemption or honors her privileges, it is above all celebrating the events of salvation in which, by God's salvific plan, the Blessed Virgin was involved in view of the mystery of Christ."

—Collection of Masses of the Blessed Virgin Mary, "General Introduction," par. 6.

Contents

Abbreviations | xi

Notes on the Bible | xv

Presuppositions | xvi

Notes on the Lectionary for Mass | xix

Introduction | xxv

Honoring the Mother of God | xxvi

An Anthology of Marian Reflections | xxviii

A Brief Mariology | xxix

Using This Book | xxxiv

1 HEBREW BIBLE (OLD TESTAMENT) AND OLD TESTAMENT (APOCRYPHA) | 1

GENESIS | 1
 Work, Enmity, Life-Giver, Trust, Righteousness, Test, Dream I

EXODUS | 8
 Fire, Wings

NUMBERS | 10
 Bless, Star

RUTH | 12
 Father

1 SAMUEL | 13
 Three, Handmaid, Barren

2 SAMUEL | 16
   House I, David

1 KINGS | 19
   Temple

1 CHRONICLES | 20
   Ark

JUDITH | 21
   Pillar, Hope I, Heart, Judith, Ransom, Mountains

ESTHER | 27
   Mercy, Mediatrix

2 MACCABEES | 29
   Commend

PSALMS | 31
   Son, Wonder, Steadfast, Tent, Sheol, Metaphors, Torah, Motherhood, Sovereign, King, House II, Refuge, Angel, Offering, Ophir, Colors, Gracious, Justice, Happy, Peace, City, Sworn, Dust, Trees, Dawn, Victory, Being, Remember, Sun, Cup, Strength, Precepts, Jerusalem, Olive, Weaned, Habitation, Meditate, Ordinances

PROVERBS | 73
   Wisdom, Seat

SONG OF (SOLOMON) SONGS | 75
   Visit, Face, Fountain,

SIRACH (ECCLESIASTICUS) | 78
   Mother, Counsel, Dwelling, Hope II, Fair, Ancestors, Tongue

ISAIAH | 86
   Announcement, Crowned, Root, Well, Good News, Pain, Teacher, Light, Consolation, Clothes I, Garments, Married, Urgency, Nursing

JEREMIAH | 102
   Gathered

EZEKIEL | 103
   Water

MICAH | 104
   Nowhereville

ZEPHANIAH | 105
   Rejoice, Unity

ZECHARIAH | 107
   Joy, Queen

MALACHI | 109
   Covenant

2 CHRISTIAN BIBLE (NEW TESTAMENT) | 111

MATTHEW'S GOSPEL | 111
   Women, Fourteen, Dream II, Fulfill, House III, Nazareth, Mourn, Disciple, Parents, Mary, Gate, Earthquake,

MARK'S GOSPEL | 125
   Family, Authority

LUKE'S GOSPEL | 127
   Name, Beatitude, Song, Abraham, Genetrix, Treasure, Shepherds, Circumcision, Home, Simeon, Anna, Praise, Sorrow, Spouse, Boyhood, Ponder, Hearing/Doing, Listening, Blessedness, Suffering

JOHN'S GOSPEL | 151
   Word, Providence, Darkness, Booths, Prophecy, Representative, Comfort, Delight, One, Church, Blood, Lamb

ACTS OF THE APOSTLES | 165
   Witness, Prayer, Spirit, Repent, Raised

ROMANS | 170
   Faith, Eve, Predestined, Love, Hospitality

1 CORINTHIANS | 177
   All, Harvest, Imperishability

2 CORINTHIANS | 180
    Mercies, Reconciliation

GALATIANS | 182
    Adoption

EPHESIANS | 184
    Chosen, Gift, Epiphany

COLOSSIANS | 187
    Completing, Clothes II

1 TIMOTHY | 190
    Mediator

TITUS | 191
    Grace, Rebirth

HEBREWS | 193
    Glory, Flesh and Blood, Obedience, Discern, Assurance

1 JOHN | 199
    Children

BOOK OF REVELATION | 200
    Presence, Michael, Bride

Appendices |
    1 The Litany of the Blessed Virgin Mary (Litany of Loreto) | 205
    2 Litany of the Blessed Virgin Mary in the "Order of Crowning an Image of the Blessed Virgin Mary" | 209
    3 List of Marian Celebrations during the Liturgical Year and Scripture Texts Assigned for Each | 211
    4 The Common of the Blessed Virgin Mary and Votive Masses of the Blessed Virgin Mary | 216
    5 Collection of Masses of the Blessed Virgin Mary and Scripture Texts Assigned for Each | 218
    Advent Season | 218
    Christmas Season | 219
    Lenten Season | 220
    Easter Season | 220

Ordinary Time: Section 1 | 221
Ordinary Time: Section 2 | 222
Ordinary Time: Section 3 | 223
Bibliography | 227
Books by Mark G. Boyer on Mariology | 229
Recent Books by Mark G. Boyer | 229

Abbreviations

BB = *Book of Blessings*
BCE = Before the Common Era (same as BC = Before Christ)
BYM = *Behold Your Mother*

CB (NT) = CHRISTIAN BIBLE (NEW TESTAMENT)
    Acts = Acts of the Apostles
    Col = Letter to the Colossians
    1 Cor = First Letter of Paul to the Corinthians
    2 Cor = Second Letter of Paul to the Corinthians
    Eph = Letter to the Ephesians
    Gal = Letter of Paul to the Galatians
    Heb = Letter to the Hebrews
    John = John's Gospel
    1 John = First Letter of John
    Luke = Luke's Gospel
    Mark = Mark's Gospel
    Matt = Matthew's Gospel
    Phil = Letter of Paul to the Philippians
    Rev = Revelation
    Rom = Letter of Paul to the Romans
    1 Tim = First Letter to Timothy
    2 Tim = Second Letter to Timothy
    Titus = Letter to Titus

CBVM = The Common of the Blessed Virgin Mary
CCC = *Catechism of the Catholic Church*
CE = Common Era (same as AD = *Anno Domini*, in the year of the Lord)
cf. = confer, compare

ABBREVIATIONS

CMBVM: Lectionary = *Collection of Masses of the Blessed Virgin Mary: Volume II: Lectionary*
CSL = Constitution on the Sacred Liturgy
DCC = Dogmatic Constitution on the Church
DPPL = Directory on Popular Piety and the Liturgy

HB (OT) = HEBREW BIBLE (OLD TESTAMENT)

1 Chr = First Book of Chronicles
Dan = Daniel
Deut = Deuteronomy
Esth = Esther
Exod = Exodus
Ezek = Ezekiel
Gen = Genesis
Hab = Habakkuk
Isa = Isaiah
Jer = Jeremiah
Judg = Judges
1 Kgs = First Book of Kings
Lev = Leviticus
Mal = Malachi
Mic = Micah
Num = Numbers
Prov = Proverbs
Ps(s) = Psalm(s)
Ruth = Ruth
1 Sam = First Book of Samuel
2 Sam = Second Book of Samuel
Song = Song of (Solomon) Songs
Zech = Zechariah
Zeph = Zephaniah

LBVM(LL) = The Litany of the Blessed Virgin Mary (Litany of Loreto)
LBVMOCIBVM = Litany of the Blessed Virgin Mary in the "Order of Crowning an Image of the Blessed Virgin Mary"
LM = *Lectionary for Mass*
MC = *Marialis Cultus*

OT (A) = OLD TESTAMENT (APOCRYPHA)
Jdt = Judith
2 Macc = Second Book of Maccabees
Sir = Sirach (Ecclesiasticus)
Wis = Wisdom (of Solomon)

par. = paragraph
pars. = paragraphs
RM = *Redemptoris Mater*
RVM = *Rosarium Virginis Mariae*

Notes on the Bible

THE BIBLE IS DIVIDED into two parts: The Hebrew Bible (Old Testament) and the Christian Bible (New Testament). The Hebrew Bible consists of thirty-nine named books accepted by Jews and Protestants as Holy Scripture. The Old Testament also contains those thirty-nine books plus seven to fifteen more named books or parts of books called the Apocrypha or the Deuterocanonical Books; the Old Testament is accepted by Catholics and several other Christian denominations as Holy Scripture. The Christian Bible, consisting of twenty-seven named books, is also called the New Testament; it is accepted by Christians as Holy Scripture. Thus, in this work:

- Hebrew Bible (Old Testament), abbreviated HB (OT), indicates that a book is found both in the Hebrew Bible and the Old Testament;
- Old Testament (Apocrypha), abbreviated OT (A), indicates that a book is found only in the Old Testament Apocrypha and not in the Hebrew Bible;
- and Christian Bible (New Testament), abbreviated CB (NT), indicates that a book is found only in the Christian Bible or New Testament.

In notating biblical texts, the first number refers to the chapter in the book, and the second number refers to the verse within the chapter. Thus, HB (OT) Isa 7:11 means that the quotation comes from Isaiah, chapter 7, verse 11. OT (A) Sirach 39:30 means that the quotation comes from Sirach, chapter 39, verse 30. CB (NT) Mark 6:2 means that the quotation comes from Mark's Gospel, chapter 6, verse 2. When more than one sentence appears in a verse, the letters a, b, c, etc. indicate the sentence being referenced in the verse. Thus, HB (OT) 2 Kgs 1:6a means that the quotation comes from the Second Book of Kings, chapter 1, verse 6, sentence 1. Also, poetry, such as the Psalms and sections of Judith, Proverbs, and Isaiah, may be noted using the letters a, b, c, etc. to indicate the lines being used. Thus, Psalm 16:4a refers to the first line of verse 4 of Psalm 16; there are two more lines of verse 4: b and c.

Because there may be a difference in the verse numbers between the New Revised Standard Version (NRSV) and the Vulgate (the Latin translation of the Septuagint, such as *The New American Bible Revised Edition* [NABRE]), alternative verse numbers appear in parentheses. This is true particularly with the Psalms, but with other books as well. Thus, NRSV Isaiah 9:2–7 is NABRE (Vulgate) Isaiah 9:1–6; NRSV Isaiah 9:2–4, 6–7 is NABRE (Vulgate) Isaiah 9:1–3, 5–6. Introductory material to Bibles usually indicates which verse-numbering is being used.

In the HB (OT) and the OT (A), the reader often sees LORD (note all capital letters). Because God's name (Yahweh or YHWH, referred to as the Tetragrammaton) is not to be pronounced, the name Adonai (meaning *Lord*) is substituted for Yahweh when a biblical text is read. When a biblical text is translated and printed, LORD (cf. Gen 2:4) is used to alert the reader to what the text actually states: Yahweh. Furthermore, when the biblical author writes Lord Yahweh, printers present Lord GOD (note all capital letters for GOD; cf. Gen 15:2) to avoid the printed ambiguity of LORD LORD. When the reference is to Jesus, the word printed is Lord (note capital L and lower case letters; cf. Luke 11:1). When writing about a lord (note all lower case letters (cf. Matt 18:25) with servants, no capital L is used.

PRESUPPOSITIONS

The HB (OT) begins as stories passed on by word of mouth from one person to another. Sometime during the oral transmission stage, authors decide to collect the oral stories and write them. A change occurs immediately. One does not tell a story the same way one writes a story. Repetition and correction occur in oral story-telling. Except for future emendations by copyists, single statements by characters and plot structure guides dominate written stories. Furthermore, in both oral and written story-telling, types or models are employed. In the CB (NT) Elizabeth becomes a type of Hannah, who is herself a type of Sarah. When orally narrating or writing a story, the teller or author consciously creates one character as a type of another in order to make the character and his or her words and actions intelligible to the hearer or reader.

In the CB (NT) the oldest gospel is Mark's account of Jesus' victory. The author of Matthew's Gospel copied and shortened about eighty percent of Mark's material into his book and then added other stories to make the work longer. The author of Luke's Gospel copied and shortened about fifty percent of Mark's material into his orderly account and then added other stories to make the work much longer. Mark's Gospel begins as oral story-telling, lasting for about forty years in that form. An unidentified author, called Mark for the sake of convenience, collects the oral stories, sets a plot, and writes the first gospel around 70 CE. Because Jesus was expected to return soon, no one had thought about recording what he had said and done until Mark came along and realized that he was not returning as quickly as had been thought. About ten years after Mark finished his gospel, Matthew needed to adopt Mark's narrative—originally intended for a peasant Gentile readership—to a Jewish audience. And about twenty years after Mark finished his gospel, Luke needed to adapt Mark's poor Gentile-intended work for a rich, upper class, urban, Gentile readership. The author of John's Gospel did not know the existence of the other three works collectively named Synoptic Gospels.

Furthermore, gospels were not first intended to be read privately as is done today. They were meant to be heard in a group. The very low rate of literacy in the first century would have never dictated many copies of texts since most people could not read, and their standard practice was to listen to another read the stories to them. Thus, what began as oral story-telling passed on by word of mouth became written story-telling preserved in gospels. A careful reading of Mark's Gospel will reveal the orality still embedded in the text, especially evident in the repetition of words and the organization of stories in three parts. In rewriting Mark, Matthew and Luke remove the last traces of oral story-telling.

Notes on the *Lectionary for Mass*

THE *LECTIONARY FOR MASS* is a collection of Scripture texts assigned for every day of the Liturgical Year. Currently, the Lectionary consists of six volumes (one for Sundays; two for Weekdays; one for Ritual, Votive, and Commons; a Supplement; and one volume for the *Collection of Masses of the Blessed Virgin Mary*).[1] There is also a *Book of the Gospels*, which, as its title suggests, contains only gospel passages for Sundays, solemnities, and feasts of the Lord and saints, along with selections for ritual Masses; all gospel selections are taken from the *Lectionary for Mass*, Volumes I, II, III, and IV and are numbered accordingly. More explanation about the *Lectionary for Mass* follows:

Collection of Masses of the Blessed Virgin Mary: Volume II: Lectionary = (CMBVM: Lectionary) The book of Scripture texts assigned to the forty-six Mass formularies in the *Collection of Masses of the Blessed Virgin Mary: Volume I: Missal*. The CMBVM: Lectionary is divided into eight sections: the Advent Season (three sets of Scripture texts, numbered 1–3), the Christmas Season (six sets of Scripture texts, numbered 4–9), the Lenten Season (five sets of Scripture texts, numbered 10–14), the Easter Season (four sets of Scripture texts, numbered 15–18), and Ordinary Time divided into Section 1 (eleven sets of Scripture texts, numbered 19–29), Section 2 (nine sets of Scripture texts, numbered 30–38), and Section 3 (eight sets of Scripture texts, numbered 39–46), along with an Appendix providing eight optional HB (OT) texts (numbered 1–8), eight CB (NT) optional texts from sources other than the gospels (numbered 9–16), and five CB (NT) optional gospel texts (numbered 17–21). Appendix 5 in this book contains the list of the Masses of the Blessed Virgin Mary and the Scripture texts assigned for each.

When the CMBVM: Lectionary presents an optional First Reading from the Appendix, it simultaneously presents an optional Responsorial

---

1. Cf. BYM, par. 94; MC, pars. 12, 80; RVM, par. 30.

Psalm from the Appendix, because every First Reading in the Appendix has a Responsorial Psalm that accompanies it. Thus, in this book the number of the Responsorial Psalm is derived from the number of the First Reading which it accompanies in the Appendix.

Common of the Blessed Virgin Mary, The = (CBVM) Common texts which may be used in Masses honoring the Blessed Virgin Mary found in the LM are numbered and divided into seven sections: 707. Reading I from the Old Testament (options 1–11); 708. Reading I from the New Testament during the Easter Season (options 1–3); 709. Responsorial Psalm (options 1–5); 710. Reading II from the New Testament (first—fourth options); 711. Alleluia and Verse before the Gospel (options 1–6); and 712. Gospel (options 1–12). Appendix 4 in this book contains the list of the Common of the Blessed Virgin Mary and the Scripture texts which may be used.

Cycles A, B, and C = This designation refers to the three-year cycle of Scripture texts assigned to every Sunday and some solemnities of the liturgical year and found in the *Lectionary for Mass*, a four-volume set (plus a Supplement) of books providing readings for Sundays, Weekdays, and other sacramental celebrations. Cycle A (Matthew's Gospel) is used in 2020, 2023, 2026, etc. Cycle B (Mark's Gospel) is used in 2018, 2021, 2024, etc. And Cycle C (Luke's Gospel) is used in 2019, 2022, 2025, etc. During the weekdays of Lent and Easter, the biblical texts remain the same every year. For the weekdays of Ordinary Time, two different sets of Scripture texts are provided: Year I (used in odd-numbered years) and Year II (used in even-numbered years).

First Reading = a Scripture text taken either from the HB (OT), OT (A), or a CB (NT) source other than gospels; sometimes an optional text and/or a longer or shorter version of a text is provided.

Gospel = a Scripture text taken from one of the CB (NT) Gospels of Matthew, Mark, Luke, or John; sometimes an optional text and/or a longer or shorter version of a text is provided.

Lectionary for Mass = (LM) a four-volume set (plus a Supplement) of books providing readings for Sundays, Weekdays, and other sacramental celebrations. Every Set of Scripture Texts is numbered. When a set lacks a text for a Mass in honor of the Blessed Virgin Mary, it refers to LM 707–712. The Common of the Blessed Virgin Mary, seven collections of texts from which Scripture passages may be chosen. Appendix 3 in this book contains a list of Marian celebrations during the liturgical year and the Scripture texts assigned for each. Appendix 4 in this book contains the list of the Common of the Blessed Virgin Mary and the Scripture texts which may be used.

Lectionary Numbers = Every set of Scripture texts in the *Lectionary for Mass* has a number, such as 572. Feast of the Visitation of the Blessed Virgin Mary, May 31, First Reading: First Option, Second Option; Responsorial Psalm; Alleluia; Gospel; or 573. Memorial of the Immaculate Heart of the Blessed Virgin Mary, Saturday following the Second Sunday after Pentecost, First Reading or 707. CBVM; Responsorial Psalm; Alleluia; Gospel.

The Litany of the Blessed Virgin Mary (Litany of Loreto) = (LBVM[LL]) This litany, a series of invocations, which are usually sung by a cantor and followed by a sung response by people, invokes Mary under various titles. Originally approved in 1587 by Pope Sixtus V, its first-known place of origin was the Shrine of Our Lady of Loreto (Italy), where its usage was recorded as early as 1558. The complete litany is found in Appendix 1 of this book.[2]

Litany of the Blessed Virgin Mary in the "Order of Crowing an Image of the Blessed Virgin Mary" = (LBVMOCIBVM) This litany, a series of invocations, which are usually sung by a cantor and followed by a sung response by people, invokes Mary under various titles. Approved in 1981 by Pope St. John Paul II, it was translated from the original Latin text into English and published in 1987. The complete litany is found in Appendix 2 of this book.[3]

Liturgical Year = The liturgical year begins with the First Sunday of Advent, usually the last Sunday of November or the first Sunday of December; the Advent Season lasts for four weeks. The Christmas Season begins on December 25, lasts three weeks, and ends with the Feast of the Baptism of the Lord, usually the second Sunday of January. The Lenten Season begins with Ash Wednesday, which can occur anytime in February or early March; it lasts six weeks and ends at the beginning of The Sacred Paschal Triduum with Thursday of the Lord's Supper, which can occur anytime from late March into early April. The Sacred Paschal Triduum ends on Easter Sunday evening. The Easter Season begins with Easter Sunday of the Resurrection of the Lord—usually falling in late March or early April—lasts fifty days, and ends with Pentecost Sunday, falling anytime between the middle of May and early June. In between

---

2. Cf. DPPL, par. 203.
3. Ibid.

the Christmas Season and the Lenten Season and in between the Easter Season and the next Advent is the Season of Ordinary Time—meaning counted weeks. The first section of Ordinary Time can be from two to ten weeks, and the second section of Ordinary Time can be from eleven to thirty-four weeks. Appendix 3 in this book contains the list of the Marian celebrations during the liturgical year and the Scripture texts assigned for each.

Mass = In *The Roman Missal*, Mass refers to the two parts of the Celebration of the Eucharist: the Liturgy of the Word and the Liturgy of the Eucharist. The word *Mass*, from the Latin *missa*—from the Latin *mittere*, meaning *to send*—means to send away. The last line of the Mass in Latin is "Ite, missa est," meaning "Go, the Mass is ended." In other words, those present are sent into the world to live what they have celebrated.

Rank = Every Marian Mass is ranked by its importance in the Liturgical Year: (1) Solemnity, (2) Feast, (3) Memorial, and (4) Optional Memorial. All Masses in the CMBVM are Optional Memorials. Solemnities, feasts, and memorials are always celebrated. Optional Memorials are the choice of the bishop or priest celebrating the Mass. In *The Roman Missal* can be found the "Table of Liturgical Days According to Their Order of Precedence."[4] That tool explains what happens when a solemnity, feast, or memorial falls on a Sunday or on another solemnity, feast, or memorial.

Responsorial Psalm = Verses from a HB (OT) Psalm or HB (OT), OT (A), or CB (NT) canticle are presented with one verse or a part of a verse used as a response. A canticle is a song found in a biblical book other than the HB (OT) book of Psalms.

Second Reading = a Scripture text taken from a CB (NT) source other than gospels; sometimes an optional text and/or a shorter or longer version of a text is provided. Second readings are provided for solemnities and for some feasts.

Set of Scripture Texts = A basic set of Scripture texts (used for Feasts, Memorials, and Optional Memorials) consists of a First Reading (taken either from the HB [OT], OT [A], or a CB [NT] source other than gospels), a Responsorial Psalm (verses from a HB [OT] Psalm or HB [OT], OT (A), or CB [NT] canticle with one verse or a part of a verse used as a response), an Alleluia Verse, and a Gospel (taken from one of the CB [NT] Gospels of Matthew, Mark, Luke, or John). On Solemnities, the First Reading (taken from the HB [OT]) with a Responsorial Psalm

---

4. *Roman Missal*, "Universal Norms," 119–120.

(verses from a HB [OT] Psalm or HB [OT], OT [A], or CB [NT] canticle with one verse or a part of a verse used as a response), is followed by a Second Reading (taken from a CB [NT] source other than gospels), then the Alleluia Verse and Gospel (taken from one of the CB [NT] Gospels of Matthew, Mark, Luke, or John). In many cases for the First Reading, the Second Reading, and the Gospel, optional texts are presented in the LM; options are presented as 1, 2, 3, or first option, second option, etc. The CMBVM: Lectionary presents options as A, B, C, etc. Sometimes there are also longer and shorter forms of a text.

Votive Mass = A Votive Mass is one that is celebrated for a special purpose or on a special occasion. In *The Roman Missal*, there is a section titled Votive Masses.[5] Section 10. The Blessed Virgin Mary presents subsections: A (Masses from the Common of the Blessed Virgin Mary, pages 1039–51, in *The Roman Missal*; Scripture texts for those Masses are chosen from LM: 707–712. The Common of the Blessed Virgin Mary); Section B. Our Lady, Mother of the Church (Scripture texts are found in LM: Volume IV: 1002. The Blessed Virgin Mary, I. The Blessed Virgin Mary, Mother of the Church); Section C. The Most Holy Name of Mary (Scripture texts are found in LM: Volume IV: 1002. The Blessed Virgin Mary, II. The Most Holy Name of Mary); Section D. Our Lady, Queen of Apostles (Scripture texts are found in LM: Supplement: 1002. The Blessed Virgin Mary, III. Our Lady, Queen of Apostles). Appendix 4 in this book contains the list of the Votive Masses for the Blessed Virgin Mary and the Scripture texts assigned for each.

---

5. *Roman Missal*, 1325–66.

Introduction

THIS BOOK

THE TITLE OF THIS book is *All Things Mary*. This book provides reflections on all Scripture texts associated with celebrations in honor of the Blessed Virgin Mary during the liturgical year. The reflections follow the order of the books in the Bible; this simultaneously serves as an index of the Scripture texts used in Marian celebrations. During the course of the usual liturgical year, twenty-seven solemnities, feasts, memorials, and optional memorials in honor of the Blessed Virgin Mary or connected to her (such as the Nativity of the Lord, Holy Family, and Saints Joachim and Anne) are presented. Most of these have their own set of biblical texts. In addition, there are thirty-five Scripture texts listed in the CBVM in the LM and twelve for Votive Masses in honor of the Blessed Virgin Mary. Add to these the many biblical texts in the CMBVM: Lectionary, and there are almost two hundred texts from Scripture associated with Marian celebrations. Since this book provides a reflection on each biblical text, it is titled *All Things Mary*.

In the course of the life of the Church, there developed the custom of keeping Saturday as Mary's Day in the same way that Sunday is kept as the Lord's Day. According to the "General Introduction" to the CMBVM: Volume I: Missal, "The custom of dedicating Saturday to the

Blessed Virgin Mary arose in Carolingian monasteries at the end of the eighth century . . . ."[1] Following the liturgical reforms initiated by the Council of Trent (1545–1547, 1551–1552, 1562–1563), "the custom of celebrating a memorial of the Blessed Virgin Mary on Saturday was incorporated into the *Missale Romanun* (*The Roman Missal*).[2] Finally, the liturgical reforms brought by the Second Vatican Council (1962–1965) "clarified the meaning of the memorial of the Blessed Virgin on Saturday and gave it new vigor by making possible a more frequent celebration of this memorial [and] increase[ed] the number of . . . biblical readings . . ."[3] "The General Instruction of *The Roman Missal*" reflects this understanding: "Particularly recommended is the Saturday commemoration of the Blessed Virgin Mary, because it is to the Mother of the Redeemer that in the liturgy of the Church firstly and before all the saints veneration is given."[4] The "Universal Norms on the Liturgical Year and the General Roman Calendar" is even more specific, stating, "On Saturdays in Ordinary Time when no Obligatory Memorial occurs, an Optional Memorial of the Blessed Virgin Mary may be celebrated."[5]

HONORING THE MOTHER OF GOD

The first subtitle for this work is *Honoring the Mother of God*. ". . . Holy Church honors the Blessed Virgin Mary, Mother of God, with a special love. She is inseparably linked with her son's saving work," states "The Constitution on the Sacred Liturgy."[6] In Mary the Church "admires and exalts the most excellent fruit of redemption, and joyfully contemplates, as in a faultless image, that which she herself desires and hopes wholly to be."[7] In other words, Mary is honored as the exemplar of the Christian life.[8] The members of the Church are invited to imitate her faith and the

---

1. "General Introduction," par. 35.
2. Ibid.
3. Ibid., cf. MC, par. 9; cf. DPPL, par. 188.
4. "General Instruction," par. 378.
5. "Universal Norms," par. 15.
6. CSL, par. 103.
7. Ibid.
8. "General Introduction," par. 15.

loving manner in which she embraced and participated in God's plan of salvation.[9]

A good Mariology begins with a good Christology, and not vice-versa. Jesus Christ, the only-begotten Son of God eternally, is one-hundred percent God. Jesus Christ, the incarnate son of Mary, is one-hundred percent human. In the one person of Jesus Christ there are two natures, namely, the divine and the human. When Mary conceived the Son of God in her womb, she simultaneously became the mother of God and the mother of the man, Jesus. She is the mother of God because Jesus Christ is God, and she is the mother of man because Jesus, who became incarnate in her womb by the Holy Spirit, took flesh in her own body.

"What the Catholic faith believes about Mary is based on what it believes about Christ," states the *Catechism of the Catholic Church*, "and what it teaches about Mary illumines in turn its faith in Christ."[10] In the "General Introduction," priests and others who have pastoral responsibilities are told "to strive above all to teach the faithful that the eucharistic sacrifice is the memorial of the death and resurrection of Christ" while not failing "to point out the power of Mary's example that can do so much for the sanctification of the faithful."[11]

In 1986 the *Collection of Masses of the Blessed Virgin Mary* was issued by the Congregation for Divine Worship in Rome to honor the mother of God. After the release of the third edition of *The Roman Missal* in English in 2012, the *Collection of Masses of the Blessed Virgin Mary* was re-issued "with revisions and adaptations"[12] the same year to conform to the third edition of *The Roman Missal*. The "General Introduction" to the forty-six Masses further emphasizes the importance of celebrating "the memorial of the Blessed Virgin on Saturday as a kind of introduction to the Lord's Day."[13] As people "prepare to celebrate the weekly remembrance of the Lord's Resurrection" on Sunday, they "look with great reverence to the Blessed Virgin, who, alone of all his disciples, on that 'great Sabbath' when Christ lay in the tomb, kept watch with full faith and hope and awaited his resurrection."[14] Thus, celebrating a memorial of the

---

9. Ibid., par. 16.

10. CCC, par. 487; cf. DPPL, pars. 101, 183; cf. MC, pars. 4, 15, 25, 46, 57; cf. RM, par. 1.

11. "General Introduction," par. 18.

12. "Foreword," *CMBVM: I: Missal*, vii.

13. "General Introduction," par. 36.

14. Ibid.

Blessed Virgin Mary on Saturday honors the mother of God and serves as "a reminder of the unfailing presence of the Blessed Virgin in the life of the Church."[15]

Besides honoring Mary on Saturdays in Ordinary Time, for "the spiritual benefit of the faithful,"[16] a Mass in honor of the Blessed Virgin Mary may be celebrated on any day when the choice of a Mass is open. However, according to the "General Introduction" to the *Collection of Masses of the Blessed Virgin Mary*, "priests and faithful should keep in mind that genuine Marian devotion does not demand the multiplication of Masses of the Blessed Virgin."[17]

AN ANTHOLOGY OF MARIAN REFLECTIONS

The second subtitle for this book is *An Anthology of Marian Reflections*. It is an anthology because it brings together Scripture texts, litanies, and catechetical teaching about Mary, the mother of God. Mary, the mother of Jesus, is known in the Church as Our Lady of Grace, Our Lady of Fatima, Our Lady of Mount Carmel, Our Lady of Sorrows, Our Lady of Guadalupe, Our Lady of Lourdes, Our Lady of the Rosary, Our Mother of Perpetual Help, and more. Her various titles describe her various functions within the Church.

Many books on Mariology, the study or doctrine relating to the Virgin Mary, treat the liturgical aspects and the devotional aspects of the topic. In this anthology they are brought together in a series of reflections based on the Scripture texts used in Marian celebrations. The liturgical aspects, which include the Marian solemnities, feasts, memorials, and optional memorials in Masses throughout a liturgical year, are viewed through the lens of the Scripture texts assigned to each celebration. Furthermore, the devotional aspects, which include the rosary, the Litany of the Blessed Virgin Mary (Litany of Loreto), the Litany of the Blessed Virgin Mary in the "Order of Crowning an Image of the Blessed Virgin Mary," and the "Order for the Blessing of an Image of the Blessed Virgin Mary" in the *Book of Blessings*, flow from the liturgical aspects.

---

15. Ibid.
16. Ibid., par. 37
17. Ibid.

A BRIEF MARIOLOGY

Chapter 8 of the "Dogmatic Constitution on the Church" of the Second Vatican Council devotes eighteen paragraphs to Mariology under the title "Our Lady." The bishops of the council make clear that they do not "intend to give a complete doctrine on Mary."[18] However, they do state that Mary "occupies a place in the Church which is the highest after Christ and also closest to [people]."[19] Furthermore, "The Church does not hesitate to profess this subordinate role of Mary, which it constantly experiences and recommends to the heartfelt attention of the faithful, so that encouraged by this maternal help they may the more closely adhere to the Mediator and Redeemer."[20] Thus, a sound Mariology flows out of a solid Christology, is grounded in a firm ecclesiology, and is intimately united with a steadfast theology of the communion of saints. The "General Introduction" emphasizes this when it states that the *Collection of Masses of the Blessed Virgin Mary* "seeks to promote celebrations that are marked by sound doctrine, the rich variety of their themes, and their rightful commemoration of the saving deeds that the Lord God has accomplished in the Blessed Virgin in view of the mystery of Christ and the Church."[21]

Christology

"... Mary is ... closely linked with the mystery of Christ," states the "General Introduction."[22] In Mayer's decree issuing the *Collection of Masses*, he writes, "In celebrating the mystery of Christ, the Church also frequently and with deep reverence honors the Blessed Virgin Mary, because of her close bond with her Son."[23] According to the "General Introduction," "In the womb of the Virgin of Nazareth, Jesus the Son of God took ... human nature and became the mediator of the old and the new covenant."[24]

---

18. DCC, par. 54.
19. Ibid.
20. Ibid., par. 62.
21. "General Introduction," par. 19.
22. Ibid., par. 24
23. Mayer, "Congregation for Divine Worship Decree," ix.
24. "General Introduction," par. 4.

Furthermore, Mary, who "entered deeply into the history of salvation,"[25] was actively present in various and wonderful ways in the mysteries of Christ's life.[26] When the Church commemorates the role of Mary in God's plan of redemption or honors her, the Church remembers the events of salvation and the involvement of the Blessed Virgin in view of the mystery of Christ.[27]

Once the first councils of the Church declared firmly who Jesus Christ was/is—*homoousios*, of the same substance of God and man—then theology began to speculate how Mary had the singular privilege of conceiving and bearing Jesus Christ, true God and true man, into the world. By a singular privilege Mary was prepared by God from the moment of her conception by her parents in the womb of her mother, traditionally known as Anne (and her father, traditionally known as Joachim) with grace to be the mother of the God-man, Jesus Christ. This means that she was saved in light of the salvation that her Son was bringing to the world; the Church refers to this as her Immaculate Conception. And the result of her giving birth to Jesus Christ and her salvation was resurrection from the dead, referred to as her Assumption into heaven.

Ecclesiology

Out of all the documents of Vatican II, the placement of the only chapter dealing with Mary within the "Dogmatic Constitution of the Church" is itself enough to speak of the necessity that Mariology be grounded in ecclesiology. The DCC declares that the mother of Jesus "is the image and beginning of the Church as it is to be perfected in the world to come."[28] The bishops add that Mary is "a sign of certain hope and comfort to the pilgrim people of God."[29] To further emphasize that Mariology is grounded in ecclesiology, Mayer explains:

> [Mary] is revered by the Church as the new Eve, who, in view of the death of her Son, received at the moment of her conception a higher form of redemption. She is revered as mother, who through the power of the Holy Spirit gave virginal birth to her

25. DCC, par. 65.
26. "General Introduction," par. 5.
27. Ibid., par. 6; cf. RM, par. 222.
28. DCC, par. 68.
29. Ibid.

Son. She is revered as the disciple of Christ, who treasured in her heart the words of Christ the master. She is revered as the faithful companion of the Redeemer, who, as God had planned, devoted herself with selfless generosity to her Son's mission.

The Church also sees in the Blessed Virgin a preeminent and unique member, graced with all virtue. The Church lovingly cherishes her and never ceases to ask for her protection, for she is the mother entrusted to [all] by Christ on the altar of the cross.[30]

The importance of ecclesiology as a mariological foundation is also found in the "General Introduction," which places Marian celebrations during the liturgical year in the life of the Church. The Season of Advent, for example, marks the work of God in preparing Mary. "God came with his grace to Mary and from the first instant of her conception preserved her from all stain of sin, filled her with the gifts of the Holy Spirit, and continued to shelter her with his love, doing great things for her . . . ."[31] During the Season of Christmas, the Church celebrates God's intervention into human history as the incarnate Word of God, born of the Blessed Virgin Mary.[32] During Lent, Mary is found standing at the foot of the cross, and during the Easter Season, she shares the joy of the resurrection while joining Jesus' disciples in prayer awaiting the gift of the Holy Spirit.[33] During the Season of Ordinary Time, the Blessed Virgin Mary is found in some of the events in Jesus' public life.[34] Thus, Mary's function does not obscure or diminish the unique mediation of Christ, but illustrates its power. Her salutary influence "originates not in any inner necessity but in the disposition of God. It flows forth from the superabundance of the merits of Christ, rests on his mediation, depends entirely on it, and draws all its power from it."[35]

In the DCC the bishops of Vatican II state that it is by reason of God's gift to Mary and her role of divine mother along with her unique graces and functions that "the Blessed Virgin is also intimately united to the Church."[36] In other words, Mary is the first member of the Church,

30. Mayer, "Congregation for Divine Worship Decree," ix.
31. " General Introduction," par. 7.
32. Ibid., par. 8
33. Ibid., par. 10.
34. Ibid., par. 9.
35. DCC, par. 60.
36. Ibid. par. 63.

and she is a type of the Church[37] in which she stands out in eminent and singular fashion as exemplar of discipleship. The "General Introduction" also notes that Mary is called a figure of the Church providing a portrait of the life of her members, and an image of the Church presenting an icon of what the Church hopes to be.[38]

Accordingly, this is best exemplified in liturgical celebration in the Church. "Because of its bonds with Mary, the Church wishes 'to live the mystery of Christ' with her and like her and, above all in the liturgy, continually finds that the Blessed Virgin is ever present as the Mother of the Church and its advocate."[39] "Thus in union with the Blessed Virgin and in imitation of her reverent devotion, the Church celebrates the divine mysteries by which 'God is perfectly glorified and the participants made holy.'"[40]

Communion of Saints

Even though Mary is "[r]edeemed in more exalted fashion, by reason of the merits of her Son and united to him by a close and indissoluble tie," and, thus, she "far surpasses all creatures, both in heaven and one earth, . . . being of the [human] race . . . , she is at the same time also united to all those who are to be saved . . . ."[41] Mayer writes: "The Church proclaims Mary as companion and sister in the journey of faith and in the adversities of life. In Mary, enthroned at Christ's side in the kingdom of heaven, the Church joyfully contemplates the image of its own future glory."[42] The DCC states, "By [Mary's] material charity, she cares for the [brothers and sisters] of her Son, who still journey on earth surrounded by dangers and difficulties until they are led into their blessed home."[43] Mary is a fellow member of the communion of saints. If there is a social hierarchy in heaven, then she has first place within it. ". . . [S]he is hailed

---

37. Ibid.
38. "General Introduction," par. 15.
39. Ibid., par. 12.
40. Ibid., par. 13.
41. DCC, par. 53.
42. Mayer, "Congregation for Divine Worship Decree," ix.
43. DCC, par. 62.

as pre-eminent and as a wholly unique member of the Church, and as its type and outstanding model in faith and charity."[44]

Summary

The three aspects of a healthy Mariology—Christology, ecclesiology, and communion of saints—is best summarized in the "General Introduction" to the *Collection of Masses of the Blessed Virgin Mary*:

> The powerful example of Mary that shines out in the celebration of the liturgy urges the faithful to become like the mother, in order that they might be fashioned more completely in the likeness of her Son. Her example also prompts the faithful to celebrate the mysteries of Christ with that same spirit of reverent devotion with which she took part in the birth of her Son, in his epiphanies, and in death and resurrection. In particular, Mary's example urges the faithful: to treasure the word of God in their hearts and dwell upon it assiduously; to praise God exultantly and thank him joyously; to serve God and neighbor faithfully and offer themselves generously; to pray with perseverance and make their petitions with confidence; to act in all things with mercy and humility; to cherish the law of God and embrace it with love; to love God in everything and above everything else; to be ready to meet Christ when he comes.[45]

Out of this sound Mariology—itself flowing out of a solid Christology, grounded in a firm ecclesiology, and intimately united with a steadfast theology of the communion of saints—there arise the liturgical and devotional aspects of the life of the Church. For example, the Blessed Virgin Mary is mentioned in the Profession of Faith (Creed), the Apostles' Creed, Prefaces, and every Eucharistic Prayer in *The Roman Missal*.[46] Where appropriate in the reflections in this book, The Litany of the Blessed Virgin Mary (Litany of Loreto) is referenced because it summarizes the attributes of Mary of Nazareth from both liturgy and devotion. Likewise, where appropriate in the reflections, the Litany of the

---

44. Ibid., par. 53

45. "General Introduction," par. 17.

46. *Roman Missal*, "Order of Mass," pars. 18, 19, 34, 62, 63, 77, 86, 99, 105, 113, 117, 122; "Appendix to the Order of Mass, Eucharistic Prayers for Reconciliation I and II," par. 7; "Eucharistic Prayer for Use in Masses for Various Needs I, II, III, and IV," par. 7; "Common of the Blessed Virgin Mary," 1039–51; "Votive Masses," 1345–52; cf. BYM, pars. 84–95; cf. MC, par. 9.

Blessed Virgin Mary in the "Order of Crowning an Image of the Blessed Virgin Mary" is referenced, because it, too, summarizes the attributes of the Blessed Virgin Mary from both liturgy and devotion. Other documents concerning Mariology are referenced as needed.

In *Solemni Hac Liturgia* (Credo of the People of God), issued in 1968, Pope St. Paul VI presents reflections on the mention of Mary in the Profession of Faith (Creed): "[B]y the Holy Spirit [the Lord Jesus Christ] was incarnate of the Virgin Mary, and became man."[47] Paul VI states that the eternal Word, born of the Father before time began, and one in substance with the Father, "was incarnate of the Virgin Mary by the power of the Holy Spirit, and was made man: equal therefore to the Father according to his divinity, and inferior to the Father according to his humanity; and himself one, not by some impossible confusion of his natures, but by the unity of his person."[48] Following this Christology is the presentation of what the Church believes about Mary set within ecclesiology:

> We believe that Mary is the Mother, who remained ever a Virgin, of the Incarnate Word, our God and Savior Jesus Christ, and that by reason of his singular election, she was, in consideration of the merits of her Son, redeemed in a more eminent manner, preserved from all stain of original sin and filled with the gift of grace more than all other creatures.
>
> Joined by a close and indissoluble bond to the mysteries of the incarnation and redemption, the Blessed Virgin, the immaculate, was at the end of her earthly life raised body and soul to heavenly glory and likened to her risen Son in anticipation of the future lot of all the just; and we believe that the Blessed Mother of God, the new Eve, mother of the Church, continues in heaven her maternal role with regard to Christ's members, cooperating with the birth and growth of divine life in the souls of the redeemed.[49]

USING THIS BOOK

This book is designed to be used by individuals for private study and prayer and by ministers for study, prayer, and preaching. The goal of this book is to foster ordinary Marian spirituality as it flows from the Bible.

---

47. *Roman Missal*, "Order of Mass," par. 18.
48. *Solemni Hac Liturgia*, par. 11.
49. Ibid., pars. 14–15.

Chapter 1 follows the order of the books in the HB (OT) with those found in the OT (A) placed among them according to the order of books found in the Vulgate. Thus, the order of HB (OT) texts with OT (A) texts indicated as (A) is: Genesis, Exodus, Numbers, Ruth, 1 Samuel, 2 Samuel, 1 Kings, 1 Chronicles, Judith (A), Esther, 2 Maccabees (A), Psalms, Proverbs, Song of (Solomon) Songs, Sirach (Ecclesiasticus) (A), Isaiah, Jeremiah, Ezekiel, Micah, Zephaniah, Zechariah, and Malachi. Abbreviations for these books can be found above in Abbreviations.

Chapter 2 follows the order of the books in the CB (NT). The order of CB (NT) texts is: Matthew, Mark, Luke, John, Acts, Romans, 1 Corinthians, 2 Corinthians, Galatians, Ephesians, Colossians, 1 Timothy, Titus, Hebrews, 1 John, and Revelation. Abbreviations for these books can be found above in Abbreviations.

An eight-part exercise is offered for the entries in both chapters.

1. **Title**: A one-word title is given to the entry. Not only does the one-word title give focus to the entry, but it imitates *Lectio Divina* (Divine Reading), the practice of reading a biblical passage and choosing a word from it for reflection, meditation, and prayer. *Lectio Divina* promotes communion with God through reflection on God's Word (Jesus Christ) and God's word (Bible). Traditionally, *Lectio Divina* has four separate steps: read, reflect, journal/meditate, and pray or contemplate.

    The one-word title is designed to promote mindfulness. According to Annemarie Scobey:

    > Mindfulness is the practice of maintaining a moment-by-moment awareness of thoughts, feelings, the body, and the surrounding environment. A person who tries to be mindful focuses on what he or she senses and feels in the present moment rather than thinking about what might need to be done later or returning to a memory. Mindfulness is the opposite of multitasking. Mindfulness is truly listening, fully tasting, deeply experiencing; it's taking our feelings as they come and not burying them or pushing them away.[50]

2. **Footnote 1**: The title contains a footnote, which lists where the Scripture passage is used in Marian Masses. The footnote indicates (1) in which Lectionary (LM or CMBVM: Lectionary) the biblical

---

50. Scobey, "Keep Prayer in Mind," 43.

passage is found; (2) the Lectionary number of the set of Scripture texts where the passage can be found; (3) the name of the Marian solemnity, feast, memorial, or optional memorial in which the biblical passage is used; (4) the date of the solemnity, feast, memorial, or optional memorial in the liturgical calendar; (5) how the Scripture passage is used (First Reading, Responsorial Psalm, Second Reading, Gospel); (6) alternate versions of the Scripture passage (longer form, shorter form); and (7) the option the biblical passage represents (A, B, C, etc.; or 1, 2, 3, etc.; or first option, second option, etc.), if there is one or if there are several.

3. **Text**: The notation for the complete biblical text as it appears in the Lectionary is given. The reader should find the text in his or her Bible and read it in its entirety. In order to understand the context of the passage, one may need to read a few verses both before and after the indicated passage. Also, it is of utmost importance to note verses that may be omitted from the flow of a biblical passage or verses selected from several chapters from a biblical book that are melded together to form a reading.

    Because of the difference in verse numbering between Bibles, as explained in "Notes on the Bible" above, alternate numbering indicating the Vulgate verse numbering is presented in parentheses and/or brackets. In some instances, there are biblical texts used in several liturgical celebrations and they differ only in a few verses. In this latter case, the word *or* is used to indicate that the passage also appears in a slightly different form in celebrations identified in footnote 1.

    While reading the text, a word other than the one presented may get the reader's attention. In this case, the reader should follow the guidance of the Holy Spirit and use his or her word for the *Lectio Divina* process of reading, reflecting, journaling/meditating, and praying or contemplating.

4. **Scripture**: Since the focus of the entry is found in the one-word title, a verse or two from the Scripture passage under consideration is presented that illustrates the focus.

5. **Reflection**: The Scripture passage is followed by a two-paragraph reflection on the biblical passage and its application to the Blessed Virgin Mary. In the reflection are found invocations from litanies and other sources—biblical and otherwise—that help to illustrate

the Scripture in light of its use in honoring Mary. The reflection is designed to present a Mariology that is grounded in Christology.

Throughout the reflections, the masculine pronoun for God, LORD, LORD God, etc. is used. The author is well aware that God is neither male nor female, but in order to avoid the repetition of nouns over and over again, he employs male pronouns, as they are also used in most biblical translations.

6. **Footnote 2**: At the end of the reflection, a footnote identifies references to various post-Vatican II documents about Mary. These do not claim to be exhaustive, but they do provide auxiliary sources for Mariology materials. Those who prepare homilies and presentations will find that the references help navigate some of the plurality of mariological documents of the past sixty years. If the references are of no concern to the reader, he or she merely ignores them. In a few entries there are no footnote 2s.

7. **Journal/Meditation**: The reflection is followed by a question for journaling and/or personal meditation. The question functions as a guide for personal appropriation of Mariology, thus leading the reader into journaling and/or personal prayer. The journal/meditation question is designed to foster a process of actively applying the reflection to one's life and further development of it. The question gets one started; where the journal/meditation goes cannot be predetermined. It may be a single statement or an idea with which one lingers for a few minutes, a few hours, or a few days. Such contemplation has no end; the reader decides when he or she has finished his or her exploration because he or she needs to attend to other things. People who like to journal—written or electronic—will find the question appropriate for that activity.

According to Scobey:

> Meditation involves quieting the mind and heart. It is a time of focusing our attention on a sacred word or on our breath; a time of letting our thoughts pass by, without holding onto them or entering into them. It is a time of deep awareness.... A common theme ... is silence and stillness. Contemplation, a cousin of meditation, was explained by St. Gregory the Great in the sixth century as "resting in God." St. Gregory went on to explain that in this "resting," the mind and heart are not so much seeking God as beginning to experience God's actual presence. The reduction of action and thought, according to St. Gregory,

allows the person practicing contemplation to sustain [his or her] consent to God's presence. In other words—without action and thought, less gets in the way of experiencing God.[51]

In RVM, Pope St. John Paul II states, "Listening and mediation are nourished by silence."[52] He continues: "A discovery of the importance of silence is one of the secrets of practicing contemplation and mediation. One drawback of a society dominated by technology and the mass media is the fact that silence becomes increasingly difficult to achieve. . . . [I]t is fitting to pause briefly after listening to the word of God, while the mind focuses on the content" of the biblical passage and the reflection.[53]

8. **Prayer:** A prayer concludes the exercise and summarizes the original word in the title, which was illustrated by the Scripture, explored in the reflection, and served as the foundation for the journal/meditation exercise.

Through this process of prayer with the focus on the Blessed Virgin Mary, the reader will come to a deeper knowledge of and a closer relationship with God through the one who gave birth to his Son, Jesus Christ, who is also the Son of Mary.

Mark G. Boyer
Feast of the Visitation of the Blessed Virgin Mary
May 31, 2018

---

51. Ibid., 43–44.
52. RVM, par. 31.
53. Ibid.

1

Hebrew Bible (Old Testament) and Old Testament (Apocrypha)

GENESIS

Work[1]

Text: Genesis 1:26—2:3

Scripture: ". . . [O]n the seventh day God finished the work that he had done, and he rested on the seventh day from all the work that he had done." (Gen 2:3)

Reflection: In order to create humankind, God works. Portraying God at work is, of course, a projection of people at work. The author of this part of the HB (OT) book of Genesis reflected on all the work he had done and imagined that God must have worked in order to create everything that exists. God even speaks to his assembly or counsel of advisors, saying, "Let us make humankind in our image, according to our likeness . . ." (Gen 1:26a). It is important to note that the image of God consists of "male and female" (Gen 1:27b). Male and female are given dominion over all other creatures that God had worked to make. Because the biblical author is reflecting on his own experience of work and projecting that onto God, he declares that God rests from his work on the seventh day. This priestly author was interested in reinforcing the command about

---

1. LM: 529. Optional Memorial of St. Joseph the Worker, May 1, First Reading, First Option.

rest on the sabbath (Exod 20:8–11; Deut 5:12–15). Furthermore, the Hebrew verb to rest, *shabat*, is the source for the word *sabbath*.

Joseph, fiancé of Mary of Nazareth, is a worker. More specifically, he is referred to as a carpenter. In Matthew's Gospel, Jesus is known as the carpenter's son (Matt 13:55a), which leads to the conclusion that Joseph was a carpenter. In chapters 1–2, Matthew provides little information about Joseph (and what he does provide is based on Joseph, son of Jacob), and his mention of him at 2:21 is the last time he is named in the First Gospel. Joseph's occupation may stem from his Markan source in which Jesus is characterized as a carpenter (Mark 6:13). The point of identifying the fiancé of Mary as a worker is to focus on the holiness of work. Some people see work as a curse; it is necessary to work in order to make money so as to survive by providing shelter, food, and clothing. But work of any kind is holy. According to Genesis, even God works. Also, according to Genesis, even God rests from all the work he does.

Journal/Meditation: What work do you consider to be holy? Explain.

Prayer: God of work and rest, after creating me in your image, you rested from all the work you had done. Give me good and healthy work that I may contribute to your world. Give me rest and healing that I may be renewed through Jesus Christ, you Son, now and forever. Amen.

Enmity[2]

Text: Genesis 3:1-6, 13-15

Scripture: "The LORD God said to the serpent, 'I will put enmity between you and the woman, and between your offspring and hers; he will strike your head, and you will strike his heel.'" (Genesis 3:14a, 15)

Reflection: When addressing the serpent in the HB (OT) book of Genesis, the LORD God declares to the snake that there will be extreme ill will or hatred between the serpent and the first woman, who is not yet named (Gen 3:20). That hatred will extend to their offspring. The enmity will cause people to strike the snake's head in order to kill it, and it will cause the snake to strike at people's heels in order to bite them and/or poison them. Christianity understands this passage to be a type of proto-gospel; this means that Jesus—Son of Mary, the new woman—has

---

2. CMBVM: Lectionary: 42. The Blessed Virgin Mary, Help of Christians, First Reading, Option B.

contended with evil, the serpent who tricked the first woman, and beaten Satan (Mark 1:13; Matt 4:1–11; Luke 4:1–13). Thus, through Mary, one of Eve's descendants—who is depicted in iconography with her foot on the snake and named Our Lady of Grace—Jesus conquered the serpent. Furthermore, Mary, as the new woman or new Eve, through her God-given sinlessness, has also struck the head of the serpent and defeated Satan's power in light of what her Son would do.

Thus, Mary is the help of Christians. In the LBVM(LL), she is invoked as help of Christians and the comforter of the afflicted, and in the LBVMOCIBVM, she is invoked as champion of God's people. Furthermore, one of her many titles is Our Lady of Perpetual Help. As the perpetual and powerful help of Christians, the Virgin Mary is asked by pray-ers to intercede with God, asking him to give the pray-er the favor which he or she needs in a given situation. Mary's role in the church flows from her union with her Son, who struck the head of the serpent with his cross and destroyed it for all time.[3]

Journal/Meditation: What help has the Blessed Virgin Mary been to you?

Prayer: Remember, O most gracious Virgin Mary, that never was it known that anyone who fled to your protection, implored your help, and sought your intersession, was left unaided. O Mother of the Word Incarnate, despise not my petitions; but in your clemency hear and answer me through Christ my Lord. Amen.

Life-Giver[4]

Text: Genesis 3:9–15, 20

Scripture: "The man named his wife Eve, because she was the mother of all living." (Gen 3:20)

---

3. References: BB, par. 1286; BYM, pars. 13–15, 19, 40–41, 55; DCC, pars. 55–56, 63; MC, pars. 56–57; RM, pars. 11, 19, 24, 37, 47.

4. LM: 572A. Memorial of the Blessed Virgin Mary, Mother of the Church, Monday after Pentecost, First Reading, First Option; LM: 689. Solemnity of the Immaculate Conception of the Blessed Virgin Mary, December 8, First Reading; LM: 707. The Common of the Blessed Virgin Mary: First Reading, Option 1; LM: 1002. The Blessed Virgin Mary, I. The Blessed Virgin Mary, Mother of the Church, First Reading, First Option; CMBVM: Lectionary: 25. The Blessed Virgin Mary, Image and Mother of the Church I, First Reading.

Reflection: In Hebrew, the name *Eve* resembles the word for living. That is why the author of the HB (OT) book of Genesis writes that the first woman was named Eve, because she became the mother of all human beings. Thus, her name describes her function as a giver of life. Mary, the mother of Jesus, is often referred to as the new Eve because she restored life to a fallen world. The first Eve gave life to the human race. The second Eve, Mary, gave birth to the giver of life, Jesus, Son of God. He, in turn, shares the gift of eternal life with everyone who is willing to follow him.

The mystery which Jesus taught is that the more life is given and shared the more there is to give away and to share. By dying on the cross, Jesus gave all of his life. But the Father raised Jesus from the dead and enabled him to give an even better gift of eternal life. Thus, Mary, who gave life to Jesus, the life-giver, received immaculate grace from the Son to whom she gave life.[5]

Journal/Meditation: In what specific instance have you experienced the mystery of life, namely, the more life you give and share the more there is to give and share?

Prayer: Heavenly Father, your servant Mary received your Word in her womb and conceived the Life-giver, through whom you created all that lives. Grant me a share in her grace that I may be more fruitful day by day through the same Jesus Christ my Lord. Amen.

Trust[6]

Text: Genesis 12:1–7

Scripture: "... [T]he LORD said to Abram, 'Go from your country and your kindred and your father's house to the land that I will show you.' So Abram went, as the LORD had told him...." (Gen 12:1, 4a)

Reflection: Abram, later to be named Abraham, the father of Israel, is remembered for his trust in God's word. When instructed by God to migrate from his own land and his own people, Abram did so; he trusted that God's promise to make of him a great nation was worthy of his confidence. In a similar way, Mary, a descendant of Abram, is remembered for

---

5. References: BB, par. 1286; BYM, pars. 13–15, 40–41, 55; CCC, pars. 411, 489, 494, 504, 508, 975, 2618; DCC, pars. 55, 56, 63; MC, pars 56–57; RM, pars. 19, 37, 47.

6. LM: 707. The Common of the Blessed Virgin Mary, First Reading, Option 2; CMBVM: Lectionary: 1.The Blessed Virgin Mary, Chosen Daughter of Israel, First Reading, Option A.

her trust in God's word. When she was instructed by God that she was to bear a child, even though she was not yet married to Joseph, she believed that God's promise to her was worthy of her trust. Thus, Mary became a chosen daughter of Israel, one of Abram's descendants.

In the LBVM(LL) Mary is invoked as the cause of joy, while in the LBVMIOCIBVM, she is invoked as the chosen daughter of the Father, the virgin daughter of Zion, and the joy of Israel. She, chosen by God like Abram before her, brings happiness into the world through her trust of God. And, again, like Abram before her, she consents to what at first glance may seem impossible.[7]

Journal/Meditation: In what specific instance of your life have you trusted God's word?

Prayer: God of Abram and Mary, your servants trusted in your word and your promise. Give me attentive ears to hear your word in the events of my day and fill me with the trust that brings happiness to all I encounter. I ask this in the name of Jesus Christ, your Son, now and forever. Amen.

Righteousness[8]

Text: Genesis 15:1-6; 21:1-3

Scripture: "... [Abram] believed the LORD; and the LORD reckoned it to him as righteousness." (Gen 15:6)

Reflection: Most people hear or see the word *righteousness* and immediately conclude with self-righteousness, the state of being sure of one's moral superiority of beliefs and actions. While there may be a lot of self-righteous or disapproving behavior around, righteousness has nothing to do with it. Righteousness indicates a relationship with God that is in good order. Abram trusts God's promise; after evaluating Abram's faith the LORD determines that all is right between him and Abram. Thus, God declares Abram a righteous man.

Abram is presented as a model for a healthy relationship with God on the Feast of the Holy Family of Jesus, Mary, and Joseph. In his letter to the Galatians, Paul employs the example of Abram, later named

---

7. References: BB, par. 1286; BYM, pars. 13, 29-30, 32-33, 47; CCC, pars. 144, 488-489, 2619; DCC, pars. 53, 55; RM, pars. 14, 21.

8. LM: 17. Feast of the Holy Family of Jesus, Mary, and Joseph, Sunday within the Octave of the Nativity of the Lord [Christmas], or, if there is no Sunday, December 30, First Reading, Year B.

Abraham, as the father of all who believe the LORD, even going so far as to say that "the scripture, foreseeing that God would justify the Gentiles by faith, declared the gospel beforehand to Abraham . . ." (Gal 3:8). Paul concludes that those who believe "are blessed with Abraham who believed" (Gal 3:9). This means that Abram's descendants are those who believe, like Abram—both Jews and Gentiles. Certainly, righteousness also describes Mary's relationship with God; she trusted the LORD to fulfill his promise.[9]

Journal/Meditation: Is your relationship with God one that can be reckoned as righteousness? Explain.

Prayer: God of Abram and Mary, because of their faith you reckoned your servants as righteous in your sight. Through the work of the Holy Spirit, bestow upon me the gift of righteousness that I may be made worthy to be in your presence now and forever. Amen.

Test[10]

Text: Genesis 22:1–2, 9–13, 15–18

Scripture: ". . . God tested Abraham. He said to him, 'Abraham!' And he said, 'Here I am.'" (Gen 22:1)

Reflection: The narrative about God testing Abraham in the HB (OT) begins with the LORD calling Abraham by name and Abraham announcing his presence. Then, God tells the patriarch to take his son Isaac, whom he loves, and make of him a burnt offering to the LORD. God is testing Abraham's trust of God; he is evaluating or judging him. While Isaac carries the wood for the burnt offering, Abraham carries the fire and the knife. Just as he is about to kill his son on the altar, the angel of the LORD—a code for God—stays his hand. Abraham has passed the test. God renews his promise to Abraham that his descendants will be numerous.

The Blessed Virgin Mary is tested by God at the cross. The new Adam, Jesus, who in John's Gospel carries the cross by himself, finds the new Eve, Mary, standing at the foot of his cross, and, thus, participating in his passion and death. After entrusting her to the care of the disciple

---

9. References: BYM, pars. 13, 20–30, 32–33, 47; CCC, pars. 144, 489, 2619; RM, par. 14.

10. CMBVM: Lectionary: 12. The Blessed Virgin Mary at the Foot of the Cross II, First Reading, Option B; CMBVM: Lectionary: Appendix, First Reading, Option 1 (Optional First Reading in Mass 12).

he loved, Jesus entrusts the disciple into her care. Then, he bows his head and dies. As she, like Abraham, suffers the death of her Son, she also receives him back through his promise to be raised from the dead by the Father (John 5:19–29). Just like Abraham received back his son, Mary will receive back her Son through resurrection.[11]

Journal/Meditation: When have you been tested by God? Did you pass the test?

Prayer: LORD God, Abraham, the father of Isaac, responded with trust when you put him to the test. Likewise, the mother of Jesus stood at the foot of the cross in hope of new life for her Son. Pour your grace upon me that I might cling to your faithfulness when confronted with daily tests of my faith. Grant my prayer in the name of Jesus, who is Lord forever and ever. Amen.

Dream I[12]

Text: Genesis 28:10–17

Scripture: "[Jacob] dreamed that there was a ladder set up on the earth, the top of it reaching to heaven, and the angels of God were ascending and descending on it." (Gen 28:12)

Reflection: In the HB (OT) account of Jacob's dream, the ladder serves to connect the top story—the heavens, where God lives—of the three-storied universe to the middle story—the earth, where people live. (The third or bottom story—the underworld or netherworld—is where the dead live.) What Jacob, son of Isaac, sees in his dream-vision of the ladder is the house of God through the gate of heaven. In biblical understanding, a rainbow, a cloud, or a tree serve the same purpose as the ladder, namely, to be a vehicle or portal for the LORD to visit the earth.

The Blessed Virgin Mary is referred to as both a house of God and a gate of heaven. As a house of God, she conceives the Son of God in her immaculate womb, becoming a true temple for the LORD. The LBVM(LL) invokes her as a house of gold in whom dwelt the unique holiness of the Son of God, and the ark of the covenant, which contained the

---

11. References: BYM, pars. 13, 29–30, 32–33, 47; CCC, pars. 144, 489, 2619; RM, par. 14.

12. CMBVM: Lectionary: 23. The Blessed Virgin Mary, Temple of the Lord, First Reading, Option C; CMBVM: Lectionary: 46. The Blessed Virgin Mary, Gate of Heaven, First Reading, Option B; CMBVM: Lectionary: Appendix, First Reading, Option 2 (Optional First Reading in Mass 23 and 46).

tablets of the Law, residing in the holiest place in the Jerusalem Temple. As the gate of heaven, closed by God to guard the way to the tree of life (Gen 3:24), Mary, invoked by the same title in the LBVM(LL), connects heaven to earth through her conception of the Son of God. She is the portal through which eternal life came to the earth.[13]

Journal/Meditation: What modern metaphor (ladder, house, gate) might you use to describe the role of the Blessed Virgin Mary?

Prayer: Heavenly Father, through the incarnation, you made the Blessed Virgin Mary the temple of the Holy Spirit, the dwelling place of your Son, Jesus Christ, and the gate of eternal life. Grant that I may one day gaze upon your face; hear my prayer through Mary's intercession. You live and reign as one God—Father, Son, and Holy Spirit—forever and ever. Amen.

EXODUS

Fire[14]

Text: Exodus 3:1–8

Scripture: "... [T]he angel of the LORD appeared to [Moses] in a flame of fire out of a bush; he looked, and the bush was blazing, yet it was not consumed." (Exod 3:2)

Reflection: The HB (OT) book of Exodus's narrative about Moses encounter with the burning bush that is not consumed on Mount Horeb (Sinai) is a theophany, a manifestation of God. While there are many other natural elements of biblical theophanic experiences, in the above passage fire mediates the LORD's voice to Moses. The burning bush draws Moses to itself while keeping him at a safe distance. Fire protects by giving heat, but fire also destroys whatever it touches. This makes fire paradoxical and, thus, a very appropriate sign of the divine presence. Thus, the LORD reveals himself as both protector and destroyer; he will protect his chosen people, and he will destroy those who have enslaved them.

Mary, the Mother of the Lord, is like Exodus's burning bush. She conceives in her womb the Son of God, the burning bush of the divine presence. After receiving the Holy Spirit and being overshadowed by the

---

13. Reference: DCC, par. 53.

14. CMBVM: Lectionary: 19. Holy Mary, Mother of the Lord, First Reading, Option B; CMBVM: Lectionary: Appendix, First Reading, Option 3 (Optional First Reading in Mass 19).

power of the Most High, the Mother of the Lord becomes a theophany, a sign of the LORD's presence. Furthermore, through her womb, she mediates the eternal Son of God to the finite earth in the person of Jesus of Nazareth. Once born, Jesus protects people by healing them and destroying whatever holds them in slavery. Mary remains a virgin, just like the bush that burns but is not destroyed. Her conception of God's Son did not destroy her virginity. This is why the LBVM(LL) invokes her as the holy virgin of virgins, the virgin most prudent, venerable, renowned, powerful, merciful, and faithful, and the LBVMOCIBVM calls her the most honored of virgins, a virgin poor and humble, and a virgin gentle and obedient.[15]

Journal/Meditation: In your home, where do you find fire that protects and destroys and reminds you of God's presence?

Prayer: As you once poured the fire of your grace upon Mary, the mother of your Son, O LORD, ignite it within me that others may recognize you in my works and words and be drawn to you, who live and reign as Father, Son, and Holy Spirit forever and ever. Amen.

Wings[16]

Text: Exodus 19:3–8a

Scripture: "... [T]he LORD called to [Moses] from the mountain, saying, 'You have seen what I did to the Egyptians, and how I bore you on eagles' wings and brought you to myself.'" (Exod 19:3–4)

Reflection: Wings are used by birds, insects, and planes for flying. Comparing himself to an eagle, God reminds Moses that he chose his people out of Egyptian slavery and flew them to Mount Horeb (Sinai). Just like an eagle that stirs up its nest, hovering over its young, spreading its wings, and bearing them aloft (Deut 32:11), God guided and brought his people to the holy mountain where he could enter into solemn covenant with them. The Israelites accepted God's offer and became a chosen people, dearer to the LORD than all other people on the earth. "Everything that the LORD has spoken we will do," they declare (Exod 19:8). With their declaration the Israelites become God's priestly kingdom and holy nation.

---

15. References: BYM, par. 13; CCC, pars. 496, 498–499, 502, 505–507, 510; DCC, pars. 52, 63, 64.

16. CMBVM: Lectionary: 9. Our Lady of Cana, First Reading.

Just as Moses served as mediator between the LORD and the Israelites, Mary, Our Lady of Cana, serves as a mediator between Jesus and the wedding guests in the unique Johannine story of the wedding at Cana. She tells the servants to do whatever Jesus tells them to do, even though he has declared that his hour has not yet come. Again, just as Moses brought God's people to his holy mountain, like an eagle that uses its wings to soar in the sky, Mary brings people to Jesus at a wedding in Cana, bearing them on eagles' wings as water becomes wine for those attending the feast.[17]

Journal/Meditation: In what one, specific instance has God bore you on eagles' wings and brought you to himself?

Prayer: God of the Exodus, on eagles' wings you bore your people from Egyptian slavery to freedom at the foot of your holy mountain, where you entered into solemn covenant with them. Give me the grace to keep your covenant that I might join the mother of Jesus in the kingdom where you live now and forever. Amen.

NUMBERS

Bless[18]

Text: Numbers 6:22–27

Scripture: "The LORD spoke to Moses, saying: Speak to Aaron and his sons, saying, Thus you shall bless the Israelites: You shall say to them, The LORD bless you and keep you. So they shall put my name on the Israelites, and I will bless them." (Num 6:22–24, 27)

Reflection: To bless is to wish well. To bless is to ask God to bestow holiness on somebody or something. Thus, when a person blesses another, the one receiving the blessing is set apart as holy or sacred. When Aaron and his sons invoke the divine name on the Israelites, they become exclusively the LORD's people for whom he cares deeply. In a manner of speaking, to bless is to ask God to smile upon somebody. God smiles upon a person who is kept safe during an accident. The LORD smiles when a tumor is discovered to be benign. God's blessing can be a clear, crisp winter's morning or a bright, breezy spring day.

---

17. References: BYM, pars. 20, 34–36, 138; CCC, par. 2618; DPPL, par. 106; MC, pars. 18, 33, 57; RM, pars. 21–22, 45; RVM, pars. 14, 16, 21.

18. LM: 18. Solemnity of the Blessed Virgin Mary, the Mother of God, January 1, First Reading.

Mary, the mother of God, is a blessed person. The LBVM(LL) refers to her as the holy mother of God, the mother most pure, the mother most chaste, the mother inviolate, the mother undefiled, the mother most amiable, and the mother most admirable. The LBVMOCIBVM calls her the holy mother of God and the mother of the Lord. God chose her, set her apart to be holy, and cared for her. From the moment of her conception she was wrapped in the LORD's grace and overshadowed by the Holy Spirit, who conceived in and brought from her womb Jesus, the Son of God, himself a blessing for the world. Mary alone bears the title of mother of God; the Holy One invoked his own name on her and blessed her. In other words, God smiled on her.[19]

Journal/Meditation: What do you consider to be the greatest blessing you have received from God?

Prayer: LORD God, I ask you to bless me and keep me, to make your face to shine upon me and be gracious to me, to lift up your countenance upon me and give me peace as you did Mary, the mother of God. Hear me in the name of Jesus Christ now and forever. Amen.

Star[20]

Text: Numbers 24:15–17a

Scripture: "The oracle of Balaam son of Beor: I see him, but not now; I behold him, but not near—a star shall come out of Jacob, and a scepter shall rise out of Israel." (Num 24:15b, 17a)

Reflection: Balaam was summoned by Balak, King of Moab, to curse the Israelites. who were camped in the plains of Moab. However, God had other plans; instead of cursing the Israelites, God instructed Balaam to bless them. In one of his oracles of blessing, Balak mentions the star that will come out of Jacob; the star is a metaphor for a king. In ancient cosmological understanding, a new star would appear in the sky when a new king was born. Balak also mentions a scepter arising out of Israel, a reference to royal authority; staffs and scepters represent leadership. Thus, Balak's oracle is about King David, who defeated Moab during his reign. The writer of the HB (OT) book of Numbers predicts

---

19. References: BB, par. 1286; BYM, pars. 2–3, 5, 62–64, 106, 109; CCC, pars. 495, 509, 963, 971, 975, 2619; CSL, par. 103; DCC, pars. 52, 53, 54, 56–57, 63, 66–67, 69; DPPL, pars. 107, 115; MC, pars. 5, 11, 14, 28, 32; RM, pars. 4, 8, 31, 39; RVM, par. 33.

20. CMBVM: Lectionary: Appendix, First Reading, Option 4.

David's appearance, knowing that at the time of writing that this has already occurred.

This optional text for any Mass of the Blessed Virgin Mary can be used in two ways. First, in the LBVM(LL) Mary is invoked as the morning star. In the LBVMOCIBVM, she is invoked as the woman crowned with stars. Thus, the star is a metaphor for Mary. Second, the star can serve as a metaphor for Jesus, Mary's Son, who reigns over the house of Jacob with a kingdom of no end (Luke 1:32–33). In either use, the star points to one who rises out of Israel.[21]

Journal/Meditation: What events—cosmological or otherwise—accompanied your birth?

Prayer: O LORD, help me to hear your words. Most High, help me to know your knowledge. Almighty, help me to see your vision with uncovered eyes. Then, understanding your will, grant me the grace to do it in the name of Jesus now and forever. Amen.

RUTH

Father[22]

Text: Ruth 2:1–2, 8–11; 4:13–17

Scripture: "... Boaz took Ruth and she became his wife. When they came together, the LORD made her conceive, and she bore a son. The women of the neighborhood gave him a name, saying, 'A [grand]son has been born to Naomi.' They named him Obed; he became the father of Jesse, the father of David." (Ruth 4:13, 17)

Reflection: The four-chapter HB (OT) book of Ruth narrates the story of women whose husbands have died, leaving three of them with no one to take care of them. In the Bible, the book is placed between the book of Judges and the First Book of Samuel; thus, it serves as a transition from when the judges ruled Israel to when the kings ruled. Because it represents a patriarchal culture, its focus is on the man born to Ruth and Boaz: Obed, the father of Jesse of Bethlehem, the father of David the king.

The Blessed Virgin Mary is like Ruth, whom the LORD enables to conceive and bear a son, who himself becomes famous in Israel. Obed,

---

21. References: DPPL, par. 102; RM, par. 3.

22. CMBVM: Lectionary: 1. The Blessed Virgin Mary, Chosen Daughter of Israel, First Reading, Option C; CMBVM: Lectionary: Appendix, First Reading, Option 5 (Optional First Reading in Mass 1).

the seventh son named in the genealogy in the book of Ruth (4:18–22), is famous for being the father of Jesse, who is the father of eight sons, the last one being David, to whom Samuel is sent to anoint as king (1 Sam 16:1–13). Biblical seven refers to completion; it is the sum of three, the number indicating the divine order, and four, the number indicating the created order. Thus, Obed's birth represents a completion of the judges. Biblical eight represents fullness because it is one more than seven, an octave, even more complete or perfect. Thus, David represents the fullness of kingship. Mary is like Ruth; she conceives in her womb and bears one of Israel's famous sons: Jesus, to whom the LORD God gives "the throne of his ancestor David" (Luke 1:32) and who will reign over Jacob's house forever with his kingdom having no end (Luke 1:33). Like Boaz chose Ruth, God chose Mary. The LBVMOCIBVM invokes Mary as the chosen daughter of the Father and the virgin daughter of Zion.[23]

Journal/Meditation: For what famous role has God chosen you?

Prayer: LORD God, give me the same grace you once gave to Ruth to follow Naomi. Wherever you lead me, I will go. You, Father, Son, and Holy Spirit, will be my God now and forever. Amen.

1 SAMUEL

Three[24]

Text: 1 Samuel 1:20–22, 24–28

Scripture: "When [Hannah] had weaned [Samuel], she took him up [to Shiloh] with her, along with a three-year-old bull, an ephah of flour, and a skin of wine. She brought him to the house of the LORD at Shiloh; and the child was young." (1 Sam 1:24)

Reflection: Hannah, wife of Elkanah, is barren. While making a trip to Shiloh, where the ark of the covenant of God was kept until David moved it to Jerusalem, she prayed that she might conceive a son, whom she would dedicate to the LORD as a nazirite until his death. A nazirite is a man consecrated to God; he drinks no wine or other intoxicants and neither does he cut his hair. Hannah's prayer is answered; she gives birth

---

23. References: BB, par. 1286; BYM, pars. 13, 15–18, 20–21; CCC, pars. 489, 712, 2619; DCC, pars. 53, 55; RM, pars. 8, 41.

24. LM: 17. Feast of the Holy Family of Jesus, Mary, and Joseph, Sunday within the Octave of the Nativity of the Lord [Christmas], or, if there is no Sunday, December 30, First Reading, Year C.

to Samuel, a priest, a prophet, the last of the judges, and the anointer of kings Saul and David. The birth of Samuel is miraculous; his dedication to God is theophanic, as indicated by the three-year-old bull offered to God. The number three refers to the spiritual order; it gives a sense of order to chaos, and it represents the LORD's presence.

The Blessed Virgin Mary is like Hannah. She conceives Jesus by the Holy Spirit, the overshadowing power of the Most High. She and Joseph take Jesus to the Jerusalem Temple for the feast of Passover when he is twelve years old; twelve is the sum of three (the divine) and four (the earth) and five (grace, the Torah) or the product of three (the divine) times four (the earth); it is also the number of Jacob's sons and Jesus' apostles. The holy family, consisting of three people, enters the Temple, built by Solomon to house the ark of the covenant and rebuilt by Ezra and Nehemiah after the Babylonian captivity, one of the signs of God's presence. Later they will find Jesus, Son of God, in the Temple, his Father's house (Luke 2:49). Clearly, a theophany is occurring; the LORD's presence is indicated by the holy family, three persons, both in and outside of the Temple.[25]

Journal/Meditation: What number signals God's presence for you?

Prayer: My heart exults in you, LORD; my strength is exalted in you, my God. There is no Holy One like you, LORD. Look with favor on me and bestow your mercy on me. I ask this in the name of Jesus, your Son, now and forever. Amen.

Handmaid[26]

Text: 1 Samuel 1:24–28; 2:1–2, 4–8

Scripture: Hannah said to Eli, "Oh, my lord! As you live, my lord, I am the woman who was standing here in your presence praying to the LORD. For this child I prayed; and the LORD has granted me the petition that I made to him." (1 Sam 1:26–27)

Reflection: Hannah, wife of Elkanah, has no child. So, during one of their yearly trips to Shiloh, where the ark of the covenant is located before David brings it to Jerusalem, Hannah prays to the LORD, asking him to look on the misery of his servant, to remember her, and to give her a male child, whom she vows to set before him (1 Sam 1:11). In other words,

---

25. References: BYM, par. 47; CCC, par. 489; DPPL, par. 101.

26. CMBVM: Lectionary: 22. Holy Mary, Handmaid of the Lord, First Reading.

Hannah declares that she is God's handmaid, his female servant, one who is, literally, at hand when needed. Once Samuel is born and dedicated to the LORD at Shiloh, he becomes a priest, the last of the judges, a prophet, and the anointer of kings Saul and David.

The Blessed Virgin Mary is like Hannah. After the angel Gabriel announces the conception of Jesus to her, she declares that she is the handmaid or servant of the LORD (Luke 1:38); what has been announced to her by the angel will take place according to the angel's word. Furthermore, after she visits Elizabeth, she declares that God has looked with favor on the lowliness of his handmaid or servant (Luke 1:48). The LBVMOCIBVM invokes Mary as the handmaid of the Lord. In words inspired by Hannah (1 Sam 2:1–10), Mary, the LORD's handmaid, praises God for all the Mighty One does through his handmaids (Luke 1:46–55).[27]

Journal/Meditation: In the past week, how have you functioned as God's handmaid?

Prayer: You, LORD, are a God of knowledge who weighs human actions. Bring me to the fullness of life by making me one of your handmaids. Thus, after knowing your will, I will serve you all the days of my life. I ask this in the name of Jesus now and forever. Amen.

Barren[28]

Text: 1 Samuel 2:1, 4–5, 6–7, 8abcd

Scripture: "The barren has borne seven, but she who has many children is forlorn. The LORD kills and brings to life; he brings down to Sheol and raises up." (1 Sam 2:5c–6).

Reflection: Usually called a canticle because it is not found in the HB (OT) book of Psalms, 1 Samuel 2:1–10 is a psalm of thanksgiving for some national Israelite victory that has been placed on the lips of Hannah, Samuel's mother. When Hannah, wife of Elkanah, is first mentioned,

---

27. References: "Apostolic Exhortation on the Renewal of Religious Life," par. 56; BB, par. 1286; BYM, pars. 20, 47, 55; CCC, pars. 489, 494, 2617; DCC, par. 61; MC, pars. 17, 21, 23; RM, pars. 13, 15, 20, 26, 38–39, 41.

28. LM: 573. Memorial of the Immaculate Heart of the Blessed Virgin Mary, Saturday following the Second Sunday after Pentecost, Responsorial Psalm; LM: 709. The Common of the Blessed Virgin Mary, Responsorial Psalm, Option 1; CMBVM: Lectionary: Appendix, Responsorial Psalm, Option 5 (Optional Responsorial Psalm in Mass 1).

she is barren; she has no children (1 Sam 1:2). So, she, whose womb has been closed by the Lord (1 Sam 1:5), prays that God will open her womb, and he does. Hannah gives birth to Samuel. In the words of the canticle, she who was barren bore—not seven but—six children (1 Sam 2:21). Again, in the words of the canticle, it is the LORD who kills and brings life (1 Sam 2:6); he is in charge of everything.

Hannah's canticle is the basis for Luke's presentation of Mary's canticle (Luke 1:46–55). Hannah's heart exults in the LORD and her strength is exalted in her God (1 Sam 2:1), while Mary's soul magnifies the Lord and her spirit rejoices in God her Savior (Luke 1:46–47). Hannah declares that the bows of the mighty are broken, but the feeble put on strength (1 Sam 2:4), while Mary sings about God showing strength with his arm and scattering the proud (Luke 1:51). Hannah sings about those who were hungry getting fat with spoil (1 Sam 2:5b), while Mary states that the Lord fills the hungry with good things (Luke 1:53). The LORD makes poor and makes rich; he brings low, he also exalts, and the poor and needy sit with princes (1 Sam 2:8), according to Hannah (1 Sam 2:7), and according to Mary, the Lord brings down the powerful and lifts up the lowly (Luke 1:52). The message is clear: "There is no Holy One like the LORD, no one beside [him]; there is no Rock like . . . God" (1 Sam 2:2; Luke 1:49).[29]

Journal/Meditation: What barrenness has God removed from you?

Prayer: Holy One, LORD, you are my rock. You break the bows of the mighty and give strength to the feeble. Hear the exultation of my heart for all the barrenness you have removed from me and bring me to life with your Son, Jesus Christ, born of the Blessed Virgin Mary, who lives and reigns with you and the Holy Spirit forever and ever. Amen.

2 SAMUEL

House I[30]

Text: 2 Samuel 7:1–5, 8b–11, 16

Scripture: ". . . [T]he word of the LORD came to Nathan: Go and tell my servant David: Thus says the LORD: Are you the one to build me a

---

29. References: CCC, pars. 722, 2619.

30. LM: 707. The Common of the Blessed Virgin Mary, First Reading, Option 3; CMBVM: Lectionary: 1. The Blessed Virgin Mary, Chosen Daughter of Israel, First Reading, Option B.

house to live in? Your house and your kingdom shall be made sure forever before me; your throne shall be established forever." (2 Sam 7:4–5a, 16)

Reflection: In the biblical world, the word *house* refers to a shelter, usually made of stone or mud brick with wooden joints and planks, within which a family eats and sleeps. Except for those with some monetary means, most houses consist of a single, all-purpose room. However, the word *house* can also refer to a dynasty. In the above passage from the Second Book of Samuel, David wants to build a house (Temple) for God, a dwelling place for the ark of the covenant, which resided in a tent in Jerusalem. However, the LORD tells Nathan, David's prophet, that he does not wish to have a house. Instead, he will establish David's house, his dynasty, kingdom, and throne forever.

This everlasting promise is terminated four hundred years later when the monarchy ends in 587 BCE. However, it is transformed into a messianic expectation that the LORD would raise up a messiah who would restore the nation of Israel to its former independence. In the CB (NT) this messianic expectation is transferred to Jesus through Joseph, fiancé of Mary (Matt 1:18; Luke 1:27), by the author of Matthew's Gospel (1:1, 20) and by the author of Luke's Gospel (1:27, 32; 2:4), even though Jesus does not fulfill the popular notion of what the messiah was supposed to do, namely, re-establish Israel as an independent nation. Mary is considered a chosen daughter of Israel because she conceives Jesus by the Holy Spirit (Matt 1:18; Luke 1:35), her womb becoming a house for God. The LBVMOCIBVM invokes her as chosen daughter of the Father.[31]

Journal/Meditation: What house has God established for you?

Prayer: From the rising of the sun to its setting may your name, O LORD, be praised. Through the Blessed Virgin Mary, you have established your house and kingdom in Jesus, your Son. Grant that I may one day join the chorus of praise where he lives and reigns as king forever and ever. Amen.

David[32]

Text: 2 Samuel 7:4–5a, 12–14a, 16

---

31. References: CCC, pars. 488, 496; DCC, par. 53.

32. LM: 543. Solemnity of St. Joseph, Spouse of the Blessed Virgin Mary, March 19, First Reading.

Scripture: "... [T]he word of the LORD came to Nathan: Go and tell my servant David: Thus says the LORD: When your days are fulfilled and you lie down with your ancestors, I will raise up your offspring after you, who shall come forth from your body, and I will establish his kingdom." (2 Sam 7:4–5a, 12)

Reflection: On March 19, the Solemnity of St. Joseph, Spouse of the Blessed Virgin Mary, the passage from the Second Book of Samuel in the HB (OT) is meant to reinforce Joseph as a descendant or son of David (Matt 1:20). Because Mary is engaged or betrothed to Joseph (Matt 1:18; Luke 1:27, 2:5), he is referred to as her husband (Matt 1:19). Even though Joseph is not the biological father of Jesus, CB (NT) authors consider him Jesus' foster father, and this makes Jesus a legal descendant or son of David. The Blessed Virgin Mary, fiancée, spouse, and wife of Joseph is the means for God's Son to be born into the world and fulfill the promise the LORD made to David through Nathan.

Adoption may be the more appropriate word to describe this biblical concept. Today, many adults adopt children from their own and other countries. Grandparents often adopt their grandchildren. Uncles and aunts may adopt their nephews and nieces. Even though the modern understanding of adoption was not operative in the biblical world, Joseph adopts Jesus as his son, and this makes Jesus a son of David. How Joseph is a descendant of David is not revealed by CB (NT) authors, especially in light of the fact that the monarchy in Judah came to an end in 587 BCE with the deportation of King Zedekiah to Babylon and ten years before that with the deportation of King Jeconiah (Jehoiachin), Zedekiah's nephew, to Babylon! Almost six hundred years later, Joseph, spouse of Mary, appears as a descendant of David to serve as foster father of Jesus.[33]

Journal/Meditation: Who has adopted (favored) you? Explain.

Prayer: LORD God, once you adopted David, son of Jesse, to be king of your people, and you promised him an heir to his throne. In the fullness of time you raised up Joseph, who adopted your Son, Jesus Christ, to fulfill the promise you made to David. Grant that I may live in your kingdom today, tomorrow, and forever. Amen.

---

33. References: BYM, pars. 23, 27; CCC, pars. 488, 496–497; DPPL, pars. 218–223; MC, par. 5; RM, par. 15.

Hebrew Bible and Old Testament

1 KINGS

Temple[34]

Text: 1 Kings 8:1, 3–7, 9-11

Scripture: "... [T]he priests brought the ark of the covenant of the LORD to its place, in the inner sanctuary of the house, in the most holy place, underneath the wings of the cherubim. And when the priests came out of the holy place, a cloud filled the house of the LORD ...." (1 Kgs 8:6, 10)

Reflection: After King David died, his son, Solomon, succeeded him to the throne. Solomon built the Temple in Jerusalem. And when it was finished, Solomon assembled all the elders of Israel, the heads of the tribes, and the leaders of the ancestral houses to bring the ark of the covenant of the LORD from the tent David had prepared for it to the Holy of Holies in the innermost part of the Temple under the wings of the cherubim. The ark, a box made from acacia wood, was overlaid with pure gold inside and outside (Exod 37:1–2) and in it were placed the two tablets of stone that Moses had placed there at Mount Horeb (Sinai). Then, just as the cloud, representing the LORD's presence, had settled upon the tent of meeting when Israel was a nation wondering in the desert, the cloud filled the Temple with the glory of the LORD. God was dwelling with his people.

The Blessed Virgin Mary is considered a temple of the Lord. The LBVM(LL) invokes her as a house of gold and an ark of the covenant because she, who was overshadowed by the power of the Most High, conceived and carried in her womb, a type of holy of holies, the Son of God. Furthermore, as an ark, Mary enshrines the author of the new covenant, Jesus Christ. Filled with the Holy Spirit, Mary is truly a temple of God's glory.[35]

Journal/Meditation: How have you experienced yourself as God's temple?

Prayer: LORD, you chose to dwell in the Temple in Jerusalem and to indicate your presence with a cloud. You chose to dwell on the earth in the temple of the Blessed Virgin Mary. Grant that I may one day enter

---

34. CMBVM: Lectionary: 23. The Blessed Virgin Mary, Temple of the Lord, First Reading, Option A.

35. References: BYM, pars. 25–27; CCC, pars. 497, 721–722; DCC, par. 53; MC, pars. 6, 26, 56.

your heavenly temple and behold your trinitarian glory, Father, Son, and Holy Spirit, one God, forever and ever. Amen.

1 CHRONICLES

Ark[36]

Text: 1 Chronicles 15:3-4, 15-16; 16:1-2

Scripture: "David assembled all Israel in Jerusalem to bring up the ark of the LORD to its place, which he had prepared for it. [The Levites] brought in the ark of God, and set it inside the tent that David had pitched for it; and they offered burnt offerings and offerings of well-being before God." (1 Chr 15:3; 16:1)

Reflection: Once King David is told by God through Nathan that God does not want David to build a Temple for him in Jerusalem, David, nevertheless, decides to consolidate his power over all the twelve tribes of Israel by brining the ark to Jerusalem, where he prepares a tent for it. In this way, David, the shepherd boy, not only lends legitimacy to his kingship, but he is able to state that the LORD chose him to be king and is with him in his capital city. Since the ark represents God's presence, the LORD resides in the same city as Israel's king.

The LBVM(LL) invokes Mary as both a house of gold and the ark of the covenant. Her womb is identified as an ark of the LORD, because it is filled with the presence of the Son of God. Thus, Mary is named the mother of the Lord by the LBVMOCIBVM. The LBVM(LL) invokes her as the mother of Christ—as does the LBVMOCIBVM—and the mother of the Savior. Just as David brought the ark to Jerusalem, so the child in Mary's womb makes his way to Jerusalem, where upon his death on a cross the curtain in the Temple is torn in two from top to bottom (Mark 15:38; Matt 27:51; Luke 23:45) to indicate that God now lives everywhere upon the earth.[37]

Journal/Meditation: Where do you locate God's presence?

---

36. LM: 621. Solemnity of the Assumption of the Blessed Virgin Mary, Vigil Mass, August 15, First Reading; LM: 707. The Common of the Blessed Virgin Mary, First Reading, Option 4; CMBVM: Lectionary: 19. Holy Mary, Mother of the Lord, First Reading, Option A.

37. References: BB, par. 1286; BYM, pars. 25-27; CCC, pars. 506, 963; DCC, pars. 52, 54, 55, 69; MC, pars. 6, 26, 56.

Prayer: LORD God, you chose to dwell with your people in a tent. Your Son, Jesus Christ, pitched his tent among people by becoming man in the womb of the Blessed Virgin Mary. Grant me a deep awareness of your presence as Trinity—Father, Son, and Holy Spirit—now and forever. Amen.

JUDITH

Pillar[38]

Text: Judith 13:14, 17–20

Scripture: "... Uzziah said to [Judith], 'O daughter, you are blessed by the Most High God above all other women on earth; and blessed be the Lord God who created the heavens and the earth, who has guided you to cut off the head of the leader of our enemies.'" (Jdt 13:18)

Reflection: The OT (A) book of Judith narrates a story about a warrior-woman named Judith, who puts into motion a plan to be captured by the leader of her people's enemy, the Assyrian Holofernes. He lures her into his tent, where, after he falls asleep, she takes his sword and beheads him! Then, after placing his head in a bag, she carries it to her people in Bethulia, exhorting them to praise God for his mercy in enabling her to destroy the enemy of Israel. Judith, a woman, is a pillar of strength in the midst of almost certain destruction. Uzziah, male leader of the magistrates of Bethulia, praises Judith as a woman blessed by God above all other women on earth.

It is not difficult to see from where the author of Luke's Gospel found the words for Elizabeth's blessing of Mary (Luke 1:42). Uzziah declares Judith blessed by God above all other women on the earth. Likewise, some of the words in Mary's response echo Uzziah's words declaring that Judith's praise will never depart from those who remember the power of God at work in her (Jdt 13:19–20; Luke 1:48b–49). The Blessed Virgin is invoked as a tower of David and a tower of ivory in the LBVM(LL). She is a stronghold, a pillar of faith, like Judith.[39]

Journal/Meditation: In your life who represents a pillar of faith? How?

---

38. CMBVM: Lectionary: 35.The Blessed Virgin Mary, Pillar of Faith, First Reading.

39. References: BYM, pars. 28–29, 142; CCC, pars. 489, 495; DPPL, par. 101; RM, pars. 13, 17–18, 25–27, 45.

Prayer: I praise you, Most High God, for not withdrawing your mercy from me. When my enemies looked to destroy me, you protected me. Keep me strong in faith and continue to shower your blessings upon me through Jesus Christ my Lord. Amen.

Hope I[40]

Text: Judith 13:17–20

Scripture: "... Uzziah said to Judith, 'Your praise will never depart from the hearts of those who remember the power of God.'" (Jdt 13:19)

Reflection: The complete tale of the exploits of the warrior-woman Judith can be found in the OT (A) book of Judith, who is remembered for having tricked Holofernes, the Assyrian army general, whose head she cut off with his sword! In a patriarchal culture, it was almost unheard of that a woman could rescue Israel from its enemies. But Judith did, and Uzziah, the male leader of the magistrates of Bethulia, reminds Judith that her praise will endure forever. Other versions of Uzziah's words to Judith declare that her hope will be remembered in the hearts of those who remember God's power.

God guides Judith in her plan to defeat Israel's enemy by instilling hope in Judith that overflows to the men of Bethulia, Judith's hometown. Like Judith, Mary was guided by God with hope, first with a pregnancy, then through the death of her Son on a cross (John 19:25–27). Furthermore, just as Judith's deed of hope lives on in the book bearing her name, so, too, does Mary's deed of hope live on in the gospel narratives. Both women are signs of hope in a world that may seem to be hopeless because they are led by the Most High God.[41]

Journal/Meditation: In what specific way is the Blessed Virgin Mary a sign of hope for you?

Prayer: Blessed are you, O God, who instill hope in people. Grant me a generous share of your power that others may see the hope I place in you and praise your name. Keep me walking in the straight path before you, LORD, following your Son, Jesus Christ, now and forever. Amen.

---

40. CMBVM: Lectionary: 12. The Blessed Virgin Mary at the Foot of the Cross II, First Reading, Option A.

41. References: CCC, pars. 489, 2619.

Heart[42]

Text: Judith 13:17–20; 15:9

Scripture: When the high priest Joakim and the elders of the Israelites "met [Judith], they all blessed her with one accord and said to her, 'You are the glory of Jerusalem, you are the great boast of Israel, you are the great pride of our nation!'" (Jdt 15:9)

Reflection: From an anatomical point of view, the heart is a hollow muscular organ located in the center of the chest that pumps blood around the body. From an emotional point of view, the heart is the source and center where people locate their deepest feelings. In the biblical world, the heart is the seat of intelligence and decision, what modern people would call mind or will. All biblical thinking is located in the heart, as is morality. In other words, heart designates character, and, as such, it is where God transforms a person with the Spirit he sends there and the love he pours there. Judith knows that only God can plumb the depths of the human heart and save the Israelites from their enemies (Jdt 8:12–17). As the leader of the magistrates of her city, Uzziah, makes clear, Judith speaks from a true heart, whose disposition is right (Jdt 8:28–29).

The Blessed Virgin Mary is presented as a type of Judith. Mary ponders events in her heart (Luke 2:19, 51). Both the LBVM(LL) and the LBVMOCIBVM invoke her as the queen conceived without original sin, that is, as one who possesses a biblical, immaculate heart. The LBVM(LL) also refers to her as the mother most pure, chaste, inviolate, undefiled, amiable, and admirable. The LBVMOCIBVM echoes those attributes with these: fountain of beauty, model of virtue, joy of Israel, and pride of the human race. Thus, it is not difficult to see how Mary is compared to Judith as the glory of Jerusalem, the great boast of Israel, and the great pride of the nation because of her true or immaculate heart.[43]

Journal/Meditation: Whom do you know possesses a heart transformed by God through the Spirit of love? Explain.

Prayer: I sing to you, my God, for you, O LORD, are great and glorious, wonderful in strength, invincible. You send your Spirit to transform the hearts of those who believe in you. Give me the Holy Spirit and create in me a new and true heart that I may please you all the days of my life.

---

42. CMBVM: Lectionary: 28. The Immaculate Heart of the Blessed Virgin Mary, First Reading.

43. References: BYM, pars. 50, 52, 141; CCC, pars. 489, 964, 973; MC, par. 8; RM, par. 20; RVM, par 11.

Hear me in the name of Jesus, your Son, who is Lord forever and ever. Amen.

Judith[44]

Text: Judith 13:18bcde, 19 or 13:18, 19, 20

Scripture: "O daughter, you are blessed by the Most High God above all other women on earth." (Jdt 13:18b)

Reflection: The OT (A) book of Judith is a sixteen-chapter novel describing the exploits of a warrior-woman named Judith, who is lured to the tent of Holofernes, the general of the Assyrian army. After he drinks himself drunk, Judith takes his sword and cuts off his head in order to bring victory to her people. King Uzziah of Judah, also known as Azariah (785–742 BCE), praises Judith's deed (Jdt 13:18) and declares that her praise will never leave the hearts of those who remember God's power at work in her (Jdt 13:19–20). Uzziah's blessing of Judith resembles another warrior-woman's blessing, namely, Deborah's blessing of Jael (Judg 5:24) and to a lesser extend Melchizedek's blessing of Abraham (Gen 14:19–20). The blessing is also the source of Elizabeth's words to Mary in Luke's Gospel: "Blessed are you among women, and blessed is the fruit of your womb" (Luke 1:42b).

Uzziah's words blessing Judith are applied to the Blessed Virgin Mary. She is a daughter of Judah who has been blessed by the Most High God (Luke 1:32) from the moment of her conception in the womb of her mother and prepared by him to be the mother of his Son, Jesus Christ. Her praise never departs from the hearts of those who remember the power of God (Jdt 13:19), because all generations call her blessed (Luke 1:48b). The perpetual honor given to Judith in memory of her deed (Jdt

---

44. LM: 531. Optional Memorial of Our Lady of Lourdes, February 11, Responsorial Psalm; LM: 613. Optional Memorial of the Dedication of the Basilica of St. Mary Major, August 5, Responsorial Psalm; LM: 690A. Feast of Our Lady of Guadalupe, December 12, Responsorial Psalm; LM: 709. The Common of the Blessed Virgin Mary, Responsorial Psalm, Option 2; LM: 1002. The Blessed Virgin Mary, I. The Blessed Virgin Mary, Mother of the Church, Responsorial Psalm; CMBVM: Lectionary: 25. The Blessed Virgin Mary, Image and Mother of the Church I, Responsorial Psalm; CMBVM: Lectionary: 31. The Blessed Virgin Mary, Fountain of Salvation II, Responsorial Psalm.

13:20) is bestowed upon Mary in memory of her deed of giving birth to the Son of God (Luke 2:11–7).[45]

Journal/Meditation: For what deed do you want people to remember you?

Prayer: Most High God, creator of the heavens and the earth, you gave your strength to your servant Judith and blessed her among all other women on earth. You gave your Holy Spirit to your servant Mary and blessed her above all other women. Grant your blessing to me as I remember your power as one God—Father, Son, and Holy Spirit—forever and ever. Amen.

Ransom[46]

Text: Judith 15:8–10; 16:13–14

Scripture: "The high priest Joakim and the elders of the Israelites said to Judith, 'You have done all this with your own hand; you have done great good to Israel, and God is well pleased with it. May the Almighty Lord bless you forever!' And all the people said, 'Amen.'" (Jdt 15:10)

Reflection: The "this" to which Joakim and the elders refer in their words to Judith is ransom Israel from the hand of Holofernes, the Assyrian army commander, by cutting off his head. Usually, the word *ransom* refers to an amount of money demanded or paid for the redemption of a person held in captivity. The OT (A) book of Judith portrays the nation of Israel in captivity before Holofernes. Judith, a widow, with a well thought-out plot lures the general into his own tent, where she removes his head with his own sword, and thus, frees Israel from his siege. The risk of her life, should her plan fail, is the ransom.

The Blessed Virgin Mary is compared to Judith. Like Judith, she is a woman in a man's world, but, again like Judith, she ransoms the world by agreeing to be the mother of Jesus while only engaged to Joseph and risking her life by being stoned to death. Through the incarnation, she gave the world the redeemer, who ransomed it through his suffering, death, and resurrection. Unlike Judith and Mary, the price paid for his ransom was his life! Judith risked her life to ransom Israel from its enemy. Mary

---

45. References: BYM, pars. 14, 18–19, 24–25, 53, 55, 118; CCC, pars. 488, 490, 511; DPPL, par. 101; MC, pars. 6, 17, 26, 28, 33, 41, 44, 46; RM, pars. 8–10, 13, 15, 27, 41; RVM, pars. 10, 16, 18, 20, 24, 33.

46. CMBVM: Lectionary: 43. Our Lady of Ransom, First Reading.

risked her life to ransom the world with the birth of Jesus. And Christ ransomed the universe by paying with his life.[47]

Journal/Meditation: How have you been ransomed during the past week? Who ransomed you? What was the price he or she paid?

Prayer: Almighty LORD, you blessed your servant Judith, who ransomed your people Israel from their enemy. You blessed your servant Mary, who gave birth to Jesus, who ransomed the world. Send forth your Spirit to bless me that I may be a faithful follower of Jesus Christ and that you may be pleased with me now and forever. Amen.

Mountains[48]

Text: Judith 16:13, 14, 15

Scripture: ". . . [T]he mountains shall be shaken to their foundations with the waters; before your glance [, O LORD,] the rocks shall melt like wax. But to those who fear you you show mercy." (Jdt 16:15)

Reflection: In biblical literature there is a genre known as the victory song. For example, after successfully crossing the Sea of Reeds and watching pharaoh's army drown in the waters, Moses and the Israelites sing a song of victory to the LORD (Exod 15:1–21). Another victory song is found in the HB (OT) book of Judges; here Deborah and Barak sing about defeating King Jabin of Canaan (Judg 5:1–31). The OT (A) book of Judith contains a seventeen-verse victory song that recounts Judith's beheading of Holofernes; the LORD foiled him with the hand of a woman (Jdt 16:5). With the beauty of her countenance, Judith undid him (Jdt 16:6d). The song gives the victory to God, who is great, glorious, strong, and invincible (Jdt 16:13). To declare how mighty the LORD is, the victor declares that the immovable mountains can be shaken and the rocks can melt like wax with God's glance (Jdt 16:15ab). And even with such power, the LORD shows mercy to those who fear him (Jdt 16:15c).

The three verses of Judith's victory song expressing the extraordinary help given by God to this warrior-woman are applied to the Blessed Virgin Mary, who helps Christians in time of need. In the CB (NT) the apocalyptic literature of the Book of Revelation presents the pregnant

---

47. References: CCC, pars. 484, 488, 495–6, 501, 504, 506, 723, 966, 973; DCC, pars. 56, 68; MC, pars. 26, 57; RM, par. 20.

48. CMBVM: Lectionary: 42. The Blessed Virgin Mary, Help of Christians, Responsorial Psalm.

woman giving birth to a son, who will rule the nations (Rev 12:1–6); the woman's son is a heavenly warrior who wins the victory over all who oppress faithful believers (Rev 12:17; 19:11–16). Thus, the son's mother protects those who wage the battle of faith by giving birth to him, just like Judith protected her people by defeating Holofernes. The Blessed Virgin Mary, invoked as the help of Christians in the LBVM(LL) and helper of the Redeemer and champion of God's people in LBVMOCIBVM, is like the unshakable mountains and their mighty rocks; only the LORD can tremble or melt them. To those who reverence him, he shows mercy.[49]

Journal/Meditation: What victory song in honor of God do you need to sing?

Prayer: O Lord, you are great and glorious, wonderful in strength and invincible. The mountains are shaken and the rocks melt like wax before your glance, yet you show mercy to those who revere you. Hear this prayer for help in all my needs; send your Spirit to guide me through your Son, Jesus Christ, Lord forever and ever. Amen.

ESTHER

Mercy[50]

Text: Esther C:12, 14–15, 25, 30

Scripture: "[Queen Esther] prayed to the Lord God of Israel, and said, 'O my Lord, you only are our king; help me, who am alone and have no helper but you.'" (Esth C:14 [Add Esth 14:3])

Reflection: Esther is a Jewess chosen by Persian King Ahasuerus to be his wife and queen. Her prayer follows her discovery that Haman, grand vizier, has a plan to eliminate all the Jews living in Ahasuerus's empire. She cannot enter the king's presence unless he summons her, so in an effort to save herself and her people she devises a plan to let the king know about Haman's scheme. Before taking her life in her hands, Esther places herself at the God of Israel's disposal because he is her true king, and only he can help her who is all alone. The full account of Esther's dilemma can be found in the HB (OT) book bearing her name or in the OT (A) book also bearing her name.

---

49. References: BB, par. 1286; CCC, pars. 494–5, 963; DCC, par. 62.

50. CMBVM: Lectionary: 39. Holy Mary, Queen and Mother of Mercy I, First Reading.

The Blessed Virgin Mary, who is invoked as queen of mercy in LBVMOCIBVM, fulfills the role of Queen Esther as one who prays for the salvation of people. Mary is also the mother of mercy because she conceived and gave birth to Jesus, the visible manifestation of the mercy of the invisible God. In John's Gospel, she shows mercy to those attending the wedding at Cana by interceding with her Son when the wine gives out. In Luke's Gospel, she declares that God's mercy is for those who fear him from generation to generation (Luke 1:50) and that God has helped Israel, his servant, in remembrance of his mercy (Luke 1:54). Just like Jesus, who teaches all to be merciful as the Father is merciful (Luke 6:36), Mary, the recipient of God's mercy, intercedes with the Mighty One to extend his mercy to all the children who call her mother.[51]

Journal/Meditation: In what specific way have you experienced God's mercy?

Prayer: Remember me, O Lord, and make yourself known in times of affliction with a generous outpouring of your mercy. Hear the prayers of Mary, the mother of your Son, and grant me help when I am alone and have no helper but you. I ask this in the name of Jesus Christ, who lives and reigns with you and the Holy Spirit, one God, forever and ever. Amen.

Mediatrix[52]

Text: Esther 8:3–8, 16–17a

Scripture: Esther said to King Ahasuerus, "If it pleases the king, and if I have won his favor, and if the thing seems right before the king, and I have his approval, let an order be written to revoke the letters devised by Haman son of Hammedatha the Agagite, which he wrote giving orders to destroy the Jews who are in all the provinces of the king." (Esth 8:5b)

Reflection: A mediatrix is a female mediator, one who works with both sides in a dispute in an attempt to help them reach an agreement. In the HB (OT) book of Esther, the queen serves this role. After she reveals the plot of the grand vizier, Haman, to kill all the Jews in King Ahasuerus's empire and the king orders Haman hanged, Queen Esther goes to

---

51. References: BYM, pars. 20, 24–36, 38; CCC, pars. 489, 964, 969, 973, 975; MC, pars. 18, 33, 57; RM, pars. 21–22, 45; RVM, pars. 14, 16, 21.

52. CMBVM: Lectionary: 30. The Blessed Virgin Mary, Mother and Mediatrix of Grace, First Reading.

the king and asks him to write a letter revoking the letters written by Haman containing his order to destroy all the Jews in the Persian empire. The king tells his queen that she and the new grand vizier, Mordecai, her uncle, can write letters revoking Haman's orders and seal them with the king's ring; any document sealed with the king's ring cannot be revoked (Esth 8:8).

With Esther as a model, the Blessed Virgin Mary is invoked as mother and mediatrix of grace. The LBVM(LL) invokes her as mother of divine grace, while the LBVMOCIBVM invokes her as full of grace. While Christ is the one mediator between people and God, his mother serves as a mediatrix, giving birth to him who gave the greatest of graces: redemption and salvation. In other words, Mary as mother gives birth to the author of all grace and, thus, serves as Jesus' companion in bringing about redemption. She is able to obtain abundant grace, like Esther, as mediatrix for all people.[53]

Journal/Reflection: In what recent way have you functioned as a mediator or mediatrix?

Prayer: God, you are gracious and bless you people with the light of your face. Grant me an abundance of your grace through the intersession of the Blessed Virgin Mary, mother of your Son, Jesus Christ, author of all grace, who lives and reigns forever and ever. Amen.

2 MACCABEES

Commend[54]

Text: 2 Maccabees 7:1, 20–29

Scripture: "The mother [of seven sons] was especially admirable and worthy of honorable memory. Although she saw her seven sons perish within a single day, she bore it with good courage because of her hope in the Lord. She encouraged each of them in the language of their ancestors. Filled with a noble spirit, she reinforced her woman's reasoning with a man's courage . . . ." (2 Macc 7:20–21)

Reflection: To commend a person is to praise him or her in a formal way. Thus, the mother of seven sons in the OT (A) Second Book

---

53. References: BYM, pars. 65–66, 68–69, 102, 107; CCC, pars. 969, 975; DCC, pars. 62–63; RM, par. 40.

54. CMBVM: Lectionary: 13. The Commending of the Blessed Virgin Mary, First Reading.

of Maccabees is praised for her noble reasoning and manly courage in counseling her seven sons not to renege on their Jewish faith in order to save their lives from the Greek ruler named Antiochus. While the much longer story about each of her sons and the mother's own death is not presented in the text, it can be found at 7:1–41. Seven, of course, is a sacred number, indicating fullness. In other words, not only are the sons full of faith, but they also represent the fullness of the presence of the Creator of the world (2 Macc 7:23).

The Blessed Virgin Mary is compared to the nameless woman in the Second Book of Maccabees. Mary is commended for having accepted the Word of God, conceived him in her womb, carried him for months, and given birth to him in the wonder of the incarnation. Her only Son, who is commended to his mother's care until he began his mission of teaching and preaching about the reign of God, commends her to the care of the disciple he loved as he hangs on the cross (John 19:25–27). And he commends the disciple he loved to his mother's care. Thus, the Blessed Virgin Mary is praised, like the mother of seven sons, for her noble reasoning and manly courage as she stood at the foot of the cross and watched her Son take his last breath.[55]

Journal/Meditation: For what great act of faith should you be commended?

Prayer: Ever-living God, your Son commended his mother to the beloved disciple's care and the beloved disciple to his mother's care. Grant that I may be counted among your adopted children and commended in your eternal reign through Jesus Christ my Lord. Amen.

---

55. References: BYM, pars. 37, 115; CCC, par. 2619; RM, pars. 23–24, 45; RVM, pars. 7, 10.

PSALMS

Son[56]

Text: Psalm 2:7–8, 10–11ab

Scripture: "I will tell of the decree of the LORD: He said to me, 'You are my son; today I have begotten you.'" (Ps 2:7)

Reflection: Psalm 2 is a royal song which was probably used during the coronation ceremony of Judah's kings, identifying them as the LORD's anointed (*messiah* in Hebrew; *christ* in Greek). In the four verses presented in the Lectionary of the CMBVM, the king is presented as the speaker; he announces the LORD's decree. The word of God the king has heard is that the king is the LORD's adopted son as of the day of his enthronement. In a manner of speaking, the king's coronation day is the day he is begotten as a son of God. Furthermore, the king is charged with representing God's universal sovereignty; therefore, all other rulers should subject themselves to the LORD's rule in the person of the King of Judah. Of course, this is hyperbole, obvious exaggeration used for effect. The tiny kingdom of Judah had great difficulty defending itself from all the other kingdoms surrounding it until it fell to the Babylonians in 587 BCE.

The first part of the LORD's decree, "You are my son," appears in the CB (NT). At the baptism scene in Mark's Gospel, the voice from heaven declares it, and at the transfiguration the voice from the cloud repeats it (Mark 1:11; 9:7). Because the author of Matthew's Gospel used Mark as one of his sources, he records the same words (Matt 3:17; 17:5), as does the author of Luke's Gospel, who also used Mark as one of his sources (Luke 3:22b; 9:35). Following Mark's lead, all three writers add material from the prophet Isaiah (42:1b) to the words spoken by the LORD. This confirms that Jesus is a Son of God, and it prepares the reader for the declaration that he is the King of Israel (Mark 15:32; Matt 27:42) and King of the Jews (Mark 15:2, 9, 12, 18, 26; Matt 2:2; 27:11, 29, 37; Luke 23:3, 37, 38). Since the Blessed Virgin Mary gives birth to Jesus, a Son of God and King of the Jews, she is honored as the queen mother. Through her, the LORD has made the nations Jesus' heritage (Ps 2:8a).[57]

---

56. CMBVM: Lectionary: 5. The Blessed Virgin Mary, Mother of the Savior, Responsorial Psalm, Option B; CMBVM: Lectionary: Appendix, Responsorial Psalm, Option 7 (Optional Responsorial Psalm in Mass 5).

57. References: BYM, pars. 8, 71; DPPL, pars. 107, 115, 119; MC, pars. 5, 11, 18, 26, 28, 57; RM, pars. 4, 31, 39; RVM, pars. 15, 21, 33.

Journal/Meditation: How did you become a son or daughter of God?

Prayer: LORD, at his baptism you named your Son the Messiah, the Christ. Anoint me with the Spirit, just like you anointed the Blessed Virgin Mary, that I may serve you all the days of my life. Grant this through Jesus Christ, who lives and reigns with you and the Holy Spirit, one God, forever and ever. Amen.

Wonder[58]

Text: Psalm 8:3–4, 5–6, 7–8 (8:4–5, 6–7a, 7b–9)

Scripture: "O LORD, our Sovereign, how majestic is your name in all the earth! (Ps 8:1a, 9 [8:2a, 10])

Reflection: Psalm 8 comes with its own refrain at the beginning and the end (Ps 8:1a, 9 [8:2a, 10]). The verse is directly addressed to God using the titles of LORD—the substitute word for Yahweh—and Sovereign—the word indicating universal reign. The verses presented above begin with the creation of the heavens and culminate with the creation of insignificant people, who live on the earth under the heavens. People are entrusted with ruling God's works on the earth. Out of his goodness, the LORD has given glory and honor to humans, even though they are lower than God on the hierarchical scale. That is why they stand in praise of the LORD.

The psalm presents wonder like that which many people do when watching the night sky away from city lights. While sitting or standing and gazing into the heavens at the stars, a person can reflect on the fact that some of those stars went out of existence ages ago, but their light is just now reaching the earth! While looking at the moon in any one of its phases, one realizes that it is like a mirror reflecting the sun's light to the earth. If the reader were to fly in a spacecraft to the outermost limits of the Milky Way Galaxy, how big would the earth look and how insignificant would its inhabitants be? Such wonder can only help but lead a person, like the psalmist, to praise the LORD, who sent Jesus, his Son, to the earth through the cooperation of the Blessed Virgin Mary.[59]

Journal/Meditation: At what do you wonder? How does it lead to praising God?

---

58. CMBVM: Lectionary: Appendix, Responsorial Psalm, Option 10.
59. References: BYM, pars. 8, 71; MC, par. 32.

Prayer: O LORD, my God, how majestic is your name in heaven and on earth. Accept my praise for all you have made and for the life that you have breathed into me. Hear me in the name of Jesus Christ, your Son, who is Lord forever and ever. Amen.

Steadfast[60]

Text: Psalm 13:5–6 (13:6ab, 6c)

Scripture: "I trusted in your steadfast love [, O LORD]; my heart shall rejoice in your salvation." (Ps 13:5 [13:6ab])

Reflection: Psalm 13 is a prayer for help. It begins by asking the LORD if he has forgotten the pray-er and how long the pray-er will have to endure pain before God answers. Just as it looks like the petitioner is about to give up, the psalmist begins to sing about trust in the LORD's steadfast love. This thought about never-ending love enables the pray-er's heart to rejoice in God's salvation and to sing to God because he has been merciful to his servant.

The word *steadfast* means firm and unwavering in purpose, loyalty, or resolve. God is steadfast in love because he is love. He is constant even when people, like the psalmist, do not think that the LORD is listening. The two verses of Psalm 13 chosen for the Feast of the Nativity of the Blessed Virgin Mary illustrate the steadfast love God bestowed upon her by preserving her from sin. They also echo her song of praise in Luke's Gospel (1:46–55).[61]

Journal/Meditation: In what specific ways have you experienced God's steadfastness?

Prayer: O LORD, I trust in your steadfast love, and my heart rejoices in your salvation. I praise you, O God, because you have dealt bountifully with me. Hear this prayer of praise in the name of your Son, Jesus Christ, born of the Virgin Mary, and Lord forever and ever. Amen.

---

60. LM: 636. Feast of the Nativity of the Blessed Virgin Mary, September 8, Responsorial Psalm.

61. References: CCC, pars. 44, 493, 508, 722, 966–7, 2619; MC, par. 7.

Tent[62]

Text: Psalm 15:2–3a, 3bc–4, 5

Scripture: "O LORD, who may abide in your tent? Who may dwell on your holy hill?" (Ps 15:1)

Reflection: Psalm 15 begins with two questions posed to God. Both questions ask exactly the same thing: Who may abide or dwell in the Jerusalem Temple? The first question uses the word *tent* to refer to the days of the Israelites' wondering in the desert. The *holy hill* refers to Mount Zion upon which Solomon built the Temple. In its earliest form, this psalm was probably used as a processional song as people entered the Temple precincts. In its current form, it answers the questions posed at the beginning by presenting the behavior that illustrates the lifestyle of those who are righteous. Thus, those who enter the Temple do what is right and speak the truth. They avoid slander, keep their promises, do not practice usury, and do not bribe. In other words, those who are devoted totally to God can abide in the LORD's tent and dwell on his holy hill.

As a mother and teacher in the Spirit, the Blessed Virgin Mary was the LORD's temple. By the power of the Holy Spirit she conceived in her womb the Son of God. He found her to be a worthy place to dwell and from which to be born. By her lifestyle, Mary of Nazareth is a model of cooperation with God. She did what was right. She spoke the truth. She did not slander her neighbor, practice usury, or bribe anyone. She kept the promise she made to the LORD. Thus, not only was she totally devoted to God and entitled to enter his Temple, but she became a dwelling place for the incarnate Word.[63]

Journal/Meditation: How does your lifestyle reflect righteousness?

Prayer: O LORD, who direct the footsteps of those who trust you, grant that I may walk blamelessly before you and be admitted to your heavenly tent. I ask this in the name of your Son, Jesus Christ, who lives and reigns with you and the Holy Spirit, one God, forever and ever. Amen.

---

62. CMBVM: Lectionary: 32. The Blessed Virgin Mary, Mother and Teacher in the Spirit, Responsorial Psalm.

63. References: BYM, pars. 25–27; MC, pars. 6, 26, 37, 56; RM, pars. 1, 4, 9, 11, 24; RVM, par. 24.

Sheol[64]

Text: Psalm 16:5 and 8, 9–10, 11

Scripture: "... [Y]ou [, LORD,] do not give me up to Sheol, or let your faithful one see the Pit. You show me the path of life. In your presence there is fullness of joy; in your right hand are pleasures forevermore." (Ps 16:10–11)

Reflection: The verses of Psalm 16 alternate between prayer and expressions of faith. It opens with the singer declaring that he or she has taken refuge in God; thus, the LORD is asked to provide protection (Ps 16:1) and counsel (Ps 16:7). This enables the singer to be glad and rejoice (Ps 16:9). The psalmist trusts that God will not let him or her enter Sheol, the Pit, the underworld, or the netherworld. Ancient cosmology presumed the world was built like a three-storied skyscraper! On the top level—the heavens—lived God. On the middle level—the earth—lived people. And on the bottom level—Sheol—lived the dead. While on the earth, the singer declares that God shows the path of life and provides the fullness of joy.

This psalm highlights some of the life of the Blessed Virgin Mary. First, she took refuge in God's protection by her willingness to trust the LORD's plan that she conceive and give birth to his Son. She chose the LORD as her portion, keeping his presence—both as LORD and Son—ever before her. Her canticle in Luke's Gospel (1:46–55) expresses the gladness of her heart and the rejoicing of her soul. And because God preserved her from all sin, she did not go to Sheol, but followed the path of eternal life blazed by her Son to the heavens, where she enjoys the fullest joy in the presence of God.[65]

Journal/Meditation: What path do you walk? Does it give you great joy?

Prayer: O LORD, you are my chosen portion, and I keep you ever before me. With the Holy Spirit guide my feet on the path of life to the kingdom where I will enjoy the fullness of your presence with your Son, Jesus Christ, forever and ever. Amen.

---

64. CMBVM: Lectionary: 12. The Blessed Virgin Mary at the Foot of the Cross II, Responsorial Psalm, Option B; CMBVM: Lectionary: 29. The Blessed Virgin Mary, Queen of All Creation, Responsorial Psalm, Option C; CMBVM: Lectionary: Appendix, Responsorial Psalm, Option 1 and Option 12 (Optional Responsorial Psalm in Mass 12 and 29).

65. References: MC, par. 18; RM, pars. 35–37; RVM, par. 20.

Metaphors[66]

Text: Psalm 18:2–3, 4–5, 6, 18–19 (18:2–3, 5–6, 7, 19–20)

Scripture: "The LORD is my rock, my fortress, and my deliverer, my God, my rock in whom I take refuge, my shield, and the horn of my salvation, my stronghold." (Ps 18:2 [18:3])

Reflection: Psalm 18 presents a list of metaphors for God; verse 2 contains at least six. First, the LORD is the psalmist's rock, the largest stone behind which he can hide for protection. Second, the LORD is the psalmist's fortress, a fortified, impenetrable military installation. Third, the LORD is the psalmist's deliverer; he rescues him. Fourth, on an individual level, the LORD is the psalmist's shield, a piece of armor carried on the arm and used as protection against weapon blows, arrows, bullets, or projectiles. Fifth, the LORD is a horn of salvation for the psalmist; a horn represents success, strength, victory, and vindication. And sixth, the LORD is the psalmist's stronghold, a place that is easily defended because of its fortifications. Thus, states the psalmist, "I call upon the LORD, who is worthy to be praised, so I shall be saved from my enemies" (Ps 18:3 [18:4]).

For the Blessed Virgin Mary, God was her rock, her fortress, her deliverer, her shield, her horn of salvation, and her stronghold. The LORD was Mary's rock behind which she could hide for protection (Luke 1:28). He was her fortress which could not be breached (Luke 1:35). He rescued her from the shame of being an unmarried, pregnant teen (Matt 1:18–25). The LORD's arm was her shield of strength (Luke 1:51), and his merciful horn of salvation did great things in her (Luke 1:49–50). The LORD was Mary's stronghold, uniquely presented in John's Gospel when Jesus commends his mother to the beloved disciple and entrusts the beloved disciple to his mother (John 19:25–27). Using the words of the psalmist, Mary can say: "[The LORD] brought me out into a broad place; he delivered me, because he delighted in me" (Ps 18:19 [18:20]).[67]

Journal/Meditation: What metaphors do you apply to God?

Prayer: I love you, O LORD, my strength, my rock, my fortress, my deliverer, my shield, the horn of my salvation, and my stronghold. When

---

66. CMBVM: Lectionary: 11. The Blessed Virgin Mary at the Foot of the Cross I, Responsorial Psalm; CMBVM: Lectionary: 13. The Commending of the Blessed Virgin Mary, Responsorial Psalm.

67. References: BYM, pars. 37, 115; CCC, par. 2619; MC, par. 20; RM, pars. 18, 23–24, 45; RVM, pars. 7, 10.

I call upon you, who are worthy of all praise, answer me through Jesus Christ my Lord. Amen.

Torah[68]

Text: Psalm 19:7–8, 9–10, 14 (19:8–9, 10–11, 15)

Scripture: "More to be desired are [the ordinances of the LORD] than gold, even much fine gold; sweeter also than honey, and drippings of the honeycomb." (Ps 19:10 [19:11])

Reflection: While the first half of Psalm 19 is a creation hymn (Ps 19:1–7 [19:1–6]), the second half is a reflection on Torah, the six hundred thirteen precepts divided into 248 commandments of what is to be done and 365 prohibitions of what is to be avoided. The synonyms for Torah employed in Psalm 19 are laws, decrees, precepts, commandments, and ordinances. According to the psalmist, Torah is to be desired more than gold, even much fine gold. In other words, God's Torah is richer than one of the most valuable minerals on the planet. Torah is also sweeter than honey dripping from a honeycomb. Since sugar was not yet available, the psalmist had nothing sweeter than honey to which to compare God's Torah.

In Israelite understanding, Torah was a basic structure of the universe. It gave order to the chaos surrounding the people. It encompassed all and made possible the preservation of life. By studying Torah one could acquire wisdom, be enlightened, and acquire a healthy, awesome fear of the LORD. Nothing surpassed its value. Mary of Nazareth was raised to appreciate Torah because it was God's word addressed to his people. As one who listened intently to the LORD's words, the Blessed Virgin Mary is a model disciple; she received and pondered the word. And just like her own people who reflected deeply on Torah, she reflected deeply on the incarnate Word she conceived in her womb. And just like her own people who discerned God's will through Torah, Mary sought to know the divine will and then to carry it out faithfully.[69]

Journal/Meditation: What is your process for determining God's will?

Prayer: O LORD, my rock and my redeemer, your Torah preserved the life of your people. Grant that the words of my mouth and

---

68. CMBVM: Lectionary: 10. Holy Mary, Disciple of the Lord, Responsorial Psalm.
69. References: BYM, pars. 78, 126; RM, pars. 1, 8, 17, 20, 45; RVM, pars. 11, 15.

the mediations of my heart on your word will be acceptable to you and bring me to eternal life with Jesus Christ, your Son, Lord forever and ever. Amen.

Motherhood[70]

Text: Psalm 22:3–5, 9–10, 22–23 (22:4–6, 10–11, 23–24)

Scripture: "... [I]t was you [, LORD,] who took me from the womb; you kept me safe on my mother's breast. On you I was cast from my birth, and since my mother bore me you have been my God." (Ps 22:9–10 [22:10–11])

Reflection: When the above two verses of Psalm 22 are taken out of context, they seem far removed from the opening line: "My God, my God, why have you forsaken me?" (Ps 22:1a) This song of lament portrays the broken relationship between the psalmist and God. To the singer God seems very far away. Verses 3–5 (4–6) declare God's holiness and remind the singer that time after time his people cried out to him and he delivered them. In the depths of his perceived forsakenness, the psalmist remembers that God delivered him of his mother and protected him at her breasts. God caught him when he emerged from the womb; this is why God has been his God—his mother—since he was born. After more lamenting, the psalmist sings about declaring God's name in praise to his brothers and sisters and the members of the congregation of Israel.

The seven verses of Psalm 22 totally removed from their original context illustrate the motherhood of God and are applied to Mary under her title of Mother of God. God's motherhood is illustrated in God's protection of the psalmist on his mother's breast. But even more so, it is demonstrated in the psalmist's words about being cast from birth on God. Just like a midwife or doctor receives the child emerging from its mother's womb and then places the child on its mother's breast, the psalmist declares that he was placed on God, who from the day of his birth has been his God. Mary is named Mother of God because she gave birth to Jesus, who was true God and true man. Because Jesus was true God, she is titled the Mother of God.[71]

---

70. CMBVM: Lectionary: 4. Holy Mary, Mother of God, Responsorial Psalm.

71. References: BYM, pars. 2–3, 62–64, 106, 109; CCC, pars. 495, 509, 963–4, 971, 973, 975, 2619; CSL, par. 103; DCC, pars. 52–54, 56–57, 63, 66–67, 69; DPPL, pars. 107, 115; MC, pars. 5, 11, 14, 28, 32; RM, pars. 4, 31, 39; RVM, par. 33.

Journal/Meditation: What mothering role has God served in your life?

Prayer: My God, you took me from my mother's womb and kept me safe on her breast. For this and all your mighty works in my life, I praise you and tell of your holy name—Father, Son, and Holy Spirit—to all the world now and forever. Amen.

Sovereign[72]

Text: Psalm 24:1–2, 3–4ab, 5–6

Scripture: "The earth is the LORD's and all that is in it, the world, and those who live in it." (Ps 24:1)

Reflection: The opening line of Psalm 24 declares the LORD's sovereignty. A sovereign is one, usually a monarch, who possesses supreme authority and power. Throughout the Bible, God is declared to be the creator; that is why Psalm 24 begins by declaring that everything—earth, world, people—belongs to the LORD. In order to further emphasize this, it declares that God founded the earth on the seas and established it upon the rivers (Ps 24:2); water represents chaos. Thus, when God creates the earth and tames the waters, he creates order out of primeval chaos. The psalmist asks who is worthy to stand before the divine, creating presence, and his answer is the clean-handed and pure-hearted. Only they may join those seeking the face of the God of Jacob (Israel).

This psalm, probably sung as accompaniment to a procession carrying the ark of the covenant into the Temple, is used to honor the Blessed Virgin Mary, who is considered a new ark of the covenant because she conceived the Word of God in her womb and carried him faithfully for nine months until he was born. She is worthy to ascend God's holy hill because she bears the Holy One of Israel. She possesses clean hands and pure heart. And there is no doubt that she received countless blessings from the LORD for her willing cooperation in bringing his salvation into the world. Never had it been heard that a creature carried within herself the sovereign Creator.[73]

---

72. CMBVM: Lectionary: 23. The Blessed Virgin Mary, Temple of the Lord, Responsorial Psalm, Option C; CMBVM: Lectionary: 46. The Blessed Virgin Mary, Gate of Heaven, Responsorial Psalm, Option B; CMBVM: Lectionary: Appendix, Responsorial Psalm, Option 2 (Optional Responsorial Psalm in Mass 23 and 46).

73. References: BYM, par. 25; CCC, pars. 144, 494, 511; MC, pars. 6, 26.

Journal/Meditation: How do you appear before the sovereign LORD?

Prayer: Divine Sovereign, Creator of everything, bestow your blessings upon me. Give me clean hands and a pure heart that I may be counted in the company of those who seek and see your face. Hear my prayer in the name of Jesus Christ my Lord. Amen.

King[74]

Text: Psalm 24:7, 8, 9, 10

Scripture: "Who is the King of glory? The LORD, strong and mighty, the LORD mighty in battle." (Ps 24:8)

Reflection: In the processional song known as Psalm 24, the priests and worshipers engage in an exchange as they approach the Temple gates. The gates are addressed as if they are persons and told to lift up their heads; likewise, the Temple doors are told to lift up their heads so that God, identified as the King of glory, can enter. Most likely, this processional song was sung when the ark of the covenant was brought into the Jerusalem Temple. The priests ask the congregation, "Who is the King of glory?" and those in procession answer, "The LORD, strong and mighty, the LORD mighty in battle" (Ps 24:8). Again, the gates and doors are told to open to receive the King of glory, and again the question is asked to identify the King of glory; the answer is that the LORD of hosts is the king of glory (Ps 24:10). The first answer about being strong and mighty in battle refers to the ordering of chaos through creation in the first half of the psalm (24:1–2). The second answer about being the LORD of hosts refers to the army of Israel and the heavenly army of divine beings surrounding the heavenly throne.

This psalm is used on the Presentation of the Lord because it compliments Luke's unique story about the child Jesus being brought to the Jerusalem Temple and presented to the LORD (Luke 2:22–40). Keeping in mind that the word *LORD* (translated from *Adonai*) is a substitute for Yahweh in the HB (OT), Jesus, the Lord, is presented to the LORD by his parents, Mary and Joseph. Not only is he presented to the LORD, but he is brought to the LORD's dwelling place, the Temple in Jerusalem. The

---

74. LM: 524. Feast of the Presentation of the Lord, February 2, Responsorial Psalm; CMBVM: Lectionary: 7. The Blessed Virgin Mary and the Presentation of the Lord, Responsorial Psalm.

Lord comes to meet the LORD, according to Luke's story. God comes to meet God. That is why in a later story, Jesus will declare the Temple to be his Father's house (Luke 2:49). Thus, the question of Psalm 24—Who is the King of glory?—now yields two answers: the LORD and the Lord.[75]

Journal/Meditation: What gate or door do you open to receive the LORD and the Lord?

Prayer: King of glory, you are strong and mighty. As I open the door of my heart, come to dwell there. You, LORD, are one God—Father, Son (Lord), and Holy Spirit—living and reigning forever and ever. Amen.

House II[76]

Text: Psalm 27:1, 3, 4, 5

Scripture: "One thing I asked of the LORD, that will I seek after: to live in the house of the LORD all the days of my life, to behold the beauty of the LORD, and to inquire in his temple." (Ps 27:4)

Reflection: After establishing the fact that the LORD is light and the stronghold of life, the psalmist expresses faith that nothing can cause him to fear. The metaphor used to counter fear is house, a place of security. That is why the singer declares that he will ask only one thing of the LORD, namely to live in the LORD's house all his days. In the Temple, the LORD's house, the psalmist finds refuge, which is similar to the safety most people associate with going home. The psalmist develops the metaphor by stating that the LORD's beauty is beheld in his house, and he can ask questions of the LORD there. Home is where people keep what they identify as beautiful—spouse, children, paintings, sculptures, furniture, etc. Home is where people inquire into each other's day—activities and words. Home provides an environment of security.

The words of Psalm 27 illustrate the faith of the Blessed Virgin Mary. The LORD, indeed, was her light of salvation, preserving her from all sin from the moment of her conception in her mother's womb. The LORD was the stronghold of her life after she said yes to conceiving his Son in her virgin womb and giving birth to him. In a way of understanding, she lived in the house of the LORD in Nazareth with her Son, Jesus, in whom

---

75. References: DPPL, pars. 107, 120, 122–3; MC, pars. 7, 20, 57; RM, par. 16; RVM, par. 20.

76. CMBVM: Lectionary: 35. The Blessed Virgin Mary, Pillar of Faith, Responsorial Psalm.

she beheld God's beauty, glory, and love. Not only did the LORD shelter her with the Holy Spirit and conceal her in the tent of his grace, but he set her high upon the heavenly rock and crowned her as queen of heaven, according to the LBVMOCIBVM.[77]

Journal/Meditation: In what ways does your home offer you security?

Prayer: LORD, you are my light and my salvation, and I have nothing to fear. Keep me safe in your earthly house and grant that I may one day behold your beauty in your heavenly home. I ask this in the name of your Son, Jesus Christ. Amen.

Refuge[78]

Text: Psalm 31:1–2a, 2b–3, 4–5, 14–15, 19 (31:2–3b, 3c–4, 5–6, 15–16, 20) or 31:1–2a, 2b–3, 4–5, 14–15, 19 (31:2 and 3b, 3cd–4, 5–6, 15–16, 20)

Scripture: "Into your hand I commit my spirit; you have redeemed me, O LORD, faithful God." (Ps 31:5 [31:6])

Reflection: The singer of Psalm 31 seeks refuge in the LORD (Ps 31:1 [31:2]). Refuge describes a sheltered or protected state rendering a person safe from something threatening, harmful, or unpleasant. The psalmist describes the LORD's refuge as a rock and strong fortress (Ps 31:2b [31:3b]). His trust in God enables him to place himself into God's hand, from which flows abundant goodness. This trust is illustrated in the Lukan Jesus' last words: "Father, into your hands I commend my spirit" (Luke 23:46). After he dies on the cross, he will await three days before the last part of the verse—you have redeemed me, O LORD, faithful God—is fulfilled by his being raised from the dead.

On the Memorial of Our Lady of Sorrows, the day after the Feast of the Exaltation of the Holy Cross on September 14, the Blessed Virgin Mary's heartache is remembered as she stood by the cross and shared in Jesus' suffering—uniquely Johannine (John 19:25–27)—and watched him die. She took refuge in the arms of the beloved disciple, but she trusted the LORD even more. It was he, her rock and fortress, who had

---

77. References: BYM, pars. 25–27; CCC, pars. 485, 490–2; 494, 508, 965, 973, 2617; MC, pars. 6, 26, 56.

78. LM: 639. Memorial of Our Lady of Sorrows, September 15, Responsorial Psalm; CMBVM: Lectionary: 12. The Blessed Virgin Mary at the Foot of the Cross II, Responsorial Psalm, Option C; CMBVM: Lectionary: Appendix, Responsorial Psalm, Option 16 (Optional Responsorial Psalm in Mass 12).

showered her with protecting grace. In him she placed her trust that on the third day the LORD, the faithful God, would redeem her Son by raising him from the dead. After entrusting her sorrows into God's hand, she experienced the abundant goodness he had prepared for her and accomplished in her because she took refuge in him (Ps 31:19 [31:20]).[79]

Journal/Meditation: How do you describe the refuge you take in the LORD?

Prayer: In you, O LORD, I take refuge. You are my rock and my fortress. For your name's sake lead me and guide me in the steps of Jesus with the Holy Spirit. Remove my sorrows with your abundant goodness and bring me to share in the life of all those you have redeemed forever. Amen.

Angel[80]

Text: Psalm 34:1-2, 5-6, 7, 8 (34:2-3, 6-7, 8, 9)

Scripture: "The angel of the LORD encamps around those who fear him, and delivers them." (Ps 34:7 [34:8])

Reflection: In the HB (OT), the *angel of the LORD* is a code phrase for God. Readers should not picture a human being with wings, as that is not what is meant by angel of the LORD. The angel of the LORD is God sending himself as a messenger. The messenger is the message! In other words, God is his own emissary; he sends himself to people for some important reason. The phrase is used to protect the transcendence of God, lest he become too imminent in his dealings with people on the earth. He directs the activities of Hagar (Gen 16:1–14), Abraham (Gen 22:1–19), Moses (Exod 3:1–6), Balaam (Num 22:15–35), Gideon (Judg 6:1–24), and Samson's parents (Judg 13:1–25), just to indicate a few. The note about the angel of the LORD encamping around those who fear him in Psalm 34:7 (34:8) refers to the angel of God who led the Israelite army out of Egypt and protected it before all the Israelites crossed the Red Sea (Exod 14:19). God not only led his people, but he also protected them from pharaoh's army.

---

79. References: CCC, par. 964; DPPL, pars. 136, 145, 151; MC, pars. 7, 11; RM, par. 16; RVM, par. 10.

80. CMBVM: Lectionary: 16. Holy Mary, Fountain of Light and Life, Responsorial Psalm.

The angel of the LORD encamped around the Blessed Virgin Mary. In Luke's Gospel, it is the angel Gabriel, whose name means *God is strong*, who brings Mary of Nazareth the gracious greeting that God wills that she conceive his Son in her womb (Luke 1:26–38). Earlier in the author's narrative, Gabriel had identified himself as one who stands in the presence of God and has been sent to speak good news (Luke 1:19). According to the psalmist, God is present to those who fear him; fear does not mean fright, but connotes trust in and dependence upon the LORD, who saves people. Certainly, Mary trusted God and tasted—experienced—how good God is (Ps 34:8 [34:9]).[81]

Journal/Meditation: How have you experienced the angel of the LORD encamping around you?

Prayer: I bless you, LORD, at all times. Praise is continually in my mouth for all you have done for me. Continue to send your angel to encamp around me and deliver me. Then, I will be happy taking refuge in you now and forever. Amen.

Offering[82]

Text: Psalm 40:6–7a, 7b–8, 9, 10 (40:7–8a, 8b–9, 10, 11)

Scripture: "Sacrifice and offering you[, O LORD,] do not desire, but you have given me an open ear. Burnt offering and sin offering you have not required." (Ps 40:6 [40:7])

Reflection: The psalmist's words about God not desiring sacrifices and offerings would come as a surprise to most Israelite ears. The HB (OT) books of Exodus, Leviticus, Numbers, and Deuteronomy are filled with prescriptions of burnt animal sacrifices and grain offerings. The psalmist is not discounting these; rather, he announces that the LORD prefers trust, offering one's whole self to him: "I delight to do you will, O my God; your law is within my heart" (Ps 40:8 [40:9]). The author of the Letter to the Hebrews in the CB (NT) uses Psalm 40:6–8 (40:7–9) to

---

81. References: BYM, pars. 14, 18, 24–25; CCC, pars. 485, 490, 494, 965, 973, 2617; DPPL, par. 101; MC, pars. 6, 17, 26, 28, 33, 41, 44, 46; RM, pars. 8–9, 13, 15, 27; RVM, pars. 10, 16, 18, 20, 24, 33.

82. LM: 545. Solemnity of the Annunciation of the Lord, March 25, Responsorial Psalm; CMBVM: Lectionary: 2. The Blessed Virgin Mary and the Annunciation of the Lord, Responsorial Psalm; CMBVM: Lectionary: 20. Holy Mary, the New Eve, Responsorial Psalm, Option B; CMBVM: Appendix, Responsorial Psalm, Option 9 (Optional Responsorial Psalm in Mass 20).

argue that God's wants obedience to his will as modeled in Jesus (Heb 10:1–10).

Five verses of Psalm 40 are sung on the Annunciation of the Lord in order to highlight the conception of Jesus in the womb of the Blessed Virgin Mary, who with an open ear listened to God and did his will. In the words of the psalm, Mary is heard to say, "Here I am; I delight to do your will, O my God" (Ps 40:7a, 8a [40:8a, 9a]). However, Jesus is also heard to say, "Here I am; I delight to do your will, O my God" (Ps 40:7a, 8a [40:8a, 9a]). This means that he takes delight in his incarnation in the womb of Mary of Nazareth and comes to abolish forever burnt offerings and sin offerings by offering himself on the cross in obedience to God once for all.[83]

Journal/Meditation: When have you most recently said, "Here I am; I delight to do your will, O my God"?

Prayer: Faithful and saving God, you take no delight in sacrifice and offering, but you exult when your people take delight in doing your will. Give me an open ear to hear your word and the strength of your Son, Jesus Christ, to do it that I may proclaim your steadfast love now and forever. Amen.

Ophir[84]

Text: Psalm 45:9b, 10, 11, 15 (45:10, 11, 12, 16)

Scripture: ". . . God, your God, has anointed you with the oil of gladness beyond your companions; at your right hand stands the queen in gold of Ophir." (Ps 45:7bc, 9b [45:8bc, 10b])

Reflection: Psalm 45 is unique not because its superscription indicates that it is a love song, and not because it was written to be used at a royal wedding of Judean or Israelite kings, but because it is addressed to the king (Ps 45:1b [45:2b]) and not to God! The handsome king (Ps 45:2 [45:3]), who is dressed militarily with sword (Ps 45:3 [45:4]) and bow and arrows (Ps 45:5 [45:6]), often victoriously rides his horse (Ps 45:4), while otherwise sitting on his throne with his scepter (Ps 45:6b [45:7]). There is no doubt that he is one of God's anointed sons (Ps 45:7bc

---

83. References: BYM, pars. 14, 18, 24–25; CCC, par. 964; DPPL, par. 101; MC, pars. 6, 17, 26, 28, 33, 41, 44, 46; RM, pars. 8–9, 13, 15, 27; RVM, pars. 10, 16, 18, 20, 24, 33.

84. LM: 622. Solemnity of the Assumption of the Blessed Virgin Mary, August 15, At the Mass during the Day, Responsorial Psalm.

[45:8bc]), dressed in royal robes and listening to stringed instruments (Ps 45:8 [45:9]), while his queen is at his right hand—the next place of power after the king's throne—clothed in fine gold mined in Ophir (Ps 45:9b [45:10b]), a gold-producing region on the southwest coast of Arabia on the Red Sea. While the king desires her for her beauty (Ps 45:11a [45:12a]), he, nevertheless, is her lord to whom she should bow (Ps 45:11b [45:12b]).

Once Jesus is declared to be the king of the universe, his mother is named queen. The Blessed Virgin Mary is declared to be the queen assumed into heaven, the queen of all the earth, the queen of heaven, and the queen of the universe in the LBVMOCIBVM. It is not difficult to see how the royal wedding song, Psalm 45, is applied to her on the celebration of her assumption or resurrection. Her wedding with God began the day she was conceived in the womb of her mother and reached a culmination with the birth of God's Son. Once she dies, is raised from the dead, and with joy and gladness enters the heavenly palace of God the King, she is crowned queen and takes her place at the right hand of her Son, who himself sits at God's right hand in glory. Because she is highly esteemed, she wears gold which highlights her virginal beauty. Her assumption into heaven completes her marriage to God.[85]

Journal/Meditation: What does each of the following invocations of Mary mean to you: Queen of Love, Queen of Mercy, Queen of Peace?

Prayer: O God, my heart overflows with a godly theme in praise of your name. With joy and gladness you led the mother of your Son to your heavenly throne and crowned her queen. Grant that I may share in the glory of your kingdom, where you live and reign with Jesus Christ and the Holy Spirit, one God, forever and ever. Amen.

Colors[86]

Text: Psalm 45:10–11a, 12c–14, 15–16, 17 (45:11–12, 14–15, 16–17, 18)

Scripture: "The princess is decked in her chamber with gold-woven robes; in many-colored robes she is led to the king." (Ps 45:13b–14a [45:14–15a])

---

85. References: BYM, pars. 36, 61; CCC, pars. 966, 969, 972, 974; MC, par. 26.

86. LM: 563A. Optional Memorial of Our Lady of Fatima, May 13, Responsorial Psalm; LM: 709. The Common of the Blessed Virgin Mary, Responsorial Psalm, Option 3; CMBVM: Lectionary: 29. The Blessed Virgin Mary, Queen of All Creation, Responsorial Psalm.

Reflection: Psalm 45 is a love song addressed to the Judean or Israelite king (Ps 45:1b [45:2b]) on his wedding day. After describing the king in military attire (Ps 45:3-5 [45:4-6]) and with enthroned accruement of his office (Ps 45:6 [45:7]), while dressed in royal robes (Ps 45:8 [45:9]), the lyrics turn to his fiancée, the queen, who stands at his right hand, dressed in precious gold robes (Ps 45:9 [45:10]). The queen is on the king's right because that is the next place of power after the king's throne. The queen is urged to forget her own people as she is joined to the king in marriage (Ps 45:10b [45:11b]). While the king desires her for her beauty (Ps 45:11a [45:12a]), he, nevertheless, is her lord to whom she should bow (Ps 45:11b [45:12b]). The queen is dressed in gold-woven and many-colored robes (Ps 45:13b-14a [45:14-15a]) as she is led in procession, followed by her virgin attendants (Ps 45:14b [45:15b]), to the king's palace (Ps 45:15 [45:16]). The psalmist promises the king sons (Ps 45:16 [45:17]) and a well-known and well-honored name (Ps 45:17 [45:18]) as a result of this union.

The LBVMOCIBVM invokes the Blessed Virgin Mary as queen of all the earth, of heaven, and of the universe. The words of Psalm 45 aptly describe her clothing as queen of all creation. However, in art Mary is depicted wearing a variety of colors. Sometimes she wears red to represent the blood of her humanity. Sometimes she is dressed in white to indicate her purity of heart. When she wears blue, the color of the heavens, the divinity of the One she carried in her womb is being indicated. A combination of red and blue presents her humanity wrapped in God's divine grace. Her renunciation of worldly values is represented by her dressed in brown. Her beauty may be depicted with floral clothing or depictions of flowers embroidered in gold. And, of course, her dignity as queen requires that she be presented wearing a gold crown.[87]

Journal/Meditation: What is your favorite color? What does it signify for you?

Prayer: With joy and gladness I praise you, O God, for having chosen the Blessed Virgin Mary to be the mother of your Son, Jesus Christ. May her radiant beauty of holiness continually inspire me to strive toward the kingdom, where you live and reign as one God—Father, Son, and Holy Spirit—forever and ever. Amen.

---

87. References: CCC, pars. 966, 969, 972, 974.

Gracious[88]

Text: Psalm 67:1–2, 4, 5, 7 (67:2–3, 5, 6, 8) or 67:1–2, 3–4, 5–6 (67:2–3, 4–5, 6–7)

Scripture: "May God be gracious to us and bless us and make his face to shine upon us." (Ps 67:1 [67:2])

Reflection: The word *may*, which introduces Psalm 67, is a modal verb (one used with other verbs to express possibility) indicating that something could be true, could have happened, or will possibly happen in the future. In the first verse of Psalm 67, *may* is used with the verbs *be*, *bless*, and *make* with a view to the future. The first possibility expressed by the psalmist is that God may be gracious; the singer asks that God display divine grace, mercy, and compassion to the community of Israel. The second possibility expressed by the psalmist is that God may bless; the singer asks that God bestow some of his holiness on the community of Israel. And the third possibility expressed by the psalmist is that God may make his face shine; the singer asks that God direct his divine light upon the community of Israel. The wishes expressed in Psalm 67:1 (67:2) echo some of the words of the priestly blessing found in the HB (OT) book of Numbers 6:24–25: "The LORD bless you and keep you; the LORD make his face to shine upon you, and be gracious to you."

These possibilities expressed by the psalmist and the author of the book of Numbers present images of graciousness, protection, and favor. Invoking the divine name LORD upon the community indicates that it belongs exclusively to God. That is why this psalm is used to honor the Blessed Virgin Mary. She was the recipient of the LORD's grace, mercy, and compassion from the moment of her conception in her mother's womb; in the words of Luke's Gospel, she is a "favored one" (Luke 1:28). Her relative, Elizabeth, addresses her as blessed among women (Luke 1:42) and as blessed for believing that the LORD would fulfill his promise (Luke 1:45); in other words, Mary is filled with holiness. God shined his face upon Mary with the Holy Spirit coming upon her and the power of the Most High overshadowing her (Luke 1:35); in other words, divine light surrounded her. Thus, all three possibilities expressed by the

---

88. LM: 18. Solemnity of Mary, the Holy Mother of God, January 1, Responsorial Psalm; CMBVM: Lectionary: 30. The Blessed Virgin Mary, Mother and Mediatrix of Grace, Responsorial Psalm.

psalmist in the opening verse of Psalm 67 become reality in the life of Mary of Nazareth.[89]

Journal/Meditation: How has God been gracious to you? How has God blessed you? How has God shined his face upon you?

Prayer: O God, I join all the peoples in praising you for the grace, blessing, and light you bestowed upon the Blessed Virgin Mary, mother of your Son, Jesus Christ. May you be gracious to me and bless me and make your face shine upon me until I come to share in your life in heaven forever and ever. Amen.

Justice[90]

Text: Psalm 72:1-2, 7-8, 10–11, 12–13 or 72:1-2, 7–8, 12–13, 17

Scripture: "Give the king your justice, O God, and your righteousness to a king's son." (Ps 72:1)

Reflection: Psalm 72 is a royal coronation song used as a prayer for the Judean king. Its opening verse petitions God to give justice and righteousness to the king. Keeping in mind that the king is the agent of God's will, the psalmist requests that God endows his earthly agent with divine justice and righteousness (Ps 72:2, 7). Biblical justice means giving to others what is due to them both morally and legally without any partiality. Biblical righteousness means doing the right thing because it is the right thing to do both morally and legally. Both of these qualities should be found in the king, who is the source of law, the administrator of justice, and an example to those he rules of God's justice and righteousness. This is why the psalm mentions the needy, poor, and weak (Ps 72:12–13); when they are protected and empowered, justice and righteousness exist.

Psalm 72 is used to portray Jesus, son of the Blessed Virgin Mary, as the new king who enacts justice and righteousness on the earth which result in peace (Ps 72:7). Throughout the gospels, Jesus enacts justice,

---

89. References: CCC, pars. 490, 493, 722, 968–9, 2617.

90. LM: 20. Solemnity of the Epiphany of the Lord, January 6 (in the United States, the Sunday after January 1), Responsorial Psalm; CMBVM: Lectionary: 2. The Blessed Virgin Mary and the Annunciation of the Lord, Responsorial Psalm, Option B; CMBVM: Lectionary: 3. The Visitation of the Blessed Virgin Mary, Responsorial Psalm, Option C; CMBVM: Lectionary: 29. The Blessed Virgin Mary, Queen of All Creation, Responsorial Psalm, Option B; CMBVM: Lectionary: 6. The Blessed Virgin Mary and the Epiphany of the Lord, Responsorial Psalm; CMBVM: Lectionary: Appendix, Responsorial Psalm, Option 4, Option 6 (Optional Responsorial Psalm in Mass 2), and Option 8 (Optional Responsorial Psalm in Mass 3 and 29).

giving to others what is due to them both morally and legally without any partiality. He heals the sick, casts out demons, feeds the poor, and raises the dead—both Jews and Gentiles. He teaches righteousness by doing the right thing because it is the right thing to do by breaking the sabbath law, ignoring purification traditions, and disrupting Temple economics. In the gospels, Jesus is presented as the new king, the new agent of God's will, who makes his epiphany, manifestation, in the world through the womb of the Blessed Virgin Mary. In the words of Psalm 72:17a: "May his name endure forever, his fame continue as long as the sun."

Journal/Meditation: How have you most recently done biblical justice? biblical righteousness?

Prayer: O God, give the rulers of nations your justice and your righteousness that they may stand as examples to the peoples of the earth. Fill me with justice and righteousness that I may serve the needy, the poor, and the weak. Grant that my name may endure forever before you. You are one God—Father, Son, and Holy Spirit—forever and ever. Amen.

Happy[91]

Text: Psalm 84:1–2, 4–5, 8–9 (84:2–3, 5–6, 9–10) or 84:2, 3, 4 and 9, 10 (84:3, 4, 5 and 10, 11)

Scripture: "Happy are those who live in your house [, O LORD,] ever singing your praise." (Ps 84:4 [84:5])

Reflection: Psalm 84 is a song sung by pilgrims as they made their way to Jerusalem on Mount Zion and the lovely Temple—God's house—in which the LORD dwells. The pilgrims express their longing for the Temple courts, while they sing this joyful song to the LORD (Ps 84:2 [84:3]). The sparrow and swallow are envied for the closeness of their nests to God. The singing establishes the theme of happiness (Ps 84:4, 5, 12 [84:5, 6, 13]); those who live in God's house are happy; those who make pilgrimage are happy; those who trust the LORD are happy. In other words, God is the source of all happiness. The song declares that a day in the Temple courts is better than a thousand anywhere else; the

---

91. LM: 17. Feast of the Holy Family of Jesus, Mary, and Joseph, Sunday within the Octave of the Nativity of the Lord [Christmas], or, if there is no Sunday, December 30, Responsorial Psalm, Cycle C; CMBVM: Lectionary: 8. Our Lady of Nazareth II, Responsorial Psalm; CMBVM: Lectionary: 23. The Blessed Virgin Mary, Temple of the Lord, Responsorial Psalm.

psalmist would rather be a doorkeeper in God's house that live in the tents of wickedness (Ps 84:10b [84:11b]).

Happiness is a theme that is presented over twenty times in the Psalter. Those are happy who take refuge in God (Pss 2:12b; 34:8 [34:9]; 40:4 [40:5]; 146:5), who do not follow the advice of the wicked (Pss 1:1; 119:1–2), who are forgiven (Ps 32:1–2), who care for the poor (Ps 41:1), who live in the Temple courts (Ps 65:4a [65:5a]), who have a just and righteous king (Pss 72:17b; 106:3), who fear the LORD (Pss 112:1; 128:1–2), who have sons (Ps 127:5), who get revenge and kill babies (Ps 137:8–9), and whom God disciplines (Ps 94:12). Likewise, the nation whose God is the Lord is happy (Pss 33:12a; 41:2a; 89:15 [89:16]; 144:15). All these references to happiness indicate that its source is centered in God. Those devoted to God find contentment and joy. The Blessed Virgin Mary's happiness is also centered in God. Her canticle of praise and joy (Luke 1:46–55) serves as a summary of all the happiness mentioned in the Psalter.

Journal/Meditation: In what specific ways does God make you happy?

Prayer: O LORD, my soul longs for your heavenly courts, while my heart and my flesh sing for joy to you. Hear my prayer of praise and bring me to your heavenly dwelling place. I ask this through my Lord Jesus Christ, who lives and reigns with you and the Holy Spirit forever and ever. Amen.

Peace[92]

Text: Psalm 85:8–9, 10–11, 12–13 (85:9ab–10, 11–12, 13–14)

Scripture: "Steadfast love and faithfulness will meet; righteousness and peace will kiss each other." (Ps 85:10 [85:11])

Reflection: Psalm 85 is a communal prayer for help from God to restore the Jewish people after the Babylonian exile (Ps 85:4 [85:5]). The psalmist hears God speaking peace to his people (Ps 85:8 [85:9]), those faithful ones who turn to him with their hearts. For those who fear the LORD, salvation is at hand, and God's glory will once again dwell in Israel (Ps 85:9 [85:10]). Throughout the Bible, steadfast love and faithfulness describe the essence of God's character (Ps 85:10 [85:11]). Steadfast love

---

92. CMBVM: Lectionary: 45. The Blessed Virgin Mary, Queen of Peace, Responsorial Psalm.

describes God's affection, which is firm, unwavering, loyal, and resolute for his chosen people. Faithfulness describes God's consistent trustworthiness, reliability, and devotion. When righteousness, the essence of God's will, kisses peace, the return of the people to their land, order is restored, and the LORD gives what is good to his people (Ps 85:12 [85:13]).

Both the LBVM(LL) and the LBVMOCIBVM invoke the Blessed Virgin Mary as the queen of peace. As such, she is one of those faithful ones who turned to God with her heart and brought salvation to the whole world by conceiving and giving birth to the Son of God. Her life bears witness to God's steadfast love and faithfulness; in love the LORD chose Mary from among all women, then he remained with her throughout her life. He made her righteous in his sight, showering her in grace, and he gave her peace. Through her Son, God restored order to the world that had devolved into chaos and saved those who listen to what the LORD spoke (Ps 85:8 [85:9]). The virgin of Nazareth listened and acted on God's word and knew profound peace.[93]

Journal/Meditation: What peace have you known from hearing and doing God's word?

Prayer: LORD, you were favorable to your land and restored order to the chaos resulting in the exile of your people. Remember your steadfast love, faithfulness, righteousness, and peace, and grant that I may walk in their path to the kingdom, where you live and reign with your Son, Jesus Christ, and the Holy Spirit, forever and ever. Amen.

City[94]

Text: Psalm 87:1–2, 3 and 5, 6–7

Scripture: "Glorious things are spoken of you, O city of God. The LORD records, as he registers the people, 'This one was born there.'" (Ps 87:3, 6)

Reflection: Psalm 87 is a hymn about the city of Jerusalem, built on the holy mountain named Zion (Ps 87:1). The psalmist declares that the LORD loves the gates of the city more than any other (Ps 87:2); thus

---

93. References: CCC, pars. 411, 144, 493–4, 508, 511, 966–7.

94. LM: 572A. Memorial of the Blessed Virgin Mary, Mother of the Church, Monday after Pentecost, Responsorial Psalm; CMBVM: Lectionary: 17. Our Lady of the Cenacle, Responsorial Psalm; CMBVM: Lectionary: 18. The Blessed Virgin Mary, Queen of Apostles, Responsorial Psalm; CMBVM: Lectionary: 26. The Blessed Virgin Mary, Image and Mother of the Church II, Responsorial Psalm.

glorious things are said about this city of God. In other words, Jerusalem is God's home, and from there he lays claim to all who know him, no matter from where they come (Ps 87:4-5). The LORD is portrayed by the psalmist as a census taker; he registers the peoples, declaring that each was born in Jerusalem (Ps 87:6).

The holy city Jerusalem, situated on the holy mountain of Zion, is an image of the Blessed Virgin Mary. She is like the city which the LORD loves and in which he dwells because the Son of God was incarnate in her womb. As Our Lady of the Cenacle—another name for the upper room—Mary is an example of peoples united in prayer, as she joins the apostles in prayer after Jesus' ascension (Acts 1:12-14), awaiting the gift of the Holy Spirit. Thus, the LBVM(LL) identifies her as queen of apostles, and the LBVMOCIBVM invokes her as queen of apostles and martyrs. Being the mother of Jesus, who entrusted her to the care of the beloved disciple (John 19:25b-27), and being found with his apostles in the upper room, Mary is an icon of the church at prayer. She is like a city founded and loved by the LORD to which all peoples are invited and in which all find a home.[95]

Journal/Meditation: What is your favorite city? How is the Blessed Virgin Mary like it?

Prayer: Most High, your servant David established Jerusalem as his capital, and on Mount Zion Solomon built the Temple in which you chose to dwell. After this earthly life, grant that I may be found to be registered in the heavenly Jerusalem, where you live with your Son, Jesus Christ, and the Holy Spirit, one God, forever and ever. Amen.

Sworn[96]

Text: Psalm 89:1-2, 3-4, 26, 28 (89:2-3, 4-5, 27, 29) or 89:3-4, 15-16, 26, 28 (89:4-5, 16-17, 27, 29)

Scripture: O LORD, "You said, 'I have made a covenant with my chosen one, I have sworn to my servant David: "I will establish your descendants forever, and build your throne for all generations."'" (Ps 89:3-4 [89:4-5])

---

95. References: BYM, par. 61; CCC, pars. 965, 2617; MC, par. 57.

96. LM: 13. Solemnity of the Nativity of the Lord [Christmas], December 25, At the Vigil Mass, Responsorial Psalm; LM: 543. Solemnity of St. Joseph, Spouse of the Blessed Virgin Mary, March 19, Responsorial Psalm.

Reflection: In 587 BCE, the Babylonians defeated Jerusalem, the capital of the southern kingdom of Judah, and ended the Davidic monarchy. According to royal Psalm 89, God declares that he made a covenant with his chosen servant David. A covenant is a sworn agreement between God and David. God swore that he would establish David's descendants forever—that someone from David's line would sit on his throne for all generations (2 Sam 7:4-16). This everlasting covenant—as it is often called—is unconditional; no matter how unfaithful a descendant of David may be, God does not terminate his agreement. However, once the monarchy ends, the meaning of the covenant is transformed into a messianic expectation; the hope is that God will provide a new anointed (messiah), who will restore the nation of Israel to its former independence and drive out the (Greek and Roman) occupation forces.

Parts of Psalm 89 are used on the Vigil of Christmas to proclaim Jesus as a descendant of David and the fulfillment of the expected anointed one (messiah). In the words of the psalm, Jesus is heard to say to God, "You are my Father, my God, and the Rock of my salvation" (Ps 89:26 [89:27]). Parts of Psalm 89 are also used on the Solemnity of St. Joseph to proclaim God's steadfast love and faithfulness (Ps 89:1-2 [89:2-3]) and to enhance Joseph's status as a descendant of David (Matt 1:6b-16, 20; Luke 1:27; 2:4); as foster-father of Jesus, this makes Jesus a descendant of David and fulfills God's sworn covenant to David that someone from his line would sit on his throne forever. In Matthew's Gospel, Joseph is presented as Jesus' legal father, but not his biological father, and the angel of the LORD directs him to take Mary, Jesus' mother, as his wife (Matt 1:18-25). In Luke's Gospel, the angel Gabriel appears to Mary, engaged to Joseph, and tells her that God has chosen her to be the mother of the Son of God (Luke 1:26-38). Thus, both on Christmas and on the Solemnity of St. Joseph, the everlasting covenant sworn to David is fulfilled in Joseph, foster-father of Jesus and fiancé of Mary, Jesus' mother.[97]

Journal/Meditation: What covenant has God sworn to you?

Prayer: I sing of your steadfast love, O LORD, and I proclaim your faithfulness to all generations. Father, you anointed your servant David and established his descendants forever. God, you anointed Jesus, David's descendant, and placed him on David's throne. Grant me a place in the kingdom, where you live and reign forever and ever. Amen.

---

97. References: BYM, pars. 23, 27; CCC, pars. 488, 497; DPPL, pars. 218-23; MC, par. 5; RM, par. 15.

Dust[98]

Text: Psalm 90:2, 3–4, 12–13, 14 and 16

Scripture: "Let your work be manifest to your servants, and your glorious power to their children." (Ps 90:16)

Reflection: Psalm 90 begins with God's eternity; God existed before he created the mountains or the earth. He is "from everlasting to everlasting" (Ps 90:2c). While God is immortal, people are not. As time passes, mortals return to the dust from which they came (Ps 90:3; cf. Gen 3:19). From God's point of view, a thousand human years are like yesterday (Ps 90:4); a divine thousand years are like a few human seconds. The wisehearted learn to count their years until they return to dust. However, they recognize that each day is a gift, a work of God revealed to people (Ps 90:16). God's steadfast love (Exod 34:6–7), God's eternity, gives them hope of seeing God's work over and over again in their lives. So, Psalm 90 ends with this plea: "Let the favor of the Lord our God be upon us, and prosper for us the work of our hands" (Ps 90:17ab).

On the Optional Memorial of St. Joseph the Worker, spouse of the Blessed Virgin Mary, the topic of the psalm is work. First, God works to create the mountains and to form the earth. Second, people, who are creations of God, work for the short time they inhabit the earth. Like Joseph, all people can do is be confident that God will show compassion and satisfy them with his steadfast love. Certainly Joseph saw and recognized God's work in his life. He heard God—in the person of an angel—speak to him in dreams (Matt 1:20–21; 2:13, 19–20). He also knew work; the author of Matthew's Gospel identifies Jesus as the Son of the carpenter and Mary (Matt 14:55). Joseph experienced the favor of the Lord. He recognized the manifestation of God's work. And God prospered the work of Joseph's hands.

Journal/Meditation: In what specific work of yours has God's work been manifested to you?

Prayer: God, you satisfy your people with your steadfast love and cause them to rejoice and be glad all their days. Let your favor be upon me and prosper the work of my hands that I may recognize the manifestation of your presence now and forever. Amen.

---

98. LM: 559. Optional Memorial of St. Joseph the Worker, May 1, Responsorial Psalm.

Trees[99]

Text: Psalm 96:1–2, 2–3, 11–12, 13 (96:1–2a, 2b–3, 11–12, 13)

Scripture: "Let the heavens be glad, and let the earth rejoice; let the sea roar, and all that fills it; let the field exult, and everything in it. Then shall all the trees of the forest sing for joy before the LORD; for he is coming, for he is coming to judge the earth." (Ps 96:11–13a)

Reflection: Psalm 96 was used in the Jerusalem Temple as attested in the First Book of Chronicles (16:8–36). It proclaims God to be king (Ps 96:10) and invites all the elements of the cosmos to acknowledge his reign. Both the top story of the three-storied universe—the heavens—and the middle story—the earth—are asked to be glad and rejoice (Ps 96:11). The sea and all the creatures living in it are told to roar their praise (Ps 96:11). The fields on the earth and everything growing in them are told to exult (Ps 96:12a). Even the trees in the forest are to sing for joy (Ps 96:12b), most likely a reference to the sound the wind makes blowing through their branches. All this gladness, rejoicing, praising, and exulting occur before the LORD who is coming (Ps 96:13).

This new song is sung to the LORD (Ps 96:1) on Christmas to announce the new birth of Jesus, born of Mary. Just as the psalmist tells of the LORD's salvation from day to day (Ps 96:1 [96:2]), an angel of the Lord announce to shepherds the birth of a Savior, who is the Messiah and Lord (Luke 2:11). Just as the heavens are invited to be glad, a multitude of heavenly host praise God by declaring glory in the highest heaven (Luke 2:14). And just as the earth is invited to rejoice, the angels declare peace on those God favors on earth (Luke 2:14). Angels in the heavens and shepherds on the earth represent the cosmic elements in Psalm 96 acknowledging God's reign come in the person of his Son, born of the Blessed Virgin Mary.[100]

Journal/Meditation: Today, what are the cosmic elements that herald the coming of God at Christmas?

Prayer: I sing a new song to you, O LORD, with the heavens and the earth for the salvation you have brought through your Son, Jesus Christ, born of the Blessed Virgin Mary. Grant me a share in that salvation that I may sing for joy in your presence now and forever. Amen.

---

99. LM: 14. Solemnity of the Nativity of the Lord [Christmas], December 25, At the Mass during the Night, Responsorial Psalm; CMBVM: Lectionary: 5. The Blessed Virgin Mary, Mother of the Savior, Responsorial Psalm.

100. Reference: DPPL, par. 109.

Dawn[101]

Text: Psalm 97:1, 6, 11–12

Scripture: "Light dawns for the righteous, and joy for the upright in heart." (Ps 97:11)

Reflection: Dawn is the first appearance of light in the sky as the sun rises at the beginning of a new day. The author of Psalm 97, an enthronement psalm declaring God to be king (Ps 97:1), uses dawn as an image of how the LORD saves his faithful people. The psalm begins with theophanic language: clouds and thick darkness, fire, lightnings, and melting mountains (Ps 97:2–5), echoing the experience at Mount Sinai (Horeb) (Exod 19:1–25). The theophanic images are meant to convey that the LORD is present to care for those who live righteous and just lives. Just as the daily dawn is reliable, God guards the righteous, those who have a healthy relationship with him. Just as the dawn brings the joy of a new day, the LORD is joy for the just, the upright of heart (Ps 97:11). Because of the mention of dawn, some verses of Psalm 97 are used for the Mass at Dawn on Christmas Day.

Another use of the image of dawn is found in Luke's Gospel. After the birth of John the Baptist, his father, Zechariah, declares that by the tender mercy of God, the dawn from on high will break upon them (Luke 1:78). The dawn from on high is a reference to the LORD liberating his people from various forms of captivity (Isa 42:7; Mal 4:2; Ps 107:10). The birth of Jesus is the dawning light for those who sit in darkness; his death and resurrection rescue those who dwell in the shadow of death (Luke 1:79). In the words of Psalm 97, Jesus, Son of Mary, is the light dawning for the righteous, and he is joy for the upright of heart.

Journal/Meditation: What does the dawn of a new day mean to you?

Prayer: You are king, O LORD, and earth rejoices at the birth of your Son, Jesus Christ. Fill me with the Spirit of righteousness and justice, the foundation of your heavenly throne. I rejoice in you and give thanks to your holy name—Father, Son, and Holy Spirit—now and forever. Amen.

---

101. LM: 15. Solemnity of the Nativity of the Lord [Christmas], December 25, At the Mass at Dawn, Responsorial Psalm.

Victory[102]

Text: Psalm 98:1, 2–3, 3–4 or 98:1, 2–3, 3–4, 5–6

Scripture: "All the ends of the earth have seen the victory of our God." (Ps 98:3b)

Reflection: In the first three verses of Psalm 98, the word *victory* appears in each verse. After stating that the LORD has done marvelous things (Ps 98:1a), the psalmist declares that God's right hand, indicating supreme power, and his holy arm, indicating his all-sufficient might and holiness, have gotten him victory (Ps 98:1b). The victory consists of saving his people from Egyptian slavery and liberating the exiles in Babylonian captivity. The LORD made know this victory to all the rest of the world (Ps 98:2), even to the ends of the earth (Ps 98:3b). Remembering his steadfast or unwavering love, he has demonstrated his faithfulness or reliability to Israel (Ps 98:3a).

This psalm is used for two victory celebrations. The first occurs on December 8, the Solemnity of the Immaculate Conception of the Blessed Virgin Mary. The Immaculate Conception is the victory of Mary's redemption from the moment of her conception in her mother's womb. This singular grace and privilege of God is understood in virtue of the merits of her Son, who saved his mother before he saved the human race. Thus, Mary is victorious over original sin. The second victory celebration is Christmas, the birth of Mary's Son. The incarnation and birth of the Son of God is a marvelous thing. All the ends of the earth have seen the saving victory of God in the person of Jesus of Nazareth. This is why the earth is invited by the psalmist to make a joyful noise to the LORD by singing joyous songs and praises using such musical instruments as the lyre and trumpets. This is exactly what the author of Luke's Gospel records at the birth of Jesus; a multitude of the heavenly host praises God, saying, "Glory to God in the highest heaven, and on earth peace among those whom he favors" (Luke 2:14).[103]

Journal/Meditation: What victory has God won for you?

---

102. LM: 16. Solemnity of the Nativity of the Lord [Christmas], December 25, At the Mass during the Day, Responsorial Psalm; LM: 689. Solemnity of the Immaculate Conception of the Blessed Virgin Mary, December 8, Responsorial Psalm.

103. References: BYM, pars. 10, 18, 21, 56, 102, 110–11; CCC, pars. 411, 490–93, 508, 966–7, 970; DPPL, pars. 101–2, 174, 195–6; MC, pars. 3, 11, 37, 56; RM, pars. 1, 3–4, 11, 24; RVM, par. 24.

Prayer: I sing a new song to you, O LORD, for you have done marvelous things. Continue to wrap me in your steadfast love, fill me with your faithfulness, and give me victory over whatever may assail me. Hear me in the name of your Son, Jesus Christ, who lives with you, Father, and the Holy Spirit, one God, forever and ever. Amen.

Being[104]

Text: Psalm 103:1–2, 3–4, 8–9, 13–14, 17–18a or 103:1–2, 3–4, 6–7, 8 and 10 or 103:1–2, 3–4, 6–7, 8 and 11 or 103:1–2, 3–4, 6 and 8, 13 and 17

Scripture: "Bless the LORD, O my soul, and all that is within me, bless his holy name." (Ps 103:1)

Reflection: Psalm 103 is a song of praise. The first two verses employ the word *bless*, which means to bestow holiness, to watch over, or to wish well. However, when the psalm was written, the word *bless* meant to kneel. Thus, the psalmist's opening words, which are addressed to himself, exhort him to acknowledge God's sovereignty by kneeling. Thus, to bless the LORD with his soul, his very being or existence—all that is within him—is the psalmist's invocation to bring his being to the knee before Being itself. He does this in recognition of the LORD's benefits: forgiveness and healing (Ps 103:3); redemption, steadfast love, and mercy (Ps 103:4); good, vindication, justice (Ps 103:5–6); grace (Ps 103:8); and compassion (Ps 103:13). Basically, because all comes from the LORD, the Creator, all human creatures should kneel before him in recognition of all he does for them.

That is why this psalm is used in the Mass honoring the Blessed Virgin Mary as the mother of reconciliation. Psalm 103 states the LORD forgives all iniquity (Ps 103:2, 10); he does not deal with people according to their sins (Ps 103:10). Rather, he removes transgression (Ps 103:12). Also, this is why this psalm is used in the Mass honoring Mary as mother of mercy. Psalm 103 uses the word *mercy* two times (Ps 103:4, 8) and the word *compassion* two times (Ps 103:13); mercy means that God does not give people what they deserve, and compassion means that he feels their

---

104. CMBVM: Lectionary: 14. The Blessed Virgin Mary, Mother or Reconciliation, Responsorial Psalm; CMBVM: Lectionary: 19. Holy Mary, Mother of the Lord, Responsorial Psalm, Option B; CMBVM: Lectionary: 39. Holy Mary, Queen and Mother of Mercy II, Responsorial Psalm; CMBVM: Lectionary: 44. The Blessed Virgin Mary, Health of the Sick, Responsorial Psalm; CMBVM: Lectionary: Appendix, Responsorial Psalm, Option 3 (Optional Responsorial Psalm in Mass 19).

weakness—the reason he shows them mercy. Psalm 103 states that the LORD "knows how we were made; he remembers that we are dust" (Ps 103:14). Finally, this psalm is used in the Mass honoring the Blessed Virgin Mary as the health of the sick. Psalm 103 states that the LORD heals all diseases (Ps 103:3) and satisfies people with good things as long as they live (Ps 103:5). Thus, because forgiveness, mercy, and healing come from the LORD, all human creatures should kneel before him in recognition of all he does for them.

Journal/Meditation: For what benefits do you need to bless (kneel before) God?

Prayer: I bless your holy name, O LORD, with all that is within me as I remember all your benefits. Continue to shower me with forgiveness, mercy, and healing. Grant that I may experience the fullness of your steadfast love in your kingdom, where you live with the Lord Jesus Christ and the Holy Spirit, one God, forever and ever. Amen.

Remember[105]

Text: Psalm 105:1-2, 3-4, 5-6, 8-9

Scripture: "Remember the wonderful works [the LORD] has done, his miracles, and the judgments he has uttered." (Ps 105:5)

Reflection: Remember is the key word to understanding the forty-five verses of Psalm 105, of which eight are used on the Feast of the Holy Family. In fact, the verses used barely get past the invitation issued by the psalmist to remember what God has done and offer grateful praise (Ps 105:1-6). The reason verses 8 and 9 are used is because they mention Abraham and Isaac, who are the focus of the reading preceding it (Gen 15:1-6; 21:1-3). Among the things that are to be remembered, according to the psalmist, are the following: God's judgment (Ps 105:7); God's covenant with Abraham, Isaac, and Jacob (Ps 105:8-11); God's protection of the people (Ps 105:12-15); Joseph saving Egypt and his family (Ps 105:16-25); Moses and Aaron leading the people out of Egyptian slavery after the plagues (Ps 105:26-38); the theophany, food, and water in the desert (Ps 105:39-42); and God's kept promise to give the land of Canaan to his people (Ps 105:43-45).

---

105. LM: 17. Feast of the Holy Family of Jesus, Mary, and Joseph, Sunday within the Octave of the Nativity of the Lord [Christmas], or, if there is no Sunday, December 30, Responsorial Psalm, Cycle B.

Psalm 105 serves as a song of memories about some of God's greater works among his chosen people. The act of recalling something or becoming aware of something that occurred in the past—remembering—is how the Hebrews, Israelites, and Jews keep their identity as God's chosen people. If they forget anything that the LORD has done for them, they also fail to remember who they are. In Luke's Gospel, the Blessed Virgin Mary is presented as one who remembers the events surrounding her Son's birth (Luke 2:19) and his being lost and found in the Temple (Luke 2:51b). In her canticle, she remembers what great things the Mighty One has done: showing mercy (Luke 1:50), scattering the proud (Luke 1:51), bringing down the powerful and lifting up the lowly (Luke 1:52), filling the hungry and sending away the rich (Luke 1:53), helping his servant Israel in remembrance of his mercy (Luke 1:54), and keeping his promise to Abraham and his descendants (Luke 1:55). Mary remembers and keeps her identity as one of God's chosen people.[106]

Journal/Meditation: What great events in your life do you remember? How do those memories create your identity?

Prayer: I give thanks to you, O LORD, calling upon your name as I make known your deeds among the peoples. I seek you to know your presence in the works you have done in my life. Hear this prayer of thanksgiving for your continual presence as Father, Son, and Holy Spirit forever and ever. Amen.

Sun[107]

Text: Psalm 113:1-2, 3-4, 5-6, 7-8

Scripture: "From the rising of the sun to its setting the name of the LORD is to be praised." (Ps 113:3).

Reflection: In ancient cosmology, the sun rose in the eastern sky every morning and set in the western sky every afternoon; it was understood to cross the heavens. In modern cosmology, the sun does not move; it is the earth that turns its face toward the sun and away from it every twenty-four hours. Psalm 113 not only reflects ancient cosmology, but

---

106. References: BYM, pars. 31, 118; CCC, pars. 144, 489, 712, 2619; MC, pars. 18, 45–6; RM, pars. 17, 20; RVM, pars. 20, 24.

107. LM: 627. Memorial of the Queenship of the Blessed Virgin Mary, August 22, Responsorial Psalm; LM: 709. The Common of the Blessed Virgin Mary, Responsorial Psalm, Option 4; CMBVM: Lectionary: 1. The Blessed Virgin Mary, Chosen Daughter of Israel, Responsorial Psalm.

it also presupposes a three-storied universe; God, who is high above all nations with his glory above the heavens (Ps 113:4), lives on the top story—seated on high (Ps 113:5)—and looks down on the heavens and the earth (Ps 113:6), the middle story. Since God is known by what he does, his name is praised because he raises the poor and lifts the needy from ashes (Ps 113:7) and he gives the barren woman a home with children (Ps 113:9). In other words, the lowering of God from above the heavens to the earth results in the raising of the poor, the needy, and the barren.

Psalm 113 makes the point that God's will is done in heaven and on earth. This is, of course, one of the petitions in the prayer that the Matthean Jesus teaches his disciples (Matt 6:10b). While the request that God's will be done on earth as it is in heaven is not in the Lukan version of the prayer (Luke 11:2-4), the Blessed Virgin Mary is presented as one who, indeed, does the will of the Most High God. She responds to the angel Gabriel, stating, "Here am I, the servant of the Lord; let it be with me according to your word" (Luke 1:38). Because Mary is the instrument for God's will to be done on earth, she is honored by the LBVM(LL) as queen of angels, patriarchs, prophets, apostles, martyrs, confessors, virgins, and all saints. The LBVMOCIBVM expands that list adding to it the invocations queen of love, mercy, peace, all the earth, heaven, and the universe. Both litanies also call Mary the queen conceived without original sin. Thus, from the rising of the sun to its setting, God is known by what he does in the life of Mary of Nazareth, mother of Jesus.[108]

Journal/Meditation: For what works of God in your life do you need to praise him today?

Prayer: I, your servant, praise you, LORD, and bless your name from this day on and forevermore for all your works. Look down on me from your heavenly throne and bestow the grace of the Holy Spirit and the wisdom of Jesus Christ upon me. You are one God worthy of all praise now and forever. Amen.

Cup[109]

Text: Psalm 116:12-13, 15-16, 17-18

---

108. References: BB, par. 1286; CCC, par. 966; RM, par. 3.

109. CMBVM: Lectionary: 11. The Blessed Virgin Mary at the Foot of the Cross I, Responsorial Psalm, Option B; CMBVM: Lectionary: Appendix, Responsorial Psalm, Option 15 (Optional Responsorial Psalm in Mass 11).

Scripture: "I will lift up the cup of salvation and call on the name of the LORD." (Ps 118:14)

Reflection: The first eleven verses of Psalm 116 set the stage for the last eight verses. The psalmist begins by expressing his love for the LORD, who has heard his voice and prayer (Ps 118:1–2). The singer recounts his near-death experience (Ps 118:3–4) and how God saved him from death, permitting him to walk in the land of the living (Ps 118:5–11). Because he was rescued from death, the psalmist asks rhetorically about what return he can make to the LORD (Ps 118:12) and answers his own question by saying he will lift the cup of salvation and call on the Lord's name in order to fulfill the vows he made (Ps 118:12–14). He will also offer a thanksgiving sacrifice and call on the LORD's name (Ps 118:17–18). The mention of the cup of salvation is a drink offering. In ancient understanding, God was given food (sacrifices of lambs, goats, bulls, etc.) with drink (wine). Jacob is the first to make a drink offering (Gen 35:14). Later, the HB (OT) book of Exodus specifies wine as a drink offering (Exod 29:40) as does Numbers (15:5, 7, 10; 28:7–8). The drink offering is poured into the fire on the altar or poured at the base of the altar.

The author of Mark's Gospel has the drink offering, the cup of salvation, in mind when he narrates that Jesus, Son of Mary, took a cup of wine after supper, saying, "This is my blood of the covenant, which is poured out for many" (Mark 14:24). Matthew's Gospel expands on his Markan source, portraying Jesus taking a cup and saying, "Drink from it, all of you [, disciples,]; for this is my blood of the covenant, which is poured out for many for the forgiveness of sins" (Matt 26:27–28). The author of Luke's Gospel also expands his Markan source, presenting two cups of wine; the first occurs before the supper (Luke 22:17), and the second occurs after the supper. Jesus tells his disciples, "This cup that is poured out for you is the new covenant in my blood" (Luke 22:20). Likewise, in his Letter to the Philippians, Paul urges his readers to remain faithful, even as he is "being poured out as a libation over the sacrifice and the offering" of their faith (Phil 2:17). The author of the Second Letter of Timothy also employs this image (2 Tim 4:6). Thus, the cup of salvation, which originally referred to a drink offering accompanying some Temple sacrifices in the HB (OT), becomes drinking the cup of Jesus' blood in the CB (NT).

Journal/Meditation: What do you return to the LORD for all his bounty to you?

Prayer: O LORD, I am your servant, whose bonds of death you have loosened through the death and resurrection of your Son. Through the intercession of the Blessed Virgin Mary, accept this thanksgiving sacrifice as I call upon your name and drink from the cup of salvation given to me by Jesus Christ, who lives and reigns with you and the Holy Spirit, one God, forever and ever. Amen.

Strength[110]

Text: Psalm 118:14–15, 16–17, 19–21

Scripture: "The LORD is my strength and my might; he has become my salvation." (Ps 118:14)

Reflection: The seven verses of Psalm 118 used as a response are only a very small part of the twenty-nine verses of this thanksgiving song to the LORD, whose steadfast love endures forever (Ps 118:1–4). The psalmist is thankful that God delivered him from some unidentified distress (Ps 118:5–13), which he compares to swarming bees or blazing fire in thorn bushes (Ps 118:12). He compares his deliverance to the exodus, quoting exactly the words that Moses and the Israelites sang to the LORD after crossing the Red Sea and being delivered from pharaoh and his army: "The LORD is my strength and my might, and he has become my salvation" (Exod 15:2). The right hand of the LORD (Ps 118:15b–16) has preserved the psalmist's life (Ps 118:18). Thus, he enters the gates of the Temple to give thanks to God for having answered his prayer (Ps 118:19–21).

The author of Luke's Gospel presents the Blessed Virgin Mary as a woman of strength. After saying yes to God's will that she conceive the Son of the Most High in her womb (Luke 1:26–38), she makes a trip to the hill country to visit Elizabeth (Luke 1:39–56). She remains engaged to Joseph (Luke 2:5) even as they make the trip to Bethlehem to register for the census, and she gives birth to Jesus (Luke 2:1–7) and watches shepherds come to see the child lying in a manger (Luke 2:8–20). She demonstrates her strength when she and Joseph present Jesus in the Temple and listen to the words of Simeon tell her that a sword will pierce her soul (Luke 2:21–35). She displays her greatest strength when she seeks to find her Son, who has stayed behind in Jerusalem (Luke 2:41–52). In other

---

110. CMBVM: Lectionary: Appendix, Responsorial Psalm, Option 13.

words, the LORD was Mary's strength and salvation, according to Luke's Gospel.[111]

Journal/Meditation: How has the LORD been your strength and salvation?

Prayer: I give thanks to you, O LORD, for you are good, and your steadfast love endures forever. You are my strength and my might; you have become my salvation in the incarnation and birth of your Son, Jesus Christ. Give me the strength of the Blessed Virgin Mary that I may do your will now and experience eternal salvation forever. Amen.

Precepts[112]

Text: Psalm 119:1-2, 10-11, 12 and 14, 15-16

Scripture: "I will meditate on your precepts, and fix my eyes on your ways." (Ps 119:15)

Reflection: Ps 119 is one hundred seventy-six verses long! As an acrostic in Hebrew—meaning that verses 1–8 begin with the first letter of the Hebrew alphabet, verses 9–16 with the second letter of the Hebrew alphabet, verses 17–24 with the third letter of the Hebrew alphabet, etc.—the psalm is a Torah song. Torah refers to the six-hundred thirteen laws found in the HB (OT) books of Genesis, Exodus, Leviticus, Numbers, and Deuteronomy. The Hebrew word *Torah* is usually translated as *law*; there are 248 commandments about what is to be done and 365 prohibitions of what is to be avoided. The word *law* appears twenty-five times in the psalm with seven synonyms: decrees, precepts, statutes, command(ment)s, ordinances, word, and promise. The psalm begins by declaring happy those who walk in the law of the LORD (Ps 119:1), recalling Psalm 1:2 about those who delight in the law of the LORD.

The verses chosen illustrate the life of the Blessed Virgin Mary. She is portrayed by the author of Luke's Gospel as one who sought the LORD with her whole heart and treasured his word in her heart (Ps 119:10-11; Luke 2:19, 51b). Likewise, Mary fixed her eyes on God's ways and did not forget his word (Ps 119:15-16; Luke 1:38). In Luke's Gospel, she is presented as the model disciple who hears God's word and does it (Luke 8:21; 11:28). Because of her presence at the unique wedding at Cana in

---

111. References: BYM, pars. 14, 18, 24–5; DPPL, par. 101; MC, pars. 6–7, 17, 26, 28, 33, 39, 41, 44, 46; RM, pars. 8–9, 12–15, 27, 36; RVM, pars. 10, 16, 18, 20, 24, 33.

112. CMBVM: Lectionary: 9. Our Lady of Cana, Responsorial Psalm.

John's Gospel (2:1–11), the mother of Jesus tells modern readers what she told the servants: "Do whatever he tells you" (John 2:5). Just as she plays her part in God's plan, readers are instructed to play their part by meditating on her Son's words and fixing their eyes on his example.[113]

Journal/Meditation: What is your favorite precept or commandment? Why?

Prayer: O LORD, happy are those who walk in your Torah and seek you with their whole heart. With the Holy Spirit guide me in seeking you with my heart and meditating upon the word of your Son, Jesus Christ, who lives and reigns forever and ever. Amen.

Jerusalem[114]

Text: Psalm 122:1–2, 3–4, 8–9

Scripture: "Our feet are standing within your gates, O Jerusalem. Jerusalem—built as a city that is bound firmly together. Pray for the peace of Jerusalem." (Ps 122:2–3, 6a)

Reflection: The city of Jerusalem, captured by King David from the Jebusites (2 Sam 5:6–10) and renamed the city of David, is more than the capital of Israel. In Jerusalem, built on Mount Zion, Solomon erected the first Temple, into which the ark of the covenant, the sign of God's presence, was enthroned. It was often called the house of the Lord (Ps 122:9). Before Jerusalem was destroyed the first time by the Babylonians in 587 BCE—it was destroyed again by the Romans in 70 CE—it became the pilgrimage site for the people of Israel. The psalmist is glad when he receives the invitation to go to the house of the LORD (Ps 122:1). After arriving there and entering the holy city, he admires the firmly-built-together walls (Ps 122:2–3) along with the city's ability to gather the people in one place to praise God. Then, he prays for the peace of Jerusalem (Ps 122:6–8); the Hebrew word for *peace* is *shalom*, a part of the name *Jerusalem*. Of course, the irony is that Jerusalem was seldom at peace with enemies often at her gate!

Just as Jerusalem served as a mother for the Israelites, housing the presence of God, Mary is a new Jerusalem containing the Son of God in

---

113. References: BYM, pars. 78, 126; CCC, pars. 494, 964, 968, 973; MC, pars. 11, 30, 35; RVM, pars. 10, 15.

114. CMBVM: Lectionary: 46. The Blessed Virgin Mary, Gate of Heaven, Responsorial Psalm.

her womb and giving birth to him. Just as the pilgrims entered Jerusalem's gates to see the Temple in which the LORD lived, Mary's womb opens to reveal the Son of God present with his people. And just as Jerusalem was the gathering place for the Israelites, Mary's Son gathers together both Jews and Gentiles into one people so that all can give thanks to the name of the LORD (Ps 122:4b). That peace for which the pilgrims prayed in Psalm 122 is the peace of doing God's will for the Virgin of Nazareth.[115]

Journal/Meditation: What is your holy city? Why is it special to you?

Prayer: O LORD, you built your house in Jerusalem on Mount Zion and invited all your people to come to Jerusalem, your holy city. You made the Blessed Virgin Mary a new Jerusalem and invited all people to come to her Son, the prince of peace. Grant that I may one day praise you in your eternal Jerusalem, where you live and reign forever and ever. Amen.

Olive[116]

Text: Psalm 128:1–2, 3, 4–5

Scripture: "... [Y]our children will be like olive shoots around your table." (Ps 128:3b)

Reflection: Psalm 128 is all about family from a patriarchal culture point of view. The man who fears—reverences—the LORD is married to a wife, who is like a fruitful vine within his house (Ps 128:3a). The vine is an image of prosperity (Zech 3:10). Furthermore, it is an image of Israel (Ps 80:8–11, 14). The metaphor switches to children, who are like olive shoots around the man's table (Ps 128:3b). The olive, an evergreen tree, possesses a thick knotted trunk which becomes many branches as it grows to heights of fifteen to thirty-five feet. It can reach a great age, counting as many as five hundred years. Besides longevity, the olive tree represents one's trust of God (Ps 52:8). The prophet Jeremiah echoes this when he reminds the people of Judah that the LORD once called them a green olive tree, fair with goodly fruit (Jer 11:16). Hosea the prophet

---

115. References: BYM, par. 61; MC, par. 57.

116. LM: 17. Feast of the Holy Family of Jesus, Mary, and Joseph, Sunday within the Octave of the Nativity of the Lord [Christmas], or, if there is no Sunday, December 30, Responsorial Psalm, Cycle A.

echoes Psalm 128 when he reminds Israel that one day his shoots shall spread like the olive tree (Hos 14:6).

On the Feast of the Holy Family, Psalm 128 is used to represent Joseph, the just man who fears the LORD and walks in his ways (Ps 128:1). His wife, Mary, is more than a fruitful vine in his house (Ps 128:3a), as she conceives and gives birth to the Most High God's Son. And Jesus, the child who is like an olive shoot at the table (Ps 128:3b), is further blessing to the man who fears the LORD (Ps 128:4). Then, the psalm takes the narrow context of family and places it within the broader one of blessing and prosperity from the LORD and peace on God's larger family of Israel (Ps 128:5–6).[117]

Journal/Meditation: What image(s) could you use to describe your family?

Prayer: O LORD, I reverence you and seek your blessing for me (and my family). Shower peace upon me (and my family) and grant me prosperity in your grace all the days of my life. I ask this in the name of Jesus Christ my Lord forever and ever. Amen.

Weaned[118]

Text: Psalm 131:1, 2, 3

Scripture: ". . . I have calmed and quieted my soul, like a weaned child with its mother; my soul is like the weaned child that is with me." (Ps 131:2)

Reflection: In the midst of a patriarchal culture, Psalm 131—composed of only three verses—shines as a song written by a woman. The historical setting for the psalm is most likely a family making a pilgrimage to Jerusalem. The woman of the family begins singing how her heart is not proud, how she exercises custody of her eyes, and how she does not step out of her role as a mother by occupying herself with things she does not understand (Ps 131:1). She compares the calm and quiet of her soul to the calm and quiet she experiences as a mother of a weaned child, one who no longer needs to nurse at her breasts, who is with her (Ps 131:2). A weaned child, while able to take solid food, still needs his or her mother

---

117. References: BYM, par. 133; DPPL, pars. 107, 112; MC, par. 5.

118. CMBVM: Lectionary: 8. Our Lady of Nazareth I, Responsorial Psalm; CMBVM: Lectionary: 40. The Blessed Virgin Mary, Mother of Divine Providence, Responsorial Psalm; CMBVM: Lectionary: Appendix, Responsorial Psalm, Option 11.

to feel secure; such is the comparison made to Israel, who feels secure in its hope in the LORD (Ps 131:3). Thus, the LORD is portrayed in Psalm 131 as a mother, who loves and nurtures her child. While the image is not unique to this psalm—it is also found in Deuteronomy 1:31; Isaiah 66:13; and Jeremiah 31:20—it is different from the usual father-son image used in a patriarchal culture.

The imagery of the psalm is perfect when honoring Mary of Nazareth. As the mother of Jesus, she made trips to Jerusalem to celebrate Jewish feasts, bringing her Son along both when he was nursing at her breasts and after he was weaned, according to Luke's Gospel (Luke 2:22–52). However, in her home in Nazareth is where her motherhood shines as she praised the LORD in song, worshiped him in silence, and honored him in her daily life by caring for her family. Honoring Mary as the mother of divine providence, one who was prepared by God from the moment of her conception to be the mother of Jesus, this psalm emphasizes her hope in the LORD with whom she cooperated. After being overshadowed by the Holy Spirit, she conceived Jesus and gave birth to the Son of God (Luke 1:26–38; 2:1–20). Just as she was generous in caring for her Son, so God, like a mother, is generous in caring for all his people and fulfilling the hope they place in him.[119]

Journal/Meditation: Other than the weaned-child imagery, what other feminine image can you use for God?

Prayer: O LORD, your works are too marvelous for me, so you calm and quiet my soul like a weaned child with its mother. Strengthen my hope in you, who are one God—Father, Son, and Holy Spirit—now and forevermore. Amen.

Habitation[120]

Text: Psalm 132:6–7, 9–10, 13–14 or 132:11, 13–14, 17–18

---

119. References: BYM, par. 14; CCC, pars. 488, 964, 973; MC, pars. 28, 34, 37; RM, pars. 1, 8, 17, 45.

120. LM: 606. Memorial of Saints Joachim and Anne, Parents of the Blessed Virgin Mary, July 26, Responsorial Psalm; LM: 621. Solemnity of the Assumption of the Blessed Virgin Mary, August 15, At the Vigil Mass, Responsorial Psalm; CMBVM: Lectionary: 19. Holy Mary, Mother of the Lord, Responsorial Psalm.

Scripture: "... [T]he LORD has chosen Zion; he has desired it for his habitation: 'This is my resting place forever; here I will reside, for I have desired it.'" (Ps 132:13–14)

Reflection: The word *habitation* refers to the occupancy of a place; in the case of Psalm 132, it refers to the place where God lives. As a royal psalm, it presents the singer articulating the reason one makes a pilgrimage to Jerusalem: That is where the ark of the covenant, a sign of God's presence, is enthroned in the Temple. The psalmist recalls David's promise to the LORD to find a dwelling place for him (Ps 132:1–5), the bringing of the ark to Jerusalem (Ps 132:6–7), and the placing of it in a tent in Jerusalem until Solomon could build the first Temple (Ps 132:8–10). Verses 11 and 12 of Psalm 132 recall God's promise to David that one of his sons would sit on his throne. Then the psalmist returns to the major theme that God has desired Zion for his habitation (Ps 132:13–14); from there he will feed the poor with bread, hear the shouts of joy of the people, provide a descendant for David, and disgrace his enemies (Ps 132:15–18).

This psalm is used on the memorial of the parents—non-biblical Joachim and Anne—of the Blessed Virgin Mary and on the solemnity of Mary's assumption to indicate that God came to live in Mary, just as the ark was brought to its habitation in a tent in Jerusalem and then in the Temple. In other words, God's habitation was the womb of the Blessed Virgin Mary; she was his resting place in the person of Jesus, God's only-begotten Son, whom the CB (NT) claims to be a descendant of David. The LORD chose Mary from the moment she was conceived by her parents, Joachim and Anne; he desired her and blessed her. Because he caused her to be conceived without original sin, he assumed her into heaven, according to the invocations in the LBVMOCIBVM. The LORD found a dwelling place in her.[121]

Journal/Meditation: In what specific ways are you a habitation for the LORD?

Prayer: Rise up, O LORD, and come to your resting place. Make me aware of your mighty Spirit at work in my life that I may shout for joy at your presence as one God—Father, Son, and Holy Spirit—forever and ever. Amen.

---

121. References: BYM, pars. 10, 18, 21, 25–27, 56, 102, 110–11; DPPL, pars. 101–2, 174; MC, pars. 6, 26, 56; RM, par. 3.

Meditate[122]

Text: Psalm 145:1–2, 4–6, 8–9

Scripture: "One generation shall laud your works to another [, LORD,] and shall declare your mighty acts. On the glorious splendor of your majesty, and on your wondrous works, I will meditate." (Ps 145:4–5)

Reflection: Psalm 145 is an invitation to meditate—to concentrate the mind on one thing—on God's works in general: graciousness, mercifulness, steadfast love, and compassion (Ps 145:8–9); upholding the falling, feeding the hungry, and being just, kind, and near (Ps 145:13b–18); hearing people's cries, saving them, watching over them, and destroying the wicked (Ps 145:19–20). The psalmist notes that one generation praises God's mighty acts to the next generation (Ps 145:4); in his meditation, he refers to these mighty acts as wondrous works (Ps 145:5), awesome deeds (Ps 145:6), abundant goodness (Ps 145:7), mighty deeds (Ps 145:12), and doings (Ps 145:17). The psalmist meditates: "All your works shall give thanks to you, O LORD" (Ps 145:10), and the faithful will "make known to all people your mighty deeds" (145:12). "The LORD is just in all his ways, and kind in all his doings" (Ps 145:17).

In applying the words of Psalm 145 to the Blessed Virgin Mary, the meditation on the LORD's works, mighty acts, wondrous works, awesome deeds, and mighty deeds would include the preservation of Mary from all original sin, the incarnation of Jesus in her womb, the birth of the Son of God, the welcoming of the magi, the flight into and out of Egypt, the circumcision, the presentation in the Temple, the finding of the boy Jesus in the Temple, her entrustment to the beloved disciple at the cross, and her assumption into heaven. Other events surrounding the life of the Virgin of Nazareth can be added to the list of God's abundant goodness. In the words of Psalm 145, these events celebrate the fame of the LORD's abundant goodness and sing aloud of his righteousness (Ps 145:7).

Journal/Meditation: What works, mighty acts, wondrous works, awesome deeds, or mighty deeds has God done for you?

Prayer: God and King, you are great and greatly to be praised for all your works from one generation to the next. Continue your awesome deeds among your people today. I give you thanks for the wondrous works you have done for me in the hope of sharing in your everlasting

---

122. CMBVM: Lectionary: 12. The Blessed Virgin Mary at the Foot of the Cross II, Responsorial Psalm.

kingdom, where your dominion endures throughout all generations forever and ever. Amen.

Ordinances[123]

Text: Psalm 147:12–13, 14–15, 19–20

Scripture: "[The LORD] declares his word to Jacob, his statutes and ordinances to Israel. He has not dealt thus with any other nation; they do not know his ordinances." (Ps 147:19–20a)

Reflection: An ordinance is a law or rule made by God. When Psalm 147 refers to the ordinances declared to Israel (Ps 147:19), the singer is praising the Torah with its six hundred thirteen precepts. He also emphasizes that the LORD has not given his ordinances to any other nation on the planet except to Jacob, another way to refer to the nation of Israel (Ps 147:20). Because of this singular, divine gift, Jerusalem is invited to praise the LORD, who strengthens the bars of the city's gates, blesses those within, grants peace within Israel's borders, and feeds the people with the finest wheat (Ps 147:12–14). By sending his command to the earth (Ps 147:15), the LORD's ordinances order the chaos of the life of God's people. Those who recognize this are considered wise.

This psalm is used to indicate the wisdom of the Blessed Virgin Mary. The LBVM(LL) invokes her as the seat of wisdom in praise of her close relationship with eternal, divine wisdom. The LORD preserved her from all sin and made her the mother of his Son. These both established her royal dignity and her wise cooperation with God's will. She contained God's wisdom in the incarnate presence of Jesus in her womb. Furthermore, as a mother, she cradled that wisdom on her lap and fed him at her breasts. In the words of Psalm 147, she listened to God's word, his ordinances declared uniquely to her and unknown to all others. Just like the earth receives the LORD's command to snow, to hail, to blow wind, and to flow water (Ps 147:16–18), Mary received his ordinances, and they became fleshly wisdom in her. Then, the LORD strengthened her, blessed her, gave her peace, and fed her. Thus, did God order her life to fulfill his purpose for all creation.[124]

Journal/Meditation: What ordinance have you received from God?

---

123. LM: 19. Second Sunday after Christmas, Responsorial Psalm; CMBVM: Lectionary: 24. The Blessed Virgin Mary, Seat of Wisdom, Responsorial Psalm.

124. References: MC, 5, 25, 57.

Hebrew Bible and Old Testament

Prayer: O LORD, you declared your word to Jacob and gave your statutes and ordinances to Israel. In the fullness of time, you sent your Word to the Blessed Virgin Mary, who welcomed your Son into her womb, gave birth to him, and nursed him at her breasts. Grant that I may imitate her wisdom in adhering to your ordinances. You are God—Father, Son, and Holy Spirit—forever and ever. Amen.

PROVERBS

Wisdom[125]

Text: Proverbs 8:17-21, 34-35

Scripture: Wisdom says: "I love those who love me, and those who seek me diligently find me. For whoever finds me finds life and obtains favor from the LORD." (Prov 8:17, 35)

Reflection: In the HB (OT) Book of Proverbs, wisdom is personified as a woman, often referred to as Lady Wisdom. This manner of presenting an abstract concept as if it were a person enables the reader to grasp the idea concretely. The abstract concept of wisdom refers to accumulated knowledge of life that has been gained through experience; a person's decisions usually reveal how wise he or she is. The book of Proverbs adds another indicator of wisdom, namely, favor shown the individual from the LORD.

The Blessed Virgin Mary is named a teacher in the Spirit because she is a woman possessing the wisdom of God. The LBVMOCIBVM invokes her as a perfect disciple of Christ, her Son. As a teacher, she hears the words of God, contemplates them in her spirit, and keeps them in her heart (Luke 2:19, 51b). Then, through her example of faithfulness to the divine word, she teaches about the spiritual life she has found through her diligent search and the favor God has bestowed upon her (Luke 1:48a). As a mother, she shares her love of wisdom by encouraging the members of the church to follow her example in imitating her Son and living by the Spirit of the gospel he proclaimed.[126]

Journal/Meditation: What life in the Spirit has flowed through you as a result of wisdom?

---

125. CMBVM: Lectionary: 32. The Blessed Virgin Mary, Mother and Teacher in the Spirit, First Reading, Option A.

126. Reference: BB, par. 1286; CCC, par. 721; MC, pars. 5, 25, 57.

Prayer: LORD God, before you created the heavens and the earth you brought forth wisdom, your master craftsperson, in whom you daily delighted and rejoiced. Through the gift of your Holy Spirit, make me truly wise in your ways that you may find delight in me now and forever and ever. Amen.

Seat[127]

Text: Proverbs 8:22–31

Scripture: Wisdom says: "The LORD created me at the beginning of his work, the first of his acts of long ago. . . . I was beside him, like a master worker; and I was daily his delight, rejoicing before him always." (Prov 8:22, 30)

Reflection: A seat is a place to sit, usually a part of a chair. In biblical understanding, a seat is a place from which a person exercises authority. Today, the pope and bishops have special seats in their cathedrals (from the Latin word for chair: *cathedra*) from which they exercise their authority. In the HB (OT) book of Proverbs, wisdom is personified as a woman, often referred to as Lady Wisdom, whom the LORD created at the beginning of his work. Wisdom sits at God's side, being the Holy One's delight, while he creates the world and everything in it. Wisdom is God's advisor.

The Blessed Virgin Mary is invoked as the seat of wisdom in the LBVM(LL). This means that she is a wise authority in terms of the spiritual life. Mary is like Lady Wisdom insofar as she conceives in her womb the Creator of the world; wisdom built himself a house, a body, in Mary's womb. Thus, the wisdom of God in the person of Jesus, eternal God born in time, speaks through the Virgin of Nazareth. In her person, Mary reveals the incomparable wisdom and prudence of the spiritual life. The wisdom, who is God's craftsperson, serves as his architect and draws the plans for the world. The Creator resides in the creature he has made, sitting at her side and delighting in his mother, after filling her with the very wisdom of God.[128]

Journal/Meditation: How are you wise in terms of the spiritual life?

---

127. LM: 707. The Common of the Blessed Virgin Mary, First Reading, Option 5; CMBVM: Lectionary: 24. The Blessed Virgin Mary, Seat of Wisdom, First Reading, Option A.

128. References: MC, pars. 5, 25, 27.

Prayer: God of wisdom, before the creation of the heavens and the earth your eternal wisdom was guiding your hand and directing your thoughts. Fill me with that Spirit of wisdom and draw me ever closer to you that you may find delight in me now and forever. Amen.

SONG OF (SOLOMON) SONGS

Visit[129]

Text: Song of (Solomon) Songs 2:8–14

Scripture: "The voice of my beloved! Look, he comes, leaping upon the mountains, bounding over the hills." (Song 2:8)

Reflection: The Song of Solomon or Song of Songs is a collection of love poems shared by a man and woman. In Song 2:8–14, the woman compares the visit of her beloved to that of a gazelle or a young stag leaping and bounding over the hills and valleys. She watches as he arrives at the city walls, then as he peers through the windows of her house. Since it is springtime, he invites her to join him in private to view the flowers blooming, the fig tree laden with figs, the grape vines laden with clusters of grapes, and to hear the turtledove cooing. His visit brings his invitation to join him in the country, where nature has burst into new life; spring's abundance represents his desire for the wealth that results from his love for this woman.

The visit of the unnamed man to his beloved, unnamed woman exudes the joy that is found in Mary's visit to Elizabeth, an event unique to Luke's Gospel. After traveling through the hill country with haste, according to Luke's Gospel (1:39), Mary enters Zechariah's and Elizabeth's home with greetings that cause John the Baptist to leap for joy in his mother's womb and provoke a double pronouncement of Mary's blessedness by Elizabeth. Such joy and gladness, signs of God's blessings, resulting from this visit are like that of the man visiting the woman in the Song of (Solomon) Songs. Not only are they signs of the presence of Holy Spirit, but they represent the fruitfulness of love brought by the same Spirit.[130]

---

129. CMBVM: Lectionary: 3. The Visitation of the Blessed Virgin Mary, First Reading, Option B.

130. References: CCC, pars. 495, 497, 721-2; MC, pars. 7, 39; RM, pars. 12-14, 36; RVM, pars. 20, 33.

Journal/Meditation: Whom have you recently visited and brought joy and gladness? Who has visited you recently and brought joy and gladness?

Prayer: God of joy and gladness, in the love of the Holy Spirit you visit me. In the silence, help me to hear your word that I may produce abundantly the new life you bestow now and forever. Amen.

Face[131]

Text: Song of (Solomon) Songs 2:10bc and 14ef; 4:8a and 9a, 11cd and 12, 15

Scripture: "Arise, my love, my fair one, and come away. . . . [F]or your voice is sweet, and your face is lovely." (Song 2:10bc, 14ef)

Reflection: The author of the Song of (Solomon) Songs presents a series of poems which describe the love between a man and woman. The man, who comes to the woman leaping upon the mountains (Song 2:8c), addresses the woman as his love, his fair one, and he invites her to arise and come away with him (Song 2:10; 13de). He desires to hear her voice and to see her face (Song 2:14cd), and he declares her voice to be sweet and her face lovely (Song 2:14ef). In another poem in chapter 4, he invites his bride to come with him from Lebanon (Song 4:8a)—the scent of her garments is like that of Lebanon (Song 4:11cd)—because she ravishes his heart (Song 4:9a). He also compares her to a garden locked and a fountain sealed, a well of living water, and flowing streams from Lebanon (Song 4:12, 15).

The pieced together verses for this Responsorial Psalm are chosen as a reflection on the fairness—the beauty, the radiance of holiness—of the Blessed Virgin Mary. The idea comes from the OT (A) book of Sirach (Ecclesiasticus) which, in a verse not found in all manuscripts of the book, portrays Wisdom saying, "I am the mother of beautiful love, of fear, of knowledge, and of holy hope" (Sir 24:18). Metaphorically, the man who comes to Mary is Gabriel in Luke's Gospel (Luke 1:26–38); he addresses her as the favored one (Luke 1:28). Gabriel invites her to accept God's request that she become the mother his Son; through Gabriel, Mary hears God's voice, and, when she gives birth to his Son, she will see God's face. With her sweet voice, she does God's will (Luke 1:38);

---

131. CMBVM: Lectionary: 36. The Blessed Virgin Mary, Mother of Fairest Love, Responsorial Psalm.

with her lovely face, she gazes upon her firstborn Son (Luke 2:7) and ponders in her heart the events surrounding his birth (Luke 2:19). She remains before, during, and after a locked garden and a fountain sealed; that is, she maintains her virginity, while at the same time giving to the world living water that flows to eternal life (John 4:10, 14). This is why the LBVMOCIBVM invokes her as the fountain of beauty.[132]

Journal/Meditation: In whom do you see the face of God?

Prayer: Heavenly Father, you have shown your face in the person of your Son, Jesus Christ, conceived in the womb and born of the Blessed Virgin Mary. You have made your voice heard in his words about eternal life. Grant that as I hear and practice his words now, I may one day see you as you are: Father, Son, and Holy Spirit, one God, forever and ever. Amen.

Fountain[133]

Text: Song of (Solomon) Songs 4:6–7, 9, 12–15

Scripture: "A garden locked is my sister, my bride, a garden locked, a fountain sealed. . . . —a garden fountain, a well of living water, and flowing streams from Lebanon." (Song 4:12, 15)

Reflection: In the LBVMOCIBVM, Mary is invoked as a fountain of beauty in the same way as she is named a fountain of salvation. A fountain is an ornamental structure featuring a jet or jets of water, often emerging from a statue into a pool. While there is also a small jet of water that releases water in a drinking fountain with the press of a button or the turning of handle, the focus is on the beauty and abundance of the life-giving liquid that emerges from the fountain. In the Song of (Solomon) Songs, the unnamed man refers to his beloved, unnamed woman as a sealed fountain—her chastity—and a garden fountain that is a well of living water with flowing streams.

The Blessed Virgin Mary is like a sealed fountain. The LBVM(LL) invokes her as the holy virgin of virgins and the virgin most faithful. The LBVMOCIBVM calls her the most honored of virgins. And yet she is also like a garden fountain flowing with streams of living water because she

---

132. References: BYM, pars. 36, 41, 44–46, 48–50; MC, pars. 5, 11, 17, 19, 36, 45, 57; RM, pars. 4, 39.

133. CMBVM: Lectionary: 31. The Blessed Virgin Mary, Fountain of Salvation II, First Reading.

bore in her womb and gave birth to the source of all life: Jesus Christ, the Son of God, who himself is the fountain of salvation. In Lourdes, France, there is a shrine at the cave where Mary appeared to St. Bernadette Soubirous for the first time on February 11, 1858, with seventeen subsequent appearances. The young peasant girl was instructed to dig in the earth where a small spring began to flow; then, she was told to drink from the water that bubbled up. Many people have been healed by drinking from or bathing in this fountain of living water. While Christ is the fountain of salvation, his mother, the sealed fountain, is also the garden fountain of living water with flowing streams.[134]

Journal/Meditation: In what specific ways is your life like a garden fountain releasing a stream of life-giving grace?

Prayer: Until the day breathes cool and the shadows lengthen, I will drink from the fountain of your grace, O LORD. Make of me a garden fountain, a well of living water flowing fresh with your Holy Spirit. I ask this in the name of your Son, Jesus Christ, the fountain of salvation, now and forever. Amen.

SIRACH (ECCLESIASTICUS)

Mother[135]

Text: Sirach 3:2–7, 12–14

Scripture: "Those who respect their father will have long life, and those who honor their mother obey the Lord." (Sir 3:6)

Reflection: While Mary shares the Feast of the Holy Family with Jesus and Joseph, the selection from the OT (A) book of Sirach (Ecclesiasticus), a collection of wisdom teachings, presents an extensive reflection upon the commandment to honor one's father and mother. The Blessed Virgin Mary is the primary focus of this book, thus only the statements about the Lord confirming "a mother's right over her children" are presented (Sir 3:2). ". . . [T]hose who respect their mother are like those who lay up treasure," states the author (Sir 3:4), in addition to "those who honor their mother obey the Lord" (Sir 3:6). Since the work emerges

---

134. References: BYM, pars. 36, 41, 44–46, 48–50; CCC, pars. 496, 498–9, 502, 505–6, 510; MC, pars. 5, 11, 17, 19, 36, 45, 57; RM, pars. 4, 39.

135. LM: 17. Feast of the Holy Family of Jesus, Mary, and Joseph, Sunday within the Octave of the Nativity of the Lord [Christmas], or, if there is no Sunday, December 30, First Reading, Cycle A.

from a patriarchal culture, it comes as no surprise that the bulk of the verses have to do with children's obligations toward their father.

Mary's right over her child, Jesus, is narrated by the author of Luke's Gospel. After searching for Jesus for three days, Mary and Joseph find him in Jerusalem's Temple, his Father's house. Luke writes that he went home with them "and was obedient to them" (Luke 2:51a). Because of the respect shown his mother, who herself treasured all the things concerning her Son (Luke 2:19, 51b), Jesus became strong in wisdom with favor both divine and human upon him (Luke 2:40, 52). Thus, did he honor his mother, Mary, and obey his Father, God. In the LBVM(LL), Mary is invoked as mother of Christ, divine grace, good counsel, the creator, and the Savior, as mother most pure, chaste, inviolate, undefiled, and mother most amiable and admirable. In LBVMOCIBVM, she is called the holy mother of God, the mother of Christ the King, and mother of the Lord. Thus, is she honored.[136]

Journal/Meditation: How do respect, honor, and obedience illustrate a holy family?

Prayer: Lord God, you have promised those who honor their father joy in their children and those who respect their mother treasure in heaven. Grant through the intersession of the holy mother of God that I may honor my father and respect my mother all the days of my life. Hear me through Christ my Lord. Amen.

Counsel[137]

Text: Sirach 14:20, 21–22, 23–25, 26–27

Scripture: "Happy is the person who meditates on wisdom and reasons intelligently, who reflects in his heart on her ways and ponders her secrets." (Sir 14:20–21)

Reflection: The poem found in the OT (A) book of Sirach (Ecclesiasticus) reminds the reader that the happy person is the one who reflects on wisdom in his heart and reasons intelligently—thinking critically—in order to discover her secrets (Sir 14:20–21). The author compares the pursuit of wisdom to that of a hunter lying in wait for her on one of her

---

136. References: BYM, pars. 2–3, 5, 8, 62–64, 71, 106, 109, 113–4, 117; CCC, pars. 495, 509, 963, 971, 975, 2619; DPPL, pars. 107, 115; MC, pars. 5, 11, 14, 16, 19, 21, 28, 32, 56; RM, pars. 4–6, 27–31, 39, 42–44, 47; RVM, par. 15.

137. CMBVM: Lectionary: 33. The Blessed Virgin Mary, Mother of Good Counsel, Responsorial Psalm.

paths (Sir 14:22). Then, switching metaphors, he compares the pursuit of wisdom to a peeping tom, who looks through windows and listens at doors (Sir 14:23). The imagery of sexual desire for wisdom continues with the pursuit compared to pitching a tent near her house in order to get as close to her as possible (Sir 14:24–25). Such a campsite is a shelter under which the pursuer lives with his children, finds relief from the heat of the day, and lives in the midst of wisdom's glory (Sir 14:26–27). In other words, male sexual desire for earthly women is redirected to Lady Wisdom by the author.

The six verses from Sirach are like a psalm, which is why they are used as a response in honor of the Blessed Virgin Mary, invoked as mother of good counsel and virgin most prudent in the LBVM(LL). Mary is portrayed as meditating on wisdom and pondering her secrets in her heart (Luke 2:19, 51b). Her unfailing yes to God's will enabled her to pursue wisdom by treasuring the words she heard from the shepherds (Luke 2:15–18) and teaching wisdom to her lost Son (Luke 2:41-51). She recognizes Jesus' wisdom at the wedding in Cana when she directs the servants to do whatever he tells them (John 2:5). She is a model of how to seek advice through critical thinking in order to know God's will and obey it faithfully.[138]

Journal/Meditation: What recent wisdom have you received from God through meditation and critical thinking?

Prayer: God of all wisdom, you reward those who reflect in their hearts and ponder your secrets with knowledge of your will. Guide me in my pursuit of wisdom with the Holy Spirit. And grant that I may one day dwell in the midst of your glory and that of your Son, Jesus Christ, in the unity of the Holy Spirit forever and ever. Amen.

Dwelling[139]

Text: Sirach 24:1–2, 8–12 or 24:1–4, 8–12, 19–21

Scripture: "... [T]he Creator of all things gave me [, Wisdom,] a command, and my Creator chose the place for my tent. He said, 'Make your dwelling in Jacob, and in Israel receive your inheritance.'" (Sir 24:8)

---

138. References: CCC, par. 721; MC, pars. 25, 57; RM, par. 20; RVM, par. 11.

139. LM: 19. Second Sunday after Christmas, First Reading; LM: 707. The Common of the Blessed Virgin Mary, First Reading, Option 6; CMBVM: Lectionary: 24. The Blessed Virgin Mary, Seat of Wisdom, First Reading, Option B. (The notation in CMBVM: Lectionary is Sirach 21:1–4, 8–12, 18–21; the chapter should be 24, not 21.)

Reflection: As in the HB (OT) book of Proverbs, Wisdom in the OT(A) book of Sirach (Ecclesiasticus) is personified as a woman who was created before anything else. Lady Wisdom tells of her glory both in the presence of the Most High and in the midst of her people, the Jews. God, her creator, commanded her to dwell among his people in the tent of meeting built by Moses and after that to dwell in the Temple in Jerusalem. She took root among the Jews, the Lord's portion, his heritage. Because Mary of Nazareth is counted among the Jewish people, she is a dwelling place for Wisdom, God's Son, Jesus Christ, and, as such, is referred to as the seat of wisdom in the LBVM(LL). In other words, through the incarnation, God came to dwell in this daughter of Jacob.

In the Bible, Lady Wisdom represents the attempt to concretize good sense, the knowledge and experience needed to make sensible decisions and judgment in terms of the things of God. Because she came forth from the mouth of the Most High from the beginning when he created her, she represents accumulated knowledge of life and the LORD that has been gained through experience. Because her Creator commanded her to dwell with people, she lives in those who write and speak about discerning the things of God. Thus, her teachings deserve careful consideration throughout all ages because she does not cease to be, nor has she abandoned God's people.[140]

Journal/Meditation: How do you experience Wisdom dwelling in you?

Prayer: Most High God, Wisdom, whom you created before the ages, in the beginning, tells of your glory. Command her to make her dwelling in me that I may be filled with the wisdom of the Holy Spirit, who lives and reigns with you, Father, and your Son, Jesus Christ, forever and ever. Amen.

Hope II[141]

Text: Sirach 24:9–12, 19–21

Scripture: "I [, Wisdom,] took root in an honored people, in the portion of the Lord, his heritage. 'Come to me, you who desire me, and eat your fill of my fruits.'" (Sir 24:12, 19)

---

140. References: CCC, par. 721; MC, pars. 5, 25, 27.

141. CMBVM: Lectionary: 37. The Blessed Virgin Mary, Mother of Divine Hope, First Reading.

Reflection: A concrete sign of hope is the planting of a tree. Wisdom, personified as a woman, in the OT (A) book of Sirach (Ecclesiasticus), declares that she took root, like a tree, in the Jews, the Lord's portion and heritage. This means that Wisdom is like a small sapling carefully planted in the earth, in which it takes root. Today, people plant trees to commemorate birthdays, anniversaries, weddings, special holidays, and deaths of ancestors. The growing tree reminds them of the special occasion when they see the tree as well as the hope-filled moment during which they planted it.

The Blessed Virgin Mary is like a tree giving hope to those who see her. Like a great tree which spreads its graceful branches, Mary offers people the shade of her hope. She, like her ancestors, hoped to see the day of a messiah, one who would deliver her people from Roman oppression and domination. In such hope she conceived the Son of God in her womb and with more hope gave birth to him in the mystery of the incarnation. In other words, Mary presents divine hope to the world. Furthermore, like Lady Wisdom, who invites all to come and eat their fill of the fruit growing on her tree of hope, the Virgin of Nazareth invites all to come and eat of her Son, who gives himself as food—bread and wine—in the hope of sharing eternal life. From Lady Wisdom and the Blessed Virgin Mary all can learn a lesson about how strong and permanent hope can be.[142]

Journal/Meditation: What serves as a sign of hope for you? How does it do that?

Prayer: Before the ages, in the beginning, you, Mighty God, created Wisdom to be the hope for all the ages and never to cease to be. In the womb of the Virgin of Nazareth, you conceived hope, made incarnate in your Son, Jesus Christ. Grant that I may eat of the fruit of his cross and share in eternal life forever and ever. Amen.

Fair[143]

Text: Sirach 24:17, 19–21 or 24:17–21

---

142. References: CCC, par. 721; MC, pars. 5, 25, 27.

143. CMBVM: Lectionary: 21. The Holy Name of the Blessed Virgin Mary, First Reading; CMBVM: Lectionary: 36. The Blessed Virgin Mary, Mother of Fairest Love, First Reading.

Scripture: "Like the vine I [,Wisdom,] bud forth delights, and my blossoms become glorious and abundant fruit." (Sir 24:17)

Reflection: One of the many definitions of the word *fair* is pleasing to the eye or beautiful to look upon. Thus, it is no accident that the holy name of Mary and her title of mother of the fairest—the highest form of pleasing to the eye or beauty—love is exemplified with a short passage from the OT (A) book of Sirach (Ecclesiasticus) that compares Lady Wisdom to the fair and rich fruit that the grapevine produces. However, the verse that honors Mary's name and identifies her as the mother of fairest hope is missing from many manuscripts of Sirach. Lady Wisdom says, "I am the mother of beautiful love, of fear, of knowledge, and of holy hope; being eternal, I am given to all my weary children . . ." (Sir 24:18). As the mother of beautiful love, Mary's spiritual fairness is a feast for the eyes and an example for the followers of her Son not to be interested in physical beauty but willingly to receive God's grace, Holy Spirit, and love, which truly honor one's name.

The Blessed Virgin Mary is fair because she was bathed in God's grace from the moment of her conception. God filled her with his own eternal life and prepared her to be the purest of mothers for his only-begotten Son. Not only was Mary's name honored by God's undeserved gift, but she was made spiritually beautiful, full of holiness. Furthermore, she is fair because she shared in the gift of the Holy Spirit, who overshadowed her, protected her, and made her radiant with the glory of her Son, Jesus. The Virgin's fairest love, like the vine that buds forth delights, is demonstrated in her acceptance of God's request that she conceive, bear, and give birth to the Son of God. Thus, from Mary, the fairest vine, blossomed the Savior of the world, who, in John's Gospel, refers to himself as the vine (John 15:1–6)[144]

Journal/Meditation: In what specific ways are you spiritually fair in God's eyes?

Prayer: Holy Father, at your command every knee bends in heaven, on earth, and under the earth when the name of your Son is spoken. Likewise, the name of his fair mother echoes on the lips of his followers throughout the ages. Grant that I may one day come before you to share in their fairness, beauty, and love. I ask this in the name of Jesus Christ, who lives and reigns with you and the Holy Spirit, one God, forever and ever. Amen.

---

144. References: CCC, pars. 488, 490, 511, 773, 963, 2030; MC, par. 57; RM, pars. 43–44, 47.

Ancestors[145]

Text: Sirach 44:1, 10–15

Scripture: "Their descendants stand by the covenants; their children also, for their sake. Their offspring will continue forever, and their glory will never be blotted out." (Sir 44:12–13)

Reflection: All descendants have ancestors. The reader is descended from parents, who are descended from parents (the reader's grandparents), who are descended from parents (the reader's great grandparents), etc. Thus, descendants stand in a long line of ancestors, who can be traced in succession for many years by those who compile family trees. Likewise, in Christian tradition, Mary, the Virgin of Nazareth, has ancestors, namely, her parents, Joachim and Anne. The names of Mary's parents are not found in biblical literature, but they come from the late second-century apocryphal *The Proto-Gospel of James*.[146] Following the usual biblical formula for famous ancestors, Joachim and Anne have no child, but pray to the Lord for one. An angel of the Lord appears both to Anne and Joachim and announces that Anne will conceive and give birth. Once the child is born, she is named Mary.

The passage from the book of Sirach (Ecclesiasticus) is from the beginning of the long section (44:1–50:24) that generically praises ancestors before honoring specific famous people of the past. Ordinary descendants of those glorious ancestors continue to stand by the covenants God made with them, according to the author. In fact, the offspring of the ancestors—the descendants—continue in a long line, and the glory of the ancestors will never be erased as long as the generations endure. On this Memorial of Saints Joachim and Anne, these words are applied to a childless couple whom God chose, according to *The Proto-Gospel of James*,[147] to be the parents of the mother of his Son: Jesus Christ.

Journal/Meditation: Who are your three most famous ancestors? What did each accomplish so that he or she is remembered by you, his or her descendant?

Prayer: God of all ancestors, you graced Joachim and Anne with the presence of the Blessed Virgin Mary, the mother of your incarnate Son. Grant that I may stand in the long line of my ancestors who have received

---

145. LM: 606. Memorial of Saints Joachim and Anne, Parents of the Blessed Virgin Mary, July 26, First Reading.

146. Ehrman, *Other Gospels*, 24–36.

147. Ibid.

your promise of salvation and share in it through Jesus Christ my Lord. Amen.

Tongue[148]

Text: Sirach 51:13–18, 20–22

Scripture: "The Lord gave me my tongue as a reward, and I will praise him with it." (Sir 51:22)

Reflection: The text for the first reading comes from the last chapter of the OT (A) book of Sirach (Ecclesiasticus) which contains a prayer of the author and some final praise of Wisdom. Verses 13–18 and 20–21 from chapter 51 contain some of Jesus son of Sirach's musings on Wisdom in which he explains how he sought Wisdom in prayer in the Temple. When his request was granted, he delighted in Wisdom and followed in her steps, finding instruction, making progress, and resolving to live according to Wisdom. His heart was stirred to seek her. And so with his God-given tongue he praises his Creator for his God-given Wisdom. In other words, Jesus son of Sirach is a disciple of Lady Wisdom, from whom he gained understanding.

Mary, the Mother of Jesus Christ, is named both mother and disciple of the Lord. The LBVMOCIBVM invokes her as the perfect disciple of Christ. She listens to the words of life he speaks and receives them. She is an example of how the inspired word speaks to one's daily life and results in a harvest of holiness. Like Jesus son of Sirach sought Wisdom, Mary sought to be the perfect disciple of her own Son. She serves as a model for those who are modern disciples of Christ to hear God's Wisdom-Word, to seek to know his will, and then faithfully to carry it out.[149]

Journal/Meditation: For what wisdom do you praise God with your tongue?

Prayer: I give you thanks, O Lord and King, and I praise you, O God my Savior, for guiding my footsteps on the straight path of wisdom. I praise your name continually with my tongue and make thanksgiving to you now and forever. Amen.

---

148. CMBVM: Lectionary: 10. Holy Mary, Disciple of the Lord, First Reading.

149. References: BYM, pars. 78, 126; CCC, pars. 494, 964, 968, 973; MC, pars. 11, 30, 35; RM, par. 41; RVM, pars. 10, 15.

ISAIAH

Announcement[150]

Text: Isaiah 7:10–14; 8:10c

Scripture: Isaiah said, ". . . [T]he Lord himself will give you a sign. Look, the young woman is with child and shall bear a son, and shall name him Immanuel." (Isa 7:14)

Reflection: Announcements concerning baby showers, wedding showers, births, graduations, marriages, and deaths arrive in the mail and in e-mail. More formal announcements arrive with a postage stamp on them; less formal ones arrive digitally. When Israel was oppressed, the prophet Isaiah made an announcement to King Ahaz of Judah (735–716 BCE) that God would fulfill his earlier promise to David by raising up a new king, who would restore the nation to its former Davidic grandeur. Isaiah offers hope in the midst of a hopeless situation. A child will be born to Ahaz's wife; in order to instill hope, the child will be named Immanuel, which means "God is with us" (Isa 8:10c). In other words, the child's name indicates his function, as do other names of biblical people.

Once the Davidic monarchy disappears in 587 BCE, the hope for a new king becomes messianic. He would be a monarch who would drive out of Palestine the Roman occupation forces and restore self-rule to the Jews. Jesus, born of the Blessed Virgin Mary, was named this new monarch, but he was not the warrior expected. The kingdom he proclaimed belongs to God. The author of Matthew's Gospel understands his name to indicate his function (Matt 1:21–23). He, Mary's child, is God with people; he saves people by announcing the kingdom of heaven (God) to them. Mary, his mother, is understood to be the prophet Isaiah's young woman with child who hears the announcement, bears a son, and names him Immanuel.[151]

Journal/Meditation: Recently, what announcement have you received from God?

---

150. LM: 545. Solemnity of the Annunciation of the Lord, March 25, First Reading; LM: 707. The Common of the Blessed Virgin Mary: First Reading, Option 7; CMBVM: Lectionary: 2. The Blessed Virgin Mary and the Annunciation of the Lord, First Reading, Option A.

151. References: BYM, pars. 14, 18, 24–25; CCC, par. 497; DPPL, par. 101; MC, pars. 6, 17, 26, 28, 33, 41, 44, 46; RM, pars. 8–9, 13, 15, 27; RVM, pars. 10, 16, 18, 20, 24, 33.

Prayer: Heavenly Father, who willed that the incarnation of your Word should take flesh in the womb of the Blessed Virgin Mary, open my ears to hear your word and give me the grace to do it. Grant my prayer through the intercession of the Mother of God and the mediation of Immanuel, her Son, who lives and reigns with you and the Holy Spirit, one God, forever and ever. Amen.

Crowned[152]

Text: Isaiah 9:2–7 or 9:2-4, 6–7 (9:1–6; 9 or 9:1–3, 5–6)

Scripture: ". . . [A]child has been born for us, a son given to us; authority rests upon his shoulders, and he is named Wonderful Counselor, Mighty God, Everlasting Father, Prince of Peace." (Isa 9:6 [9:5])

Reflection: Isaiah 9:2–7 (9:1–6) is a coronation hymn—much like Psalm 2—marking the enthronement of a new Judean king, who would reverse the harm done by King Ahaz (735–716 BCE). It is difficult to know for whom the coronation hymn was composed, but its purpose is clear: God is restoring David's royal house to its former honor and fame and giving the new king the authority he needs to renew Judah. Thus, the people who walked in the darkness of King Ahaz have a new light for which the people of the kingdom are rejoicing. The yoke of their oppressor has been broken. At his coronation—his birth—the new king is given several important names to indicate his function. He is Wonderful Counselor to stress his wisdom in offering advice in the act of ruling his kingdom. He is Mighty God to indicate that he has been anointed by God and named a son of God, as is made clear in Psalm 2:7. He is Everlasting Father, that is, he is father and protector of his people. And, finally, he is Prince of Peace; he is responsible for security within the borders of his kingdom.

This hymn is applied to Jesus at the Mass during the night for Christmas because he was anointed by God at his baptism (Mark 1:9–11; Matt

---

152. LM: 14. Solemnity of the Nativity of the Lord (Christmas), December 25, At the Mass during the Night, First Reading; LM: 627. Memorial of the Queenship of the Blessed Virgin Mary, August 22, First Reading; LM: 707. The Common of the Blessed Virgin Mary: First Reading, Option 8; CMBVM: Lectionary: 5. The Blessed Virgin Mary, Mother of the Savior, First Reading, Option A; CMBVM: Lectionary: 29. The Blessed Virgin Mary, Queen of All Creation, First Reading, Option A; CMBVM: Lectionary: 33. The Blessed Virgin Mary, Mother of Good Counsel, First Reading, Option A; CMBVM: Lectionary: 45. The Blessed Virgin Mary, Queen of Peace, First Reading.

3:13–17; Luke 3:21–22) and, in Mark's Gospel, by an unnamed woman (Mark 14:3–9). Furthermore, it is easy to see that he is the light that has come into the world, as expressed by the author of John's Gospel (John 1:5; 8:12; 9:5). Isaiah's coronation hymn is also applied to Jesus' mother. She is hailed as queen on August 22; in the LBVM(LL) she is invoked as queen of angels, patriarchs, prophets, apostles, martyrs, confessors, virgins, all saints, and of the rosary not to mention as queen conceived without original sin. In the LBVMOCIBVM she is named queen of love, mercy, angels, patriarchs and prophets, apostles and martyrs, or, confessors and virgins, and all saints, not to mention as queen conceived without original sin, queen assumed into heaven, queen of all the earth, queen of heaven, and queen of the universe. In other words, Mary is queen of all creation. Because Mary is queen mother of the Savior, whom Isaiah called Wonderful Counselor, she is also mother of good counsel, as noted in the LBVM(LL), and like her son who is called Prince of Peace, she is the queen of peace, as found in the LBVM(LL) and in LBVMOCIBVM.[153]

Journal/Meditation: In what ways do your share in God's kingdom, where Christ is King and Mary is Queen?

Prayer: Almighty and eternal God, you chose the Blessed Virgin Mary to bring forth your Son, Jesus Christ, the light of the world, by pouring the Holy Spirit upon her. He humbled himself and accepted death, but you crowned him with glory and honor. Accept my fitting praise of the greatness of your name for all your wonderful works through the Prince of Peace now and forever. Amen.

Root[154]

Text: Isaiah 11:1–5, 10

Scripture: "A shoot shall come out from the stump of Jesse, and a branch shall grow out of his roots." (Isa 11:1)

Reflection: The root is that part of a plant having no leaves or buds that usually spreads underground, anchors the plant, and absorbs water and nutrients from the soil. The prophet Isaiah uses the analogy of a tree root to write about the state of Judah after the Babylonians conquered

---

153. References: CCC, par. 966; MC, pars. 5, 11; RM, par. 41; RVM, par. 21.

154. CMBVM: Lectionary: 2. The Blessed Virgin Mary and the Annunciation of the Lord, First Reading, Option B. CMBVM: Lectionary: Appendix, First Reading, Option 6 (Optional First Reading in Mass 2).

the Kingdom of Judah and, for all practical purposes, put an end to the Davidic monarchy. Isaiah sees David's father, Jesse, as being like a tree stump, which often sprouts branches after a tree has been cut. Isaiah's hope is that one of Jehoiachin's descendants, a branch from Jesse's root, will return to Judah to rule. However, once King Jehoiachin (597 BCE) and the rest of the royal family were taken as captives to Babylon, they did not ever return. Later, in Jewish history this hope took the shape of a messianic expectation and, ultimately, was applied to Jesus. This is why this reading is employed as one option for the first reading in a Mass honoring the Blessed Virgin Mary.

She gave birth to the man identified as the messiah, the LORD's anointed, whom gospel writers attempt to connect to David (Mark 10:47, 11:10; Matt 1:1, 20, 20:31, 21:9; Luke 1:27, 2:4, 32, 18:38–39) in order to prove that he is the hoped-for savior of Israel. However, no matter how hard a writer tries to link Jesus to David through Joseph or Mary, the claim that God (Holy Spirit) is his Father immediately cancels the connection in a patriarchal culture which traced genealogy from father to son. His crime may be the claim that he was king of the Jews (Mark 15:26; Matt 27:37; Luke 23:38; John 19:19), but he was not a direct descendant of David, if God is his Father. Furthermore, in popular understanding, he was defeated by the very people—the Romans—he was expected to defeat! While paradoxical and ironic truth may spill all over, family-history truth trumps the empirical evidence. This is why Judaism still awaits its messiah.[155]

Journal/Meditation: Whom do you consider the root of your family tree? What branches have emerged from him or her? What branches have died?

Prayer: Father, through your prophet Isaiah, you declared that the root of Jesse would stand as a signal to the people. While he was not of David's line, your Spirit rested upon Jesus of Nazareth with the spirit of wisdom, understanding, counsel, might, knowledge, fear, and delight. Grace me with that same Spirit now and forever. Amen.

---

155. References: BYM, pars. 23, 27, 133; CCC, pars. 488, 4967; DPPL, pars. 218–23; MC, par. 5; RM, par. 15.

Well[156]

Text: Isaiah 12:1, 2–3, 4bcd, 5–6 or Isaiah 12:2–3, 4bcd, 5–6

Scripture: "With joy you will draw water from the wells of salvation." (Isa 12:3)

Reflection: The six-verse psalm in chapter 12 of the HB (OT) book of the prophet Isaiah concludes the second section of this six-section book. As a song of thanksgiving, it offers praise to God for the future salvation he will bring to Jerusalem. At the time the poem was composed, the author declares that the LORD was angry, but he turned it away (Isa 12:1). The hoped-for salvation is based in trust of the LORD GOD, who is all strength and might (Isa 12:2). The image of a well is introduced into the song. A well is a very important community source for water among those whose history involves desert living. The shaft that is dug in the ground to the water table is a source of life. Isaiah's poem calls it the well of salvation from which Israel can draw life (Isa 12:3).

Isaiah's song becomes the basis for the unique Johannine story about Jesus meeting a Samaritan woman at Jacob's well (John 4:5–6). Jesus tells the woman about living water (John 4:10), although she still thinks about how deep the well is (John 4:11). Jesus promises her water gushing up to eternal life (John 4:14). Isaiah's psalm is used on the Feast of the Visitation to compare Mary's womb, which houses the source of eternal life, to a well. Elizabeth recognizes this when she declares to Mary, ". . . [B]lessed is the fruit of your womb" (Luke 1:42). In the words of Isaiah, great in their midst is the Holy One of Israel (Isa 12:6b) in the person of Jesus, God's Son. He is the LORD's anointed sent to bring comfort (Isa 61:2), and this makes Mary the mother of consolation and comforter of the afflicted, according to the LBVM(LL). From her people joyfully draw water from the well of salvation opened by her Son.[157]

Journal/Meditation: What are the wells from which you draw the spiritual water of salvation?

Prayer: I give thanks to you, O LORD, and I call upon your name, making known your deeds among the nations and proclaiming that your

---

156. LM: 572. Feast of the Visitation of the Blessed Virgin Mary, May 31, Responsorial Psalm; CMBVM: Lectionary 3: The Visitation of the Blessed Virgin Mary, Responsorial Psalm; CMBVM: Lectionary: 27. The Blessed Virgin Mary, Image and Mother of the Church III, Responsorial Psalm; CMBVM: Lectionary: 31. The Blessed Virgin Mary, Fountain of Salvation I, Responsorial Psalm; CMBVM: Lectionary: 41. The Blessed Virgin Mary, Mother of Consolation, Responsorial Psalm.

157. References: CCC, par. 495; MC, par. 57; RM, pars. 40, 43–44; RVM, par. 25.

name is exalted. I praise you for the well of salvation, your Son, from whom I draw living water for eternal life. He lives and reigns with you, Father, and the Holy Spirit, one God, forever and ever. Amen.

Good News[158]

Text: Isaiah 52:7–10

Scripture: "How beautiful upon the mountains are the feet of the messenger who announces peace, who brings good news, who announces salvation, who says to Zion, 'Your God reigns.'" (Isa 52:7)

Reflection: Zion is the mountain (hill) upon which the city of Jerusalem is built. Before King David captured its inhabitants and made it his capital, it was a city-state protected by walls. In the ancient world, when one king left his walled city to fight against another king, who left his walled city, the king who won the battle sent a runner back to his city with the good news of the victory. The inhabitants of the city of the victorious king would prepare quickly for his triumphant return. This is the image Isaiah is employing in his poem about watchmen patrolling the city walls of Jerusalem and seeing a messenger bringing good news of deliverance from Babylon. The messenger's beautiful feet bring him to the city, where he announces peace, salvation from enemies, and the LORD's return to Zion to be with his people; and all the ends of the earth are seeing the salvation of God.

This text from the prophet Isaiah is used on Christmas Day because the Blessed Virgin Mary is portrayed as a type of Jerusalem in whom the LORD dwelled in the person of Jesus, who was the good news of God's victory over death. While Christmas marks his birth—when all the ends of earth see the salvation of God—it also finds Christians being like watchmen waiting for his return in glory. Meanwhile, they enjoy the kingdom of God he proclaimed. The Virgin of Nazareth welcomed the messenger, the angel Gabriel, who announced peace, who brought good news, who announced salvation, who said to her, "Your God reigns," and who told her that she would conceive and give birth to God's Son.[159]

---

158. LM: 16. Solemnity of the Nativity of the Lord [Christmas], December 25, At the Mass during the Day, First Reading.

159. References: BYM, pars. 14, 18, 24–25, 61; CCC, pars. 484, 488, 495–6; 501, 504, 506, 723, 966, 973; DPPL, par. 101; MC, pars. 6, 17, 26, 28, 33, 41, 44, 46, 57; RM, pars. 8–9, 13, 15, 27; RVM, pars. 10, 16, 18, 20, 24, 33.

Journal/Meditation: What messenger has God sent to you? What did he or she proclaim to you: peace, good news, salvation, the kingdom of God, etc.?

Prayer: God of Zion, how beautiful upon the mountains are the feet of the messenger who announces peace, who brings good news, who announces salvation, and proclaims your reign. Grant that I may be as receptive as the Blessed Virgin Mary and lift up my voice in a song of joy through Christ Jesus my Lord. Amen.

Pain[160]

Text: Isaiah 53:1–5, 7–10

Scripture: "Surely [the servant] has borne our infirmities and carried our diseases; yet we accounted him stricken, struck down by God, and afflicted. But he was wounded for our transgressions, crushed for our iniquities; upon him was the punishment that made us whole, and by his bruises we are healed." (Isa 53:4–5)

Reflection: In this last of four unique servant passages—found in the prophet Isaiah—which describe Israel's fate as God's servant, the reader finds an emphasis on the suffering endured by the LORD's servant as he fulfills his mission. According to the prophet, he is despised, rejected, and known as a man of suffering (Isa 53:3). Furthermore, he is oppressed, afflicted, and killed (Isa 53:7, 8b). The prophet adds: ". . . [I]t was the will of the LORD to crush him with pain" (Isa 53:10a). A longer portion containing this passage from Isaiah is read every year on Friday of the Passion of the Lord [Good Friday] (Isa 52:13–53:12) with the obvious connection made to Jesus' suffering and death (John 13:1–2; 17:1–5). Through his suffering, death, and resurrection, Jesus has become God's servant whose punishment made whole all people; his bruises healed all people.

Because Mary gave birth to Jesus, who healed the sick, she is invoked as health of the sick in LBVM(LL). In John's Gospel, she shares in her Son's pain as she stands near his cross (John 19:25b–27) and, thus, becomes a sign of health, healing, and hope for the sick, especially in her role of accepting God's will for herself and for her Son. Because Mary is invoked as health for the sick, many sick people make pilgrimage to

---

160. CMBVM: Lectionary: 44. The Blessed Virgin Mary, Health of the Sick, First Reading.

her shrines—such as Fatima, Portugal; Lourdes, France; Guadalupe, Mexico—to be healed through her intercession. Thus, human weakness, manifested as sickness in mind or body, has been made holy; it is an experience of God's presence in suffering and in healing. Suffering does not erode humanity; it enhances it. Suffering of any kind gradually transforms one into the image of Jesus, who did his Father's will through his suffering and death on the cross. Mary did not devalue his suffering; she chose to participate in it.[161]

Journal/Meditation: How do you view human sickness? How have you experienced God's healing touch?

Prayer: LORD God, like a lamb led to the slaughter, like a sheep before its shearers is silent, your Son did not open his mouth when he suffered and poured out himself to death on the cross. Give me the vision of the Blessed Virgin Mary that, like her, I may find you present in my suffering all the days of my life. I ask this in the name of Jesus Christ. Amen.

Teacher[162]

Text: Isaiah 56:1, 6–7

Scripture: "Thus says the LORD: . . . [T]he foreigners who join themselves to the LORD . . . I will bring to my holy mountain, and make them joyful in my house of prayer; . . . for my house shall be called a house of prayer for all peoples." (Isa 56:1a, 6a, 7ac)

Reflection: This short passage from the prophet Isaiah comes from the first chapter of what biblical scholars refer to as Third Isaiah (56:1–66:24), written sometime after the Jews had begun to return to Jerusalem (520–500 BCE), that is, after their time of captivity in Babylon. As the opening verse states, God's salvation is coming soon; the city of Jerusalem is about to be delivered (Isa 56:1). The prophet's vision of Jerusalem is broader than Judaism, since he includes foreigners, anyone not Jewish commonly called Gentiles. He sees the rebuilt Temple as a house of prayer for all peoples. That is quite a universal perspective for a Jewish prophet!

---

161. References: BYM, pars. 99–100; CCC, pars. 964, 969; DPPL, par. 102; MC, pars. 7–8, 11, 57; RM, par. 16; RVM, par. 10.

162. CMBVM: Lectionary: 32. The Blessed Virgin Mary, Mother and Teacher in the Spirit, First Reading, Option B.

Such universalism is what a teacher in the spirit offers to students. Mary, both mother and teacher in the spirit, is honored as such. She is mother of Jesus, having carried him in her womb and having fed him from her own breasts. She is also a teacher in the spirit, having nourished him spiritually in the tradition and scriptures of their Jewish ancestors, not to mention forming him in the ways of God. She must have taught him how to pray, that is, how to listen to God's word and ponder it in the heart. The LBVM(LL) invokes Mary as mother of Christ, divine grace, good counsel, of the Creator, of the Savior, and mother most pure, chaste, inviolate, undefiled, amiable, and admirable, while the LBVMOCIBVM invokes her as the mother of Christ and of the Lord, the model of virtue, the untarnished image (mother) of the church, and the splendor of the church.[163]

Journal/Meditation: In what specific ways have you served as a mother (or father) and as a teacher in the spirit of the ways of God?

Prayer: LORD, you have named your house one of prayer for all peoples. Widen my understanding of your vision and help me to listen to those who serve as mother and teacher in the spirit for me. Grant this through Christ, your Son, my Lord. Amen.

Light[164]

Text: Isaiah 60:1–6

Scripture: "Arise, shine; for your light has come, and the glory of the LORD has risen upon you." (Isa 60:1)

Reflection: Light is often opposed to darkness; however, often in the Bible God is found both in light and in darkness. The first seven verses of chapter 60 in the prophet Isaiah is an invitation to the Jews living in Babylon (darkness) to arise and return to Jerusalem (light). The vision of a great return of the exiles had not occurred; only a few of the deported people were ready and willing to go back to Jerusalem and rebuild the city walls and the Temple. Where they should not have found light—Babylon—some Jews had found God; Babylon was supposed to be the place of darkness. Where God's light should have been found—Jerusalem—some

---

163. References: CCC, pars. 507, 773, 829, 963, 967, 972, 975, 2619; RVM, par. 14.

164. LM: 20. Solemnity of the Epiphany of the Lord, January 6 (in the United States, the Sunday after January 1), First Reading; CMBVM: Lectionary: 6. The Blessed Virgin Mary and the Epiphany of the Lord, First Reading.

Jews saw only the darkness of the destroyed city and its Temple. What all came to recognize, ultimately, is that God is found in both light and darkness.

Such is the case with Mary, the mother of Jesus. In the CB (NT), she is one of the first to experience this seeming contradiction. She conceived the light of the Son of God in the darkness of her womb! She gave birth to this light in the darkness of the night. Then, she watched as the darkness of death consumed the light of her Son on the cross, only to experience the light of resurrection emerge from the darkness of the tomb. Later, she herself would participate in death's darkness and resurrection's light through her assumption into heaven. Sometimes it is easier to see in the dark than it is to see in the light; other times it is easier to see in the light than it is to see in the dark. No matter the case, God is found in both.[165]

Journal/Meditation: In what experience of your life did you find God in darkness? In what experience of your life did you find God in light?

Prayer: God of light and God of darkness, you shine your glory upon me and reveal yourself in the thick darkness that covers me. Make my heart thrill and rejoice at your presence now and forever. Amen.

Consolation[166]

Text: Isaiah 61:1–3, 10–11

Scripture: "The spirit of the Lord GOD is upon me, because the LORD has anointed me . . . to provide for those who mourn in Zion—to give them a garland instead of ashes, the oil of gladness instead of mourning, the mantle of praise instead of a faint spirit." (Isa 61:1a, 3a)

Reflection: The Blessed Virgin Mary is presented as a source of comfort for those who may be upset, disappointed, or distressed. The word *consolation* is derived from the Latin *solari*, meaning *to sooth*. Thus consolation implies one person soothing another. The LBVM(LL) invokes Mary as comforter of the afflicted because through her, God sent his Son, Jesus Christ, to be the consolation of his people. Even after her assumption into heaven, the Virgin Mary remains a sign of consolation

---

165. References: DPPL, pars. 106, 118; MC, par. 5.
166. CMBVM: Lectionary: 41. The Blessed Virgin Mary, Mother of Consolation, First Reading, Option A.

for the pilgrim people of God. In other words, she incarnates the words of the prophet Isaiah.

As a mother, she consoles those who mourn the loss of a spouse through old age. She offers consolation to parents whose child dies of an incurable disease because she lost her Son on the cross. Instead of letting the upset wallow in their disappointment, Mary offers hope of a better day and time when crisis occurs. To the distressed, Mary is the image of one who chose to live in the strength of the Spirit and praise God for those he anointed with the Spirit to announce his kingdom here and now. At one time in history, the LORD had come to the aid of his oppressed people in Egypt and led them from slavery to freedom through Moses. At another time in history, he had consoled his people captive in Babylon and led them back to the land he promised them. Through Mary, mother of consolation, he brought forth Jesus to heal and console the brokenhearted.[167]

Journal/Meditation: Who has consoled you? How did he or she do it?

Prayer: God of all consolation, through the Blessed Virgin Mary, you sent Jesus Christ to be the consolation for all people. Grant that through Mary's intercession, I may be graced with the consolation of the Spirit and willingly share it with others. Grant this in the name of Jesus my Lord. Amen.

Clothes I[168]

Text: Isaiah 61:9–11

Scripture: "I will greatly rejoice in the LORD, my whole being shall exult in my God; for he has clothed me with the garments of salvation, he has covered me with the robe of righteousness, as a bridegroom decks himself with a garland, and as a bride adorns herself with her jewels." (Isa 61:10)

Reflection: According to the prophet Isaiah, the LORD offers special clothes to people, namely, salvation and righteousness. The uniqueness

---

167. References: CCC, par. 969; RM, pars. 43–44; RVM, par. 25.

168. LM: 563A. Optional Memorial of Our Lady of Fatima, May 13, First Reading; LM: 573. Memorial of the Immaculate Heart of the Blessed Virgin Mary, Saturday after the Second Sunday after Pentecost, First Reading; LM: 707. The Common of the Blessed Virgin Mary: First Reading, Option 9; CMBVM: Lectionary: 34. The Blessed Virgin Mary, Cause of Our Joy, First Reading, Option B.

of those clothes is compared to ancient marriage customs in which the bridegroom wore a garland and the bride wore precious jewels on their wedding day. The garment of salvation is God's power to save his people from Babylonian captivity by raising up Cyrus, King of Persia, who defeated the Babylonians, and by bringing them back to Jerusalem. The robe of righteousness is God's ability to restore people's relationship with him. Thus, the person wrapped in these clothes is chosen and protected by God and discloses the great things that the LORD does in the world.

God chose to dress the Blessed Virgin Mary in the garment of salvation and the robe of righteousness. She was wrapped in saving grace from the moment of her own conception in the womb of her mother, Anne. She was clothed in the robe of righteousness because the LORD chose her to be the worthy mother of his own Son. Thus, Mary was formed into the image of Jesus, her own Son, before he was conceived in her womb. Through the death and resurrection of Mary's Son, God has made it possible for all people to be wrapped in the garment of salvation and clothed in the robe of righteousness. What the LORD did for Mary, he also did for all.[169]

Journal/Meditation: In what ways have you experienced being clothed in the garment of salvation and covered with the robe of righteousness?

Prayer: I greatly rejoice in you, O LORD; my whole being exults in you, my God. You have clothed me with the garment of salvation, and you have covered me with the robe of righteousness. My rejoicing is like that of a bridegroom decked with a garland and as a bride adorned with jewels through Jesus Christ my Lord. Amen.

Garments[170]

Text: Isaiah 61:10a–d and f, 11; 62:2–3

Scripture: "I will greatly rejoice in the LORD, my whole being shall exult in my God; for he has clothed me with the garments of salvation,

---

169. References: CCC, pars. 411, 492–3, 508, 966–7, 970; MC, pars. 14, 25, 57; RM, pars. 7–10, 24, 39.

170. CMBVM: Lectionary: 15. The Blessed Virgin Mary and the Resurrection of the Lord, Responsorial Psalm; CMBVM: Lectionary: 20. Holy Mary, the New Eve, Responsorial Psalm; CMBVM: Lectionary: Appendix, Responsorial Psalm, Option 14 (Optional Responsorial Psalm in Mass 20).

he has covered me with the robe of righteousness, and as a bride adorns herself with her jewels." (Isa 61:10a–d and f)

Reflection: A garment is a piece of clothing. The prophet Isaiah rejoices that the LORD has clothed him with the garments of salvation (Isa 61:10c) and covered him with the robe of righteousness (Isa 61:10d). The salvation about which the prophet writes is liberation from Babylonian captivity and the return of the exiles to Jerusalem to rebuild the city and its walls (Isa 62:2), what Isaiah refers to as vindication. The righteousness about which the prophet writes is doing the right thing, observing Torah. He compares his vesting in salvation and righteousness to clothes worn by a groom and bride on their wedding day (Isa 61:ef). Then, changing metaphors, the prophet compares righteousness and praise to the first shoots of spring in a garden (Isa 61:11); God will cause them to spring up. Then, with a third metaphor, the prophet tells his readers that they will be like a beautiful crown, a royal diadem, held in God's hand (Isa 62:3).

This canticle is applied to the Blessed Virgin Mary. The words about rejoicing in the LORD and one's whole being exulting in God (Isa 61:10ab) are echoed in Mary's canticle about her soul magnifying the Lord and her spirit rejoicing in God her Savior (Luke 1:46–47). From the moment of her conception in her mother's womb, she was clothed with grace; in the words of the LBVM(LL) and the LBVMOCIBVM, she is the queen conceived without original sin. She is a new Eve, or what the old Eve was supposed to be. God put the robe of righteousness around her when he chose her to be the mother of his only-begotten Son. Like a garden in spring, she gave birth to Jesus, named by the mouth of the LORD (Isa 62:2b). She received her royal diadem from the hand of her God when he raised her from the dead and assumed her into heaven (Isa 62:3) to be with her Son, who died and rose for the salvation of the world.[171]

Journal/Meditation: With what type of garments has God clothed you? With what robe has he covered you?

Prayer: I greatly rejoice in you, O LORD, and my whole being rejoices in you. Through the death and resurrection of your Son, Jesus Christ, you have clothed me with the garments of salvation and covered me with the robe of righteousness. Hear the praise I voice this day, and grant that I may one day receive the crown of beauty in the kingdom where you live and reign forever and ever. Amen.

---

171. References: BYM, pars. 31, 118; CCC, pars. 411, 489–90, 493–4, 504, 508, 958–9, 975, 2617–8; MC, pars. 14, 18, 22, 57; RM, pars. 7–10, 24, 35–37, 39.

Married[172]

Text: Isaiah 62:1–5

Scripture: "You [, Zion,] shall no more be termed Forsaken, and you land shall no more be termed Desolate; but you shall be called My Delight Is in Her, and your land Married; for the LORD delights in you, and your land shall be married." (Isa 62:4)

Reflection: Coming near the end of the book of the prophet Isaiah in the HB (OT), the above passage is meant to strengthen the few Jews returning or thinking about returning to Jerusalem from Babylonian captivity after King Cyrus of Persia has defeated Babylon. Isaiah desires to assure Zion that she is not forsaken by God nor is her land desolate, as Jerusalem and Judah had been described after 587 BCE. The prophet declares that he cannot remain silent nor can he rest until the city and the land are vindicated and the kings of nations surrounding Judah see it happen. Using the image of a man marrying a woman, Isaiah declares that the LORD, the groom, will call Jerusalem, his bride, his delight, and Judah, also his bride, married. Thus, will God delight in both.

The birth of Jesus, Son of God, from Mary, his mother, is understood as God delighting in people and marrying them by becoming one of them. If the earth were considered to be without God, the LORD in the person of Jesus has removed her desolation. Isaiah's words demonstrate God's intense love for Jerusalem and his people. Christmas celebrates God's intense love for all people in the birth of God's Son. Jesus' nativity represents the wedding of heaven and earth, and Mary is the means for this union to occur.[173]

Journal/Meditation: Besides the metaphor of marriage used to describe the union of God and people, what other metaphors do you consider appropriate?

Prayer: O LORD, the nativity of your Son brings together heaven and earth. As I remember this beginning of my redemption through the Blessed Virgin Mary, grant me the grace to recognize the nearness of your divine presence as Father, Son, and Holy Spirit forever and ever. Amen.

---

172. LM: 13. Solemnity of the Nativity of the Lord [Christmas], December 25, At the Vigil Mass, First Reading.

173. References: CCC, pars. 484, 488, 495–6, 501, 504, 506, 723, 966.

Urgency[174]

Text: Isaiah 62:11–12

Scripture: "The LORD has proclaimed to the end of the earth: Say to Daughter Zion, 'See, your salvation comes; his reward is with him, and his recompense before him.'" (Isa 62:11)

Reflection: The last two verses—11–12—of chapter 62 in the prophet Isaiah express urgency. Verse 10 is a command from the prophet to go through Jerusalem's gates and prepare the way for the Jews' return from Babylonian captivity. He tells the reader to build up the road, to clear it of stones, and to repair it for the holy people, the LORD's redeemed, who are traveling home. Salvation is about to descend upon Zion, which will become a city sought out, a city not forsaken by God, and a city in which people want to live. The LORD's promises do not fail.

This immediate need for action and attention declared by Isaiah is focused on the birth of Mary's Son on Christmas Day. Salvation has descended upon the earth, and he should be sought because God has not forsaken his people. Just as the LORD promised redemption for the inhabitants of Jerusalem and fulfilled it by bringing home the Jews, so now he fulfills his promise to save all people by bringing to birth his Son, born of the Blessed Virgin Mary, who herself is like Jerusalem prepared to welcome God's descent. One cannot help but urgently proclaim to the end of the earth the deeds of salvation brought about at God's hands.[175]

Journal/Meditation: What deed of salvation has God brought about in you? What urgency do you feel to proclaim it?

Prayer: All the ends of the earth have seen your saving power, LORD God. In the womb of the Blessed Virgin Mary, you conceived your only-begotten Son, and she gave birth to the Savior of the world. Fill me with the urgency of proclaiming salvation through Jesus Christ now and forever. Amen.

Nursing[176]

Text: Isaiah 66:10–14

---

174. LM: 15. Solemnity of the Nativity of the Lord [Christmas], December 25, At the Mass at Dawn, First Reading.

175. References: BYM, par. 61; MC, par. 57.

176. LM: 531. Optional Memorial of Our Lady of Lourdes, February 11, First Reading; CMBVM: Lectionary: 40. The Blessed Virgin Mary, Mother of Divine Providence, First Reading.

Scripture: "Rejoice with Jerusalem, and be glad for her, all you who love her; rejoice with her in joy, all you who mourn over her—that you may nurse and be satisfied from her consoling breast; that you may drink deeply with delight from her glorious bosom." (Isa 66:10–11)

Reflection: The prophet Isaiah compares Jerusalem to a woman who has just given birth to a child. Indeed, the Jews returning from Babylonian captivity are like mother Jerusalem's children, whom the prophet urges to be glad and to rejoice. He tells them to nurse at her breast, like any child sucks milk from his or her mother's nipples. He tells them to drink deeply with delight from her large bosom. The milk that mother Jerusalem produces is prosperity and wealth—spread over the city by God—which will comfort the returning exiles and cause them to rejoice. In Jerusalem they will flourish, and their flourishing will be a demonstration that the LORD's hand is with his people.

Mary, either as Our Lady of Lourdes or Mother of Divine Providence, sucked fully of God's providential grace and conceived and gave birth to Jesus, who nursed at her breasts. Thus, like Jerusalem before, Mary is the source of the LORD's great providence and a generous mother to all her children—sisters and brothers of Jesus—providing for them through her intercession with God. In this regard, the Virgin Mary is like a mother holding her hungry child and suckling him or her to her breast and sharing her own life with her child. She, the conduit of God's grace, offers it to all who come to her.[177]

Journal/Meditation: In what three ways have you nursed on God's grace?

Prayer: LORD God, you established your dwelling place in Jerusalem, naming her mother of all your chosen people and inviting all to come and suck fully of the milk of prosperity and comfort. Grant through the intercession of the Blessed Virgin Mary that I may nurse always on your grace and come to share eternal life through her Son, Jesus Christ, now and forever. Amen.

---

177. References: CCC, pars. 488, 490, 511; MC, par. 8.

JEREMIAH

Gathered[178]

Text: Jeremiah 31:10, 11–12ab, 13–14

Scripture: "Hear the word of the LORD, O nations, and declare it on the coastlands far away; say, 'He who scattered Israel will gather him, and will keep him as a shepherd a flock.'" (Jer 31:10)

Reflection: The five verses chosen from chapter 31 of the poetry of the prophet Jeremiah are a part of greater section of Jeremiah (chapters 30–33) which depict a harmonious future for Israel and Judah. Jeremiah envisions a future in which the northern kingdom of Israel and the southern kingdom of Judah—both destroyed when he was writing—are restored and reunited as one country with one shepherd (Jer 31:10). Jeremiah sees a day when the Jews will be gathered together on Mount Zion and enjoy the goodness of the LORD, the grain, the wine, the oil, and the young of flock and herd (Jer 31:12). There will be unity between the young women dancing and the young men being merry (Jer 31:13). Thus, everyone will participate in unity. However, this vision never became reality in history!

Unity among people remains a goal to be achieved. Since the Blessed Virgin Mary gave birth to Jesus, who desired that all nations be gathered together (John 17:20–26), she is hailed as the mother of unity; in her womb the divine and human natures of Jesus were united in an unbreakable bond. Invoking her intercession to achieve the unity desired by God and modeled by the Trinity—Father, Son, and Holy Spirit in perfect unity—remains a task on the level of congregation, church, city, state, and nation. Gathering the sheep under one shepherd—"that they may all be one" (John 17:21a)—remains a goal to be achieved. "As you, Father, are in me and I am in you, may they also be in us, so that the world may believe that you have sent me" is Jesus' prayer (John 17:21b). The message is still proclaimed and the prayer continues through the intercession of the mother of unity, Mary.[179]

Journal/Meditation: What unity do you experience now? What unity in your congregation, church, neighborhood, city, state, nation do you think is possible?

---

178. CMBVM: Lectionary: 38. Holy Mary, Mother of Unity, Responsorial Psalm.
179. Reference: BYM, 116.

Prayer: LORD, once you permitted your chosen people to be scattered, but in time you desired that they be gathered, like a shepherd gathers the sheep of his flock. Through the work of the Holy Spirit, the cooperation of people, and the intercession of the Blessed Virgin Mary, mother of your Son, Jesus Christ, bring together all your people. And grant that I may be among them singing aloud your praise in the heavenly Zion, where you live in perfect unity as Father, Son, and Holy Spirit, one God, forever and ever. Amen.

EZEKIEL

Water[180]

Text: Ezekiel 47:1–2, 8–9, 12

Scripture: "On the banks, on both sides of the river, there will grow all kinds of trees for food. Their leaves will not wither nor their fruit fail, but they will bear fresh fruit every month, because the water for them flows from the sanctuary. Their fruit will be for food, and their leaves for healing." (Ezek 47:12)

Reflection: The prophet Ezekiel records a vision of the newly-rebuilt Temple in Jerusalem after the Babylonian captivity of the Jews. The water flows from the Temple because the LORD's house is envisioned as the center of creation, just like the garden of Eden was in the beginning of the HB (OT) book of Genesis. Wherever the water flows, it makes fresh and abundant life. The water is so powerful that fruit trees growing along the bank of the river produce fresh fruit every month for food and healing. In other words, the water is effective; it brings about God's blessing, life, and grace.

Because Mary conceived God's only Son and gave him human life, she can be called the water or fountain of salvation. Prompted by grace, she gave the world the source of its new life. She, who had been prepared for this deed by God, received his stream of grace to her from the moment of her conception. Jesus was like a stream from God; whoever believes in him and follows him finds the way to the water of eternal life. Drinking from this stream flowing from Christ results in abundance for those who are thirsty. From the water flowing from the sanctuary in

---

180. CMBVM: Lectionary: 31. The Blessed Virgin Mary, Fountain of Salvation I, First Reading.

Ezekiel's vision, God brings abundance for people today, just like he did for Mary and her Son, Jesus.[181]

Journal/Meditation: What abundance has God brought from you because you drink the water of eternal life?

Prayer: Ever-living God, you share your water of life with your people, especially the Blessed Virgin Mary. Grant that I may drink from the stream of your grace and faithfully follow your Son to the joy of eternal life forever and ever. Amen.

MICAH

Nowhereville[182]

Text: Micah 5:1–4a (5:2–5)

Scripture: "... [Y]ou, O Bethlehem of Ephrathah, who are one of the little clans of Judah, from you shall come forth for me one who is to rule in Israel, whose origin is from of old, from ancient days." (Mic 5:1 [5:2])

Reflection: The HB (OT) prophet Micah declares that a new ruler will restore Israel after the Jews return from Babylonian Captivity to Jerusalem. The prophet does this by declaring that the new leader will come from King David's hometown, Bethlehem, and will be a descendant of David's clan, Ephrathah. Thus, the Davidic dynasty, which ruled in Jerusalem until 587 BCE, will be restored. Of course, this never occurred, but the hope lived on, nevertheless, for an anointed (messiah, christ) of the LORD who would restore self-rule to God's people. The reader doesn't want to miss the prophetic irony: Bethlehem was a Nowhereville; it was so small that the entering and leaving sign could have been placed on the same pole!

This is why the same irony is transferred to Mary and Joseph, who live in Bethlehem in Matthew's Gospel, and who travel there for a census in Luke's Gospel. It is one of the ways that the two gospel writers attempt to tie Jesus to David by portraying him being born in David's hometown,

---

181. References: CCC, pars. 411, 488, 490–3, 508, 511, 966–7.

182. LM: 636. Feast of the Nativity of the Blessed Virgin Mary, September 8, First Reading, First Option; LM 707. The Common of the Blessed Virgin Mary: First Reading, Option 10; CMBVM Lectionary: 5. The Blessed Virgin Mary, Mother of the Savior, First Reading, Option B; CMBVM: Lectionary: Appendix, First Reading, Option 7 (Optional First Reading in Mass 5).

Bethlehem. Mary gives birth to Jesus, the hoped-for messiah, in Nowhereville. When celebrating the nativity of the Blessed Virgin Mary or her role as Jesus' mother, the reader becomes aware of the irony that the messiah, God's Son, was conceived in the womb of a virginal maiden from Nazareth and born in Bethlehem, where he was not expected to be. This is precisely the point, of course: God is found where God chooses to live, not where people expect him to be: Nowhereville.

Journal/Meditation: Where have you found God but did not expect to find God there?

Prayer: LORD God, you made fruitful the virginity of Mary by bringing forth your Son, Jesus Christ. Grant that I may experience her intersession, be enlightened by the Holy Spirit, and share the eternal life of your Son, who lives and reigns forever and ever. Amen.

ZEPHANIAH

Rejoice[183]

Text: Zephaniah 3:14–18a

Scripture: "Sing aloud, O daughter Zion; shout, O Israel! Rejoice and exult with all your heart, O daughter Jerusalem! The LORD, your God, is in your midst . . . ." (Zeph 3:14, 17a)

Reflection: There is a lot of shouting in the HB (OT) prophet Zephaniah. He tells Zion, the hill upon which is built the city of Jerusalem, to sing aloud. He tells Israel to shout. And he tells Jerusalem to rejoice and exult. All this shouting, rejoicing, and display of great happiness is because the LORD will, hopefully, defeat Judah's enemies—the Babylonians—and he, the king of Israel, will once again live in the holy city among his people, who will have returned from Babylonian exile. Zephaniah declares that the LORD will rejoice over the people and the city, renewing them in his love and exulting over them with loud singing (Zeph 3:17). Thus, the people will rejoice upon their return to Zion and Jerusalem, and God will rejoice over his people.

The Blessed Virgin Mary, the mother of Jesus, rejoiced over the LORD's presence in her life. She was visited by him in the person of the angel Gabriel and asked to be the mother of his only-begotten Son. She

---

183. LM: 572. Feast of the Visitation of the Blessed Virgin Mary, May 31, First Reading, First Option; CMBVM: Lectionary: 3. The Visitation of the Blessed Virgin Mary, First Reading, Option A.

conceived Jesus by the power of the LORD's Spirit (Luke 1:26–38). Thus, not only was God in her midst, but he found residence in flesh in her womb. As a daughter of Zion and a daughter of Jerusalem, she rejoiced over the renewing love of God being given to her, and she exulted over the LORD, who had come to dwell within her.[184]

Journal/Meditation: What has God recently done for you that caused you to rejoice?

Prayer: LORD God, King of Israel, because you are in my midst, I do not fear. Awaken me to the daily power of the Holy Spirit at work within me that I may sing, shout, rejoice, and exult in your praise, Father, Son, and Holy Spirit, forever and ever. Amen.

Unity[185]

Text: Zephaniah 3:14–20

Scripture: "... I will save the lame and gather the outcast.... At that time I will bring you home, at the time when I gather you; for I will make you renowned and praised among all the peoples of the earth, when I restore your fortunes before your eyes, says the LORD." (Zeph 3:19b–20)

Reflection: Unity is the state of being one. Unity results from the combining of separate people, things, or entities to form one whole in harmony with singleness of purpose. The HB (OT) prophet Zephaniah illustrates a biblical truth that is found from Genesis to Revelation: God desires unity among people. Jacob's (Israel's) twelve sons are a family united. Moses leads the tribes out of Egyptian slavery to freedom as one. David unites the tribes into a confederacy, a single nation. While unity is often achieved for a while, disunity also appears. That is why the prophet Zephaniah depicts the LORD declaring that he will save the lame, gather the outcast, and bring home to Jerusalem from Babylon all his people. The result is that they will be renowned and praised for their unity throughout all the earth.

The Blessed Virgin Mary is a model of unity. She bore in her womb the Word of God, Jesus Christ, who united in one person the divine and human natures. Christ is presented as the bridegroom of the church, his bride; he nourishes and takes care of her, the many members of his

---

184. References: BYM, par. 22; CCC, par. 495.

185. CMBVM: Lectionary: 38. Holy Mary, Mother of Unity, First Reading, Option A.

body (Eph 5:29–32). Likewise, Mary is the image of the church, the many members who have become one body of Christ. The LBVMOCIBVM invokes her as the untarnished image of the church and splendor of the church. She forms a unity in prayer with Jesus' disciples and other women (Acts 1:14). Thus, Christians of any kind gathered together in prayer of any kind are a sign of the hoped-for unity represented by the Virgin Mary and the prophet Zephaniah.[186]

Journal/Meditation: Where do you find traces of Christian unity among churches today? Where do you find unity within yourself?

Prayer: Holy Father, your Son, Jesus Christ, chose Mary to be his mother in whose womb divinity and humanity were united. He chose the united church for his bride and desired that all scattered people be gathered into unity. Send upon me and all people the Spirit of unity that we may praise you in one glorious song now and forever. Amen.

ZECHARIAH

Joy[187]

Text: Zechariah 2:10–13 (2:14–17)

Scripture: "Sing and rejoice, O daughter Zion! For lo, I will come and dwell in your midst, says the LORD. Be silent, all people, before the LORD; for he has roused himself from his holy dwelling." (Zech 2:10, 13 [2:14, 17])

Reflection: The LBVM(LL) invokes the Blessed Virgin Mary as the cause of people's joy, and the LBVMOCIBVM invokes her as the joy of Israel. Joy describes an emotion which gives pleasure to the person experiencing it, and it can refer to satisfaction, gladness, delight, or happiness, as the HB (OT) prophet Zechariah makes clear. God urges the Babylonian exiles, who have returned to Jerusalem, to have joy because he has come to dwell in their midst. Once the citizens of Jerusalem recognize the LORD's presence, the prophet tells them to be silent. While joy and

---

186. Reference: BYM, par. 22.

187. LM: 601. Optional Memorial of Our Lady of Mount Carmel, July 16, First Reading; LM. 680. Memorial of the Presentation of the Blessed Virgin Mary, November 21, First Reading; LM. 690A. Feast of Our Lady of Guadalupe, December 12, First Reading, First Option; LM: 707. The Common of the Blessed Virgin Mary: First Reading, Option 11; CMBVM: Lectionary: 34. The Blessed Virgin Mary, Cause of Our Joy, First Reading, Option A.

silence may not seem to be compatible, they represent the paradoxical nature of biblical literature, that is, awe-filled joy expressed in awe-filled silence when the divine presence is recognized.

There can be no doubt that Mary represents this joy-silence awe, since this text is used for celebrations honoring her as Our Lady of Mount Carmel and Our Lady of Guadalupe and on the memorial of her presentation in the Temple from the apocryphal *The Proto-Gospel of James* (7:1–3).[188] Mary is the cause of joy because she cooperated with God in the incarnation of the Word, who came to dwell within her. Her Son fulfills God's promise to dwell with people, bringing them news of great joy. In Luke's Gospel, the angel of the Lord declares to the shepherds, "I am bringing you good news of great joy for all the people" (Luke 2:10). Even greater joy was brought to the world through Jesus' resurrection from the dead. In the midst of such joy, a somber silence descends as people bask in the awe resulting from an awareness of the divine presence.[189]

Journal/Meditation: What causes you to be joyful? How has God's work in your life given you joy?

Prayer: God of joy, the birth of Mary brought joy to the world, but even more joy emerged when she conceived and gave birth to your Son, Jesus Christ. Through the gift of the Holy Spirit, fill me with the same joy that I may stand in silence before your divine presence—Father, Son, and Holy Spirit—now and forever. Amen.

Queen[190]

Text: Zechariah 9:9–10

Scripture: "Rejoice greatly, O daughter Zion! Shout aloud, O daughter Jerusalem! Lo, your king comes to you; triumphant and victorious is he, humble and riding on a donkey, on a colt, the foal of a donkey." (Zech 9:9)

Reflection: The prophet Zechariah offers hope to the exiles who have returned from Babylon to Jerusalem in the midst of ruin. He offers hope by telling the newly-returned citizens of Jerusalem that they should

---

188. Ehrman, *Other Gospels*, 24–36.
189. Reference: CCC, par. 495.
190. CMBVM: Lectionary: 3. The Visitation of the Blessed Virgin Mary, First Reading, Option C; CMBVM: Lectionary: 29. The Blessed Virgin Mary, Queen of All Creation, First Reading, Option B; CMBVM: Lectionary: Appendix, First Reading, Option 8 (Optional First Reading in Mass 3 and 29).

rejoice and shout aloud because a new king is coming. He will revive the Davidic dynasty that had ended in 587 BCE with the deportation of the last king of Judah to Babylon. He will enter the city riding on a donkey, the traditional transportation for gods and kings in the ancient world. His first act will be to forbid chariots and war-horses so that there will be peace among the nations. It comes as no surprise that Zechariah's words underlie Jesus' entry into Jerusalem in Mark's Gospel (11:1–10) and Luke's Gospel (19:29–38) and are (mis)quoted by the author of Matthew's Gospel (21:1–9) and the author of John's Gospel (12:12–15) in order to identify Jesus as the hoped-for king and messiah.

Thus, if Jesus is the king, then Mary is the queen mother. As a daughter of Zion, she welcomes the Word, Jesus Christ, into her womb, where he dwells for nine months. The LBVM(LL) hails her as a spiritual vessel, a vessel of honor, and a singular vessel of devotion. The LBVMOCIBVM hails her as the virgin daughter of Zion, the chosen daughter of the Father, and the mother of Christ the King. She is invoked as queen of angels, patriarchs, prophets, apostle, martyrs, confessors, virgins, all saints, and peace in the LBVM(LL), and as queen of love, mercy, peace, angels, patriarchs and prophets, apostles and martyrs, confessors and virgins, all saints, all the earth, heaven, and the universe in the LBVMOCIBVM. She receives her honor from the king, who comes riding on a donkey and, after death on a cross, rises triumphantly and victoriously.[191]

Journal/Meditation: What does the title of queen mother for Mary mean for you?

Prayer: I rejoice greatly and shout aloud in praise of you, LORD God. Your daughter of Zion, Mary, gave birth to Christ my king, who came triumphant and victorious, humble and riding on a donkey before he was crucified and you raised him from the dead. Grant me a share in his new life now and forever. Amen.

MALACHI

Covenant[192]

Text: Malachi 3:1–4

---

191. References: CCC, pars. 489, 722, 966, 2619.

192. LM: 524. The Feast of the Presentation of the Lord, February 2, First Reading; CMBVM: Lectionary: 7. The Blessed Virgin Mary and the Presentation of the Lord, First Reading.

Scripture: "See, I am sending my messenger to prepare the way before me, and the Lord whom you seek will suddenly come to his temple. The messenger of the covenant in whom you delight—indeed, he is coming, says the LORD of hosts." (Mal 3:1)

Reflection: A covenant is a solemn agreement that is binding on all parties. The HB (OT) prophet Malachi announces the appearance of the messenger of the covenant made between God and Abraham (Gen 15:7–21; 17:1–14) and renewed by Moses at Mount Sinai (Horeb) (Exod 24:3–8). While the identity of the messenger of the covenant is not stated, the end of the prophet's book states that Elijah will be sent (Mal 4:5 [3:23]), and the CB (NT) tradition associates the messenger of the covenant with John the Baptist (Mark 9:13; Matt 11:13–14, 17:11–12; Luke 1:17). In Malachi, the messenger of the covenant is sent to the Temple priests, the descendants of Levi, who have not been making the proper offerings to the LORD (Mal 3:3).

The Blessed Virgin Mary can be considered a messenger of the covenant. Like a temple, she received the sudden Word of God in her womb, where Jesus was made flesh. And she delighted in bearing him for nine months and prepared the way for his birth into the world. Uniquely in Luke's Gospel, Mary, herself a messenger of the covenant, brings the messenger of the new covenant to Jerusalem to present him to the LORD in the Temple and to make the appropriate offering, unlike the priests making improper offerings (Luke 2:22–40). Thus, she fulfills the words of the prophet Malachi; the LORD in the person of Jesus has suddenly come to his Father house (Luke 2:49), which he will later designate a den of robbers (Luke 19:45–46; Mark 11:15–17; Matt 21:12–13). God sends messengers of the covenant suddenly and often to awaken people to his presence.[193]

Journal/Meditation: Recently, who has been a messenger of the covenant to you?

Prayer: God of the covenant, once you entered into a solemn agreement with Abraham and Sarah and renewed it with Moses. Through the cross and resurrection of your Son, Jesus, born of Mary of Nazareth, you established a new covenant. Continue to send messengers of your covenant that I may hear their proclamation and know what you desire of me. I ask this through Jesus Christ my Lord. Amen.

---

193. References: MC, pars. 7, 20, 57; RM, par. 16; RVM, par. 20.

2

Christian Bible (New Testament)

MATTHEW'S GOSPEL

Women[1]

Text: Longer Form: Matthew 1:1–16, 18–24; Shorter Form: Matthew 1:18–23

Scripture: "An account of the genealogy of Jesus the Messiah, the son of David, the son of Abraham.... Judah [was] the father of Perez and Zerah by Tamar ... and Salmon the father of Boaz by Rahab, and Boaz the father of Obed by Ruth .... And David was the father of Solomon by the wife of Uriah ... and Jacob the father of Joseph the husband of Mary, of whom Jesus was born, who is called the Messiah." (Matt 1:1, 3, 5, 6b, 16)

Reflection: In Matthew's unique genealogy of Jesus, the names of five women are mentioned; they are interspersed among an otherwise all-male list of names! Tamar, Judah's daughter-in-law, dressed like a harlot and seduced her father-in-law; through their union, she conceived and bore twins. Rahab was the manager of a brothel in Jericho. When Joshua sent spies to reconnoiter the land, Rahab hid them from the king of Jericho. Ruth was the mother of Obed, whose father was Boaz. After dressing

---

1. LM: 636. Feast of the Nativity of the Blessed Virgin Mary, September 8, Gospel; LM: 712. The Common of the Blessed Virgin Mary: Gospel, Option 1; CMBVM: Lectionary: 2. The Blessed Virgin Mary and the Annunciation of the Lord, Gospel, Option B (Shorter Form); CMBVM: Lectionary: Appendix, Gospel, Option 17 (Optional Gospel in Mass 2).

in her finest robes, she placed herself at Boaz's feet in order to convince him to marry her and raise up heirs to her dead husband's name. Obed, her son—father of Jesse—became the grandfather of David, and she was David's great-grandmother. The wife of Uriah was Bathsheba; King David saw her bathing on the roof, desired her, and conceived a child with her. Later, in order to cover up his sin, David sent Uriah into the front line of battle, where he was slain. David's and Bathsheba's child was born and died, but Bathsheba conceived again and gave birth to Solomon, David's successor.

These four women, unique to Matthew's Gospel, bear sons through irregular and unexpected situations. Even though their reputations are colored, to say the least, they are remembered by Matthew for doing God's will. They prepare for the supreme irregularity of birth, Jesus, the Son of God, from Mary, a virgin, found to be with child through the Holy Spirit before she and Joseph, her fiancé, live together. Matthew understands that the irregular birth of the Messiah, foreshadowed in the other four women, is brought about by God, who works his will in the lives of some people most would least expect.[2]

Journal/Meditation: How has God been able to work his will through some irregularity in your life? in your family?

Prayer: God of Abraham and David, you accomplished your will in Tamar, Rahab, Ruth, and Bathsheba and brought forth the ancestors of your Son. Of Mary was born the Messiah, Jesus Christ. Fill me with the Spirit so that I may know your will and do it today, tomorrow, and forever. Amen.

Fourteen[3]

Text: Matthew 1:1–17

Scripture: "So all the generations from Abraham to David are fourteen generations; and from David to the deportation to Babylon, fourteen generations; and from the deportation to Babylon to the Messiah, fourteen generations." (Matt 1:17)

Reflection: Before Arabic numerals were invented sometime in the late seventh or early eighth century CE, letters were used to indicate

---

2. References: CCC, pars. 488, 496-9, 502, 505–7, 510.

3. CMBVM: Lectionary: 1. The Blessed Virgin Mary, Chosen Daughter of Israel, Gospel.

amounts. The most common form of this is Roman numerals where I equals one, V equals five, C equals one hundred, etc. The same method was used in Hebrew. If the Hebrew letters in David's name are added, they yield fourteen, which the author of Matthew's Gospel uses to divide the ancestors of the Messiah into three groups of fourteen each, even though the last set of names contains only thirteen! Thus, the point of the three sets of fourteen names—some of which are known and some unknown—is to connect Jesus to David, to whom God (represented by the number three) made the promise that his line would endure forever. Matthew conveniently ignores the conclusion that if God is Jesus' father, then Joseph is not, rendering the genealogical connection to David null and void. However, when Joseph marries Mary, he does become Jesus' legal father; nevertheless, he is not his blood father, and that is what a genealogy traces: blood!

The names in the genealogy are divided into three sets, and three is a sacred number. Three refers to the spiritual order. It is used extensively throughout biblical literature to indicate the divine presence. Thus, from the point of view of the author of Matthew's Gospel, the LORD has been at work for generations from Abraham to Joseph preparing for the birth of the Messiah. The five women display a righteousness that is higher than the men with whom they are associated. In other words, the five of them—the same number as the books in the Torah—do God's will even though from a human perspective they are sinners! Joseph, like the women, is declared righteous because, instead of having pregnant Mary stoned according to the Torah, he takes her as his wife; he considers it the right thing to do. As the LBVMOCIBVM declares, Mary is the chosen daughter of the Father, the virgin daughter of Zion, and the mother of the Lord, three invocations like the three sets of fourteen names each. According to Matthew, God works through human generation even though humans may not be aware of it.[4]

Journal/Meditation: What recent set of three have you noted in your daily life? How was God at work?

Prayer: Father of Abraham, David, and Jesus, you accomplish your will from one generation to the next through your chosen people. Make me aware of your presence and guide me with the Spirit to know your will and to do it. I ask this in the name of your Son, Jesus Christ, born of Mary and Lord forever and ever. Amen.

---

4. References: BYM, par. 133; CCC, pars. 144, 488–9, 497, 2619; MC, par. 56.

Dream II[5]

Text: Matthew 1:16, 18–21, 24a

Scripture: "When Joseph awoke from sleep, he did as the angel of the Lord commanded him; he took [Mary] as his wife." (Matt 1:24)

Reflection: Because Matthew's Gospel is written for (Christian) Jews, it features Joseph, son of Jacob and "the husband of Mary, of whom Jesus was born, who is called the Messiah" (Matt 1:16). Joseph is depicted by the author of the gospel as a dreamer; the angel of the Lord appears to him in dreams and directs his actions (Matt 1:20, 24; 2:13, 19, 22). The reader should be suspicious when he or she realizes that the CB (NT) Joseph looks like the HB (OT) Joseph, son of Jacob, who not only had dreams (Gen 37:5–11) but also interpreted them (Gen 40:1–41:57). Furthermore, just like the HB (OT) Joseph saved his people from famine, so the CB (NT) Joseph saves Mary from public disgrace and stoning and becomes the legal father of the Son he named Jesus, who saves his people from their sins (Matt 1:21).

When CB (NT) Joseph takes Mary as his wife or spouse, he breaks Torah (Deut 22:23–24) but is, nevertheless, declared to be righteous by the author. Because he finds his virgin fiancée to be pregnant and he knows that he is not the father, Joseph should see that Mary is stoned to death. However, the angel of the Lord, a code name for God, appears to him in a dream and informs him not to be afraid to take Mary as his wife, "for the child conceived in her is from the Holy Spirit" (Matt 1:20). The LORD is in charge of this pregnancy, and, just as he has worked righteousness out of apparent sinfulness in past generations, he is at work bringing righteousness out of breaking Torah in the present. That is the lesson learned by Joseph, spouse of Mary.[6]

Journal/Meditation: What experience have you had of God working righteousness out of your sinfulness or law-breaking?

Prayer: LORD God, you made your will known to Joseph through an angel while he dreamed. Fill me with the Holy Spirit of discernment while I dream and help me to carry out you will. I ask this in the name of Jesus, Emmanuel, God-with-me now and forever. Amen.

---

5. LM: 543. Solemnity of St. Joseph, Spouse of the Blessed Virgin Mary, March 19, Gospel, Option A.

6. References: BYM, par. 133; CCC, pars. 488, 496–7; DPPL, pars. 218–23.

Fulfill[7]

Text: Longer Form: Matthew 1:1–25; Shorter Form: Matthew 1:18–25

Scripture: "All this took place to fulfill what had been spoken by the Lord through the prophet: 'Look, the virgin shall conceive and bear a son, and they shall name him Emmanuel,' which means, 'God is with us.'" (Matt 1:22–23)

Reflection: The author of Matthew's Gospel likes to use a literary device known as prediction-fulfillment. The author predicts something to happen, often using a HB (OT) quotation, and the proceeds to announce its fulfillment. The author uses this technique in his attempt to convince his Jewish audience that Jesus is the messiah they have hoped for. His first use of the prediction-fulfillment literary device is found in his narrative about the conception and birth of Jesus to Mary and Joseph. After the angel of the Lord appears in a dream to Joseph to inform him that Mary's pregnancy is by the Holy Spirit, the narrator states that the prediction fulfills what the LORD spoke through the prophet Isaiah about a virgin conceiving and bearing a son and naming him Emmanuel. However, Isaiah does not write about a virgin, but about a young woman, a wife of King Ahaz of Judah, whose kingdom is under attack. The birth of a son to the king is announced by Isaiah in order to give him hope that he will not be defeated by his enemies. That is why the son will be named Immanuel, which means "God is with us." The son will be the living sign of God's presence with the king and the people of Judah.

The author of Matthew's Gospel removes from its original context the quote from Isaiah and interprets it in reference to Jesus, whom he declares to be God with his people. Thus, the prediction (from Isaiah) is fulfilled in Jesus, according to Matthew. And this prediction-fulfillment should convince his readers that Jesus is the messiah for whom they longed. Matthew echoes this fulfillment again at the end of his book when Jesus declares to his followers, ". . . [R]emember, I am with you always, to the end of the age" (Matt 28:b). Jesus, conceived by the Holy Spirit in the womb of the Virgin Mary, crucified, and raised remains with his followers until the end of time. He is the fulfillment of Isaiah's prediction: Immanuel.[8]

---

7. LM: 13. The Solemnity of the Nativity of the Lord (Christmas), December 25, At the Vigil Mass, Gospel.

8. References: BYM, pars. 19–20; MC, pars. 26, 56–7; RM, pars. 7, 9.

Journal/Meditation: What event in your life do you consider to be one of prediction-fulfillment? How was God at work in it?

Prayer: Almighty God, your evangelist Matthew wrote about the fulfillment of your words to your prophet Isaiah. The Virgin Mary conceived and bore a son and named him Emmanuel, because he is a sign of your presence with your people. Make me even more aware of your divine presence through Jesus Christ, who lives and reigns with you and the Holy Spirit, one God, forever and ever. Amen.

House III[9]

Text: Matthew 2:1–12

Scripture: "On entering the house, [the magi] saw the child with Mary his mother; and they knelt down and paid him homage. Then, opening their treasure chests, they offered him gifts of gold, frankincense, and myrrh." (Matt 2:11)

Reflection: The Scripture above may spark memories of singing "We Three Kings," a popular Christmas carol that explains the meaning of the three gifts presented by the magi, astrologers, or magicians. However, Matthew's unique story about wise men from the East coming to Bethlehem to find Mary and Jesus—Joseph being conspicuously absent—does not indicate how many of them there are; the story only names three gifts they present to Jesus, who lives with his parents in Bethlehem. Like he did with Joseph—creating him in the image of the HB (OT) Joseph, who was a dreamer and interpreter of dreams—Matthew employs the running narrative of Moses and pharaoh to craft Jesus into a new Moses and Herod into a new pharaoh, who is frightened upon hearing about the birth of a new king of the Jews (Matt 2:3) and decides that he must be eliminated (Matt 2:16).

And that is the purpose of the three gifts. In the ancient world, gold, frankincense, and myrrh are gifts one brings to a funeral, not to a baby shower! Gold coins were placed on the eyes of the deceased to keep them closed. Frankincense was burned in order to cover the stench. And myrrh was a perfumed oil used to anoint the body before burial. In other words, this narrative is the end of the story told at the beginning!

---

9. LM: 20. The Solemnity of the Epiphany of the Lord, January 6 (in the United States, the Sunday after January 1), Gospel; CMBVM: Lectionary: 6. The Blessed Virgin Mary and the Epiphany of the Lord, Gospel; CMBVM: Lectionary: 24. The Blessed Virgin Mary, Seat of Wisdom, Gospel, Option A.

It predicts what will happen to the child, and it invites the reader to continue reading the story to the end to discover that it comes true: Jesus dies on a cross. The epiphanic dimension is his childhood manifestation to Gentile magi—and not Jews—in Bethlehem—the Jewish hometown of King David—and the death that awaits him in Jerusalem at the hand of another pharaoh—Pilate. All this is presented by the gospel's author while the child sits on his mother's knee in their home in Bethlehem.[10]

Journal/Meditation: What gift have you received from another that has multiple levels of meaning for you, like the gold, frankincense, and myrrh in Matthew's story?

Prayer: Holy Father, wise men, guided by your grace find the house in Bethlehem with Mary and the child Jesus and, after declaring him king, worship him and offer him gifts. Grant me the same grace that I may find him in all I meet and offer him the gift of praise now and forever. Amen.

Nazareth[11]

Text: Matthew 2:13-15, 19-23

Scripture: ". . . [A]fter being warned in a dream, [Joseph] went away to the district of Galilee. There he made his home in a town called Nazareth, so that what had been spoken through the prophets might be fulfilled, 'He will be called a Nazorean.'" (Matt 2:22b-23)

Reflection: Because Matthew understands Jesus through the lens of Moses, Jesus must go to Egypt, like Moses, to escape the death-trap of Herod, like Moses escaped pharaoh's order that all Hebrew boys be drowned in the Nile River. Once Herod is dead, Joseph brings the child and his mother out of Egypt to the land of Israel, but instead of settling in Bethlehem, where they had lived previously, he takes them to the district of Galilee in the north of what had once been the Kingdom of Israel and settles in a town named Nazareth. The author justifies this move with a quote that cannot be found in any prophet in the HB (OT): "He will be called a Nazorean" (Matt 2:23). Since he is known as Jesus of Nazareth (Mark 1:9, 24, 47; 16:6; Matt 26:71; Luke 4:34, 18:37; 24:19; John 1:45;

---

10. References: DPPL, pars. 106, 118; MC, par. 5; RM, par. 16.

11. LM: 17. Feast of the Holy Family of Jesus, Mary, and Joseph, Sunday within the Octave of the Nativity of the Lord [Christmas], or, if there is no Sunday, December 30, Gospel, Cycle A; LM: 712. The Common of the Blessed Virgin Mary, Gospel, Option 2; CMBVM: Lectionary: 8. Our Lady of Nazareth II, Gospel.

18:5, 7; 19:19), Matthew must get him to that town before continuing his story.

Throughout the narrative of the angel of the Lord appearing in a dream and telling Joseph to take the child Jesus and his mother to Egypt and his going to Egypt, to the narrative of the angel of the Lord appearing in a dream to Joseph and telling him to take the child and his mother to the land of Israel and his going to Israel, the only voice heard—other than the narrator—is that of the angel of the Lord (and the prophet Hosea 11:1 quoted in Matt 2:15b). Just like the LORD directed the events in Moses' life, so he directs the events in Jesus' life in Matthean understanding. In Luke's Gospel, the angel Gabriel is sent by God to Mary engaged to Joseph who live in Nazareth (Luke 1:26–27). No matter how the couple get to Nazareth—after a trip to Egypt or found already living there—Mary and Joseph (who, in Matthew's Gospel, disappears from the narrative), take care of their Son, a new Moses, who will save his people.[12]

Journal/Meditation: From what town to what town has God led you? Make a list of the towns you have called home and identify the work of God in you in each.

Prayer: All-holy Father, once you directed that your Son, born of Mary, live and grow in Nazareth. Direct all my moves from one town to another and grant that I may one day be escorted by his Blessed Mother to my final home in heaven. I ask this in the name of Jesus Christ my Lord. Amen.

Mourn[13]

Text: Matthew 5:1–12

Scripture: ". . . [Jesus] began to speak, and taught [his disciples], saying: 'Blessed are those who mourn, for they will be comforted.'" (Matt 5:2, 4)

Reflection: While it may be possible, it is not probable that a person can live a whole life and not experience mourning. A person who mourns expresses sadness at the death of a loved one or because something that was treasured was lost or no longer exists. There is also a mourning for

---

12. References: BYM, pars. 14, 131; CCC, par. 488; MC, pars. 28, 34, 37; RVM, par. 15.

13. CMBVM: Lectionary: 41. The Blessed Virgin Mary, Mother of Consolation, Gospel, Option A.

the passing of years; an elderly person may mourn getting older. In the Matthean beatitudes, Jesus, paradoxically, calls blessed—that is, in a healthy relationship with God—those who mourn; they will be comforted in God's kingdom. This is like wishing someone, "Happy mourning!" In a parallel in Luke's Gospel, the same paradox is present. Jesus states, "Blessed are you who weep now, for you will laugh" (Luke 6:21b). In effect, "Happy weeping!" states Jesus. What at first seems contradictory in these beatitudes, however, is full of truth once it is mined.

Mourning or weeping leads to comfort and laughter; the rhythm of mourning and comfort is part of the paradox of life. Likewise, the rhythm of weeping and laughter is a part of the paradox of life. The Blessed Virgin Mary, invoked as comforter of the afflicted in the LBVM(LL), conceived and gave birth to the incarnation of mourning and comfort. Furthermore, she achieved blessedness through mourning the death of Jesus and being comforted by his resurrection from the dead. She stands as a model of those who become living paradoxes of mourning and comfort, weeping and laughter. And, as such, she is a sign of hope for God's pilgrim people.[14]

Journal/Meditation: Where do you find the intersection of mourning and comfort (weeping and laughter) in your life?

Prayer: Through the Blessed Virgin Mary, LORD God, you sent the consolation of your people, Jesus Christ. Fill me with your Spirit of consolation that I may share it with those who mourn and weep. Grant this in the name of Jesus now and forever. Amen.

Disciple[15]

Text: Matthew 12:46–50

Scripture: ". . . [P]ointing to his disciples, [Jesus] said, 'Here are my mother and my brothers! For whoever does the will of my Father in heaven is my brother and sister and mother.'" (Matt 12:49–50)

---

14. References: CCC, par. 969; MC, par. 57; RM, pars. 16, 40; RVM, par. 25.

15. LM: 601. Optional Memorial of Our Lady of Mount Carmel, July 16, Gospel; LM: 680. Memorial of the Presentation of the Blessed Virgin Mary, November 21, Gospel; LM: 712. The Common of the Blessed Virgin Mary, Gospel, Option 3; LM: 1002. The Blessed Virgin Mary, III. Our Lady, Queen of Apostles, Gospel, First Option; CMBVM: Lectionary: 10. Holy Mary, Disciple of the Lord, Gospel, Option B; CMBVM: Lectionary: 32. The Blessed Virgin Mary, Mother and Teacher in the Spirit, Gospel, Option A.

Reflection: The origin of the Matthean passage about Jesus rejecting his biological family (Matt 12:46–50) is Mark's Gospel (2:31–35). In Mark's Gospel, Jesus' biological family members doubt his sanity and go to his home to restrain him (Mark 3:20–21), details left out of Matthew's Gospel! The Markan Jesus replaces his family with the family of faith, those who are sitting around him, whoever does the will of God. In Mark's Gospel, this is the only time Jesus' mother is mentioned, but not named, and she is rejected by her Son. Later, she is named Mary (Mark 6:3) in the passage narrating Jesus rejection in Nazareth. In Matthew's Gospel, this is the first reference to her since the nativity (1:16–2:23). While the display of Mary's faith—as one who does the will of the Father in heaven (Matt 12:50)—in the nativity material is contrasted with her rejection as biological kin in Matthew 12:46–50, the author's focus follows his Markan source: ". . . [W]hoever does the will of my Father in heaven is my brother and sister and mother" (Matt 12:50). In other words, in his copying of Mark's basic idea, Matthew seems to have forgotten that he has already presented Mary as one who, indeed, does the will of Jesus' Father!

This passage is used to show that Mary not only did the will of her heavenly Father by conceiving and giving birth to his only-begotten Son, but it was a greater thing for her to be a disciple of Jesus than to be his mother. Mary is more blessed in being a disciple than in being Jesus' mother, and that is why this passage is proclaimed on the Optional Memorial of Our Lady of Mount Carmel, on the Memorial of the Presentation of the Blessed Virgin Mary, is found in The Common of the Blessed Virgin Mary, is used in the Votive Mass of Our Lady, Queen of Apostles, is used in the Masses named Holy Mary, Disciple of the Lord, and The Blessed Virgin Mary, Mother and Teacher in the Spirit. This is also why the LBVMOCIBVM invokes her as the finest fruit of the redemption. As the perfect disciple of Christ, she lives by the spirit of the gospel after being wrapped in the power of the Holy Spirit to conceive the Word of God. As a disciple of the very incarnate Word she conceives in her womb, she seeks to know the heavenly Father's will and to do it faithfully.[16]

Journal/Meditation: In what specific ways have you done the will of your Father in heaven?

Prayer: Heavenly Father, you have presented the Blessed Virgin Mary as a model disciple of your Son. Open my mind and heart to hear

---

16. References: BYM, pars. 78, 126; CCC, pars. 494, 964, 968, 973; MC, pars. 11, 30, 35; RM, par. 41; RVM, pars. 10, 15.

your word so that with the guidance of the Holy Spirit I may do it. I ask this through Christ my Lord. Amen.

Parents[17]

Text: Matthew 13:16–17

Scripture: Jesus said to his disciples, "Truly I tell you, many prophets and righteous people longed to see what you see, but did not see it, and to hear what you hear, but did not hear it." (Matt 13:17)

Reflection: The parents of Mary—Joachim and Anne—are not biblical. Their names come from the late-second-century apocryphal book called *The Proto-Gospel of James*.[18] In this work that purports to be the gospel before the gospel—that is, an account of the events preceding Jesus' birth, namely, his mother's miraculous birth from aged parents, her upbringing, her young life, and her engagement to Joseph—Joachim and Anne are presented as a biblically barren couple to whom an angel of the Lord appears and announces the birth of Mary. In the ancient world, God was understood to be the one who opened or closed a woman's womb. Circumcision of the male is the sign that reminds God to make the woman fertile. Sometimes, as in the case of biblical couples—like Abraham and Sarah, Jacob and Rachel, Elkanah and Hannah—the LORD forgets his obligation! Thus infertility is not a human shortcoming, but it is a divine one. Such is the case for wealthy Joachim and barren Anne, who miraculously conceive the child they name Mary.

The two-verse passage from Matthew's Gospel is presented because Joachim and Anne are considered to be among the righteous people who longed to see the messiah, but did not see him, and to hear him, but did not hear him. As close as they came was to give birth to his mother, hailed as mirror of justice, that is, one who reflects righteousness; mystical rose, that is, a spiritual blossom from God through Joachim and Anne; and morning star, that is, the brightest object in the sky, in the LBVM(LL). In the LBVMOCIBVM, she is a woman transformed from the moment of her conception by her parents, Joachim and Anne, the grandparents of Jesus.

---

17. LM: 606. Memorial of Saints Joachim and Anne, Parents of the Blessed Virgin Mary, July 26, Gospel.

18. Ehrman, *Other Gospels*, 24–36.

Journal/Meditation: What do you consider to be the greatest thing or person you have seen that people in the past longed to see, but did not see?

Prayer: God of my grandparents, you granted Joachim and Anne the grace to give birth to Mary, the mother of your incarnate Son. Grant that I may share in the adoption brought through the ministry of Jesus Christ, who lives and reigns forever and ever. Amen.

Mary[19]

Text: Matthew 13:54–58

Scripture: "[Jesus] came to his hometown and began to teach the people in their synagogue, so that they were astonished and said, 'Where did this man get this wisdom and these deeds of power? . . . Is not his mother called Mary?'" (Matt 13:54, 55b)

Reflection: This passage from Matthew's Gospel is one of only a few that mentions the Blessed Virgin Mary but is not assigned to any given celebration. It may be used in place of any assigned gospel text in the library of biblical texts from which passages are chosen for Marian celebrations. This Matthean passage (13:54–58) comes from Mark's Gospel (6:1–6). Following his Markan source, he narrates the story about Jesus going to his hometown of Nazareth, to which he will not return, and teaching in the synagogue. His hearers are astounded because Jesus has no teacher yet teaches well; they question the source of his wisdom, asking each other if he is not the son of the carpenter (Joseph) and is not his mother Mary. The Markan hometown crowd asks if Jesus is not the carpenter, the son of Mary (Mark 6:3); no mention is made of his father! Unlike Mark, Matthew has presented a righteous Joseph, spouse of Mary, in his nativity story (Matt 1:1–2:23).

The narrator of Matthew's Gospel explains that Jesus did not do many deeds of power in Nazareth because of the people's lack of faith. His Markan source states that he could do no deed of power because of their unbelief (Mark 6:5–6). Thus, the Markan Jesus' inability becomes the Matthean Jesus' lack of volition. It is important to note that in the Synoptic Gospels (Mark, Matthew, and Luke) people who come to Jesus already have faith. Once a deed of power is finished, Jesus praises people

---

19. LM: 559. Optional Memorial of St. Joseph the Worker, May 1, Gospel; CMBVM: Appendix: Gospel, Option 18.

for their faith. However, in John's Gospel, Jesus does deeds of power in order to evoke faith in people. They see signs, and they come to believe. In Matthew's unique nativity material, Mary (and Joseph) is portrayed as a believer. She listens to Joseph narrate the messages of the angel of the Lord in many dreams and travel from Bethlehem to Egypt and, then, to Nazareth, Jesus' hometown, where the crowd rejects him.[20]

Journal/Meditation: Do you believe in Jesus and experience deeds of power? Or do you need to see Jesus' deeds of power before you believe?

Prayer: Heavenly Father, you sent Jesus, born of Mary, to teach the people in his hometown of Nazareth about your kingdom, but they rejected him. Grant that I may hear every word he speaks and follow him faithfully now and all the days of my life. Amen.

Gate[21]

Text: Matthew 25:1–13

Scripture: "... [W]hile [the foolish bridesmaids] went to buy [oil], the bridegroom came, and those who were ready went with him into the wedding banquet, and the door was shut." (Matt 25:10)

Reflection: The unique Matthean parable of the ten bridesmaids or virgins—five of whom are wise and bring oil for their lamps and five of whom are foolish and bring no oil for their lamps—represent the members of the church, the bride, since there is no bride in this wedding parable. Some are prepared and waiting for the bridegroom, Jesus, to return in glory, and some are not prepared and not waiting for his arrival. The oil, which cannot be shared, represents righteous deeds. This contrast between wisdom and foolishness is presented to emphasize the importance of being wise; it is as simple as taking a supply of oil for one's lamp. It is as simple as storing good deeds in preparation to meet the bridegroom when he comes.

The Blessed Virgin Mary, invoked as the gate of heaven in the LBVM(LL), is presented as one of the wise virgins. Not only did she conceive the bridegroom in her womb and greet him when he was born, but she has already entered through the gate or door into the heavenly banquet with her Son. She is a model of vigilance and wisdom, showing God's pilgrim people how to stay watchful with lighted lamps and plenty

---

20. References: BYM, pars. 8, 71; CCC, pars. 964, 973; MC, pars. 28, 32, 34, 37, 56.
21. CMBVM: Lectionary: 46. The Blessed Virgin Mary, Gate of Heaven, Gospel.

of oil so that when the bridegroom comes and the door or gate is opened, they can enter the kingdom of heaven and share in the feast with the Blessed Virgin Mary.

Journal/Meditation: Do you consider yourself wise or foolish? If you are wise, what kind of oil to have for your lamp? If foolish, what do you need to do?

Prayer: Heavenly Father, because I know neither the day nor the hour of the bridegroom's arrival, fill me with the Spirit of wisdom and keep me watchful for the coming in glory of Jesus Christ, your Son, who is Lord forever and ever. Amen.

Earthquake[22]

Text: Matthew 28:1–10

Scripture: "... [S]uddenly there was a great earthquake; for an angel of the Lord, descending from heaven, came and rolled back the stone and sat on it.... [T]he angel said to [Mary Magdalene and the other Mary], 'Do not be afraid. I know that you are looking for Jesus who was crucified. He is not here; for he has been raised, as he said.'" (Matt 28:2, 5–6a)

Reflection: An earthquake is caused by volcanic or tectonic activity. Molten lava is coughed up from deep inside the stomach of the earth, and this retching causes the earth to quake. Or the great plates of the crust of the earth begin to shift and slide one against another; this rubbing makes the earth quake. The Matthean report of an earthquake in the account of the empty tomb is unique to the First Gospel. It is an element of a theophany, that is, a manifestation of God in history. And just as the angel of the Lord was present when Emmanuel, the incarnate Word, first took flesh and became a manifestation of God in human form, so is the angel of the Lord present at the earthquake to make sure that the women understand that God has manifested himself again in Jesus' resurrection from the dead.

The Blessed Virgin Mary shared in her Son's resurrection. She, who had been chosen to be the mother of God, had already experienced the earthquake of his conception. God manifested himself in a dream to Joseph and told him that his fiancée was about to give birth to the Spirit-conceived One, who would save people from their sins. Because God

---

22. CMBVM: Lectionary: 15. The Blessed Virgin Mary and the Resurrection of the Lord, Gospel.

prepared her for this singular privilege, she was also deemed acceptable to share in the new life God brought about through the resurrection of Jesus by her own assumption into heaven. She is a sign that God continues to manifest himself in earthquakes today. These manifestations may not find the earth quaking, but people suddenly becoming aware of the divine presence.[23]

Journal/Meditation: What earthquake have you recently experienced?

Prayer: God, you gladden the world with the resurrection of your Son, Jesus Christ, born of the Blessed Virgin Mary. Through her intercession may I share the joys of everlasting life, where you are one God—Father, Son, and Holy Spirit—forever and ever. Amen.

MARK'S GOSPEL

Family[24]

Text: Mark 3:31–35

Scripture: "... [L]ooking at those who sat around him, [Jesus] said, 'Here are my mother and my brothers! Whoever does the will of God is my brother and sister and mother.'" (Mark 3:34–35)

Reflection: The full impact of Jesus' words about whoever does God's will is his brother, sister, and mother are lost without the unique words of the Markan narrator: "When his family heard it, they went out to restrain him for people were saying, 'He has gone out of his mind'" (Mark 3:21). In other words, in Mark's Gospel, Jesus' family doubts his sanity and sets out to restrain him. This explains why his family is left standing outside of the place where Jesus was teaching, calling him, while the members of the crowd sitting around him are told that they, who do God's will, are the members of his family. Thus, the Markan Jesus rejects his biological family in favor of his family of faith. In Mark's Gospel, the family of believers trumps all of Jesus' other relationships.

In Mark's Gospel, Jesus' mother appears unnamed in 3:31–35 and named only in 6:3. Unlike the focus on her as a model disciple in other gospels, in Mark she is replaced by the community of faith. After being named in 6:3, she never appears again in the original story ending at 16:8.

---

23. References: BYM, pars. 10, 57–60, 104, 110–11; DPPL, pars. 147, 149, 180–1, 196; MC, pars. 6, 45; RM, pars. 40–41, 50; RVM, pars. 10, 23.

24. CMBVM: Lectionary: 10. Holy Mary, Disciple of the Lord, Gospel, Option C.

Furthermore, she seems to be grouped with all his disciples who, after he is arrested, flee and are never seen again in the story (Mark 14:50–52). The author of this narrative may be reacting to those readers and believers who thought that one had to be a member of Jesus' family in order to believe in him. Thus, the author makes it clear that true followers are those who do God's will even if it means denying self, taking up the cross, and following Jesus (Mark 8:34). In other words, real believers reject human standards and personal glory, like Jesus, in order to do the will of God.[25]

Journal/Meditation: What human standards have you rejected in order to do the will of God?

Prayer: God, through the teaching and example of Jesus, Son of Mary, you announce that believers are those who do your will even if it means denying self, carrying the cross, and dying upon it. Give me the strength to follow Christ with the hope of sharing in his resurrection. He is Lord forever and ever. Amen.

Authority[26]

Text: Mark 6:1–6

Scripture: ". . . [Jesus] came to his hometown, and his disciple followed him. On the sabbath he began to teach in the synagogue, and many who heard him were astounded. They said, 'Where did this man get all this? What is this wisdom that has been given to him? What deeds of power are being done by his hands?'" (Mark 6:1–2)

Reflection: Throughout Mark's Gospel, the role of the scribes and Pharisees is to question Jesus' authority to teach. In the ancient world, a teacher taught in the name of his teacher. In Mark's Gospel, Jesus merely appears from Nazareth at the Jordan to be baptized by John; he has no teacher, and, consequently, he has no authority to teach. The narrator of this gospel tells the reader that after Jesus enters the synagogue in Capernaum and teaches that his listeners "were astounded at this teaching, for he taught them as one having authority" (Mark 1:22). Later, they are amazed at this new teaching with authority (Mark 1:27a). The narrator informs the reader that the chief priests and the scribes were looking for

---

25. References: BYM, pars. 78, 126, 134; CCC, pars. 144, 494, 511, 967; MC, pars. 11, 30, 35; RM, par. 41.

26. CMBVM: Lectionary: Appendix, Gospel, Option 20.

a way to kill Jesus; "for they were afraid of him, because the whole crowd was spellbound by his teaching" (Mark 11:18b). Finally, the chief priests, the scribes, and the elders ask Jesus, "By what authority are you doing these things? Who gave you this authority to do them?" (Mark 11:28) Jesus does not answer them except with a riddle, and, ultimately, refuses to tell them by what authority he is doing things (Mark 11:33). The Markan Jesus does not speak on the authority of his teachers; he speaks on his own authority!

The passage presented above as a gospel to be used in any Marian celebration is assigned specifically to none! It is an option because it is the only place in Mark's Gospel where Jesus' mother is named Mary (Mark 6:3). However, the use of her name is used in a slur; in the ancient world a man is not known as the son of his mother; he is known as the son of his father. The passage also echoes—and may even serve as a duplicate of Mark 3:19b–35—the reaction of the people in Jesus' hometown to his teaching, namely, to take offense at him (Mark 6:3b). Once Jesus has rejected his family and the people of his hometown have rejected him, the narrator informs the reader that Jesus "could do no deed of power there, except that he laid his hands on a few sick people and cured them. And he was amazed at their unbelief" (Mark 6:5–6). In other words, their lack of faith prevents miracles.

Journal/Meditation: If Jesus were to appear and walk into your place of worship today, would he have the authority to teach, and would the people have the faith for him to enact deeds of power? Explain.

Prayer: God of wisdom, you endowed your only-begotten Son, born of Mary, with the authority to teach about your kingdom. Open my ears to hear his words that they may take root in my heart and reveal your kingdom come upon the earth. I ask this through Christ my Lord. Amen.

LUKE'S GOSPEL

Name[27]

Text: Luke 1:26–38

---

27. LM: 545. Solemnity of the Annunciation of the Lord, March 25, Gospel; LM: 627. Memorial of the Queenship of the Blessed Virgin Mary, August 22, Gospel; LM: 653. Memorial of Our Lady of the Rosary, October 7, Gospel; LM: 689. Solemnity of the Immaculate Conception of the Blessed Virgin Mary, December 8, Gospel; LM: 690A. Feast of Our Lady of Guadalupe, December 12, Gospel, First Option; LM: 712.

Scripture: ". . . [T]he angel Gabriel was sent by God to a town in Galilee called Nazareth, to a virgin engaged to a man whose name was Joseph, of the house of David. The virgin's name was Mary." (Luke 1:26–27)

Reflection: In verse 27 of chapter 1, the author of Luke's Gospel introduces the virgin engaged to Joseph to whom the angel Gabriel has been sent in Nazareth: Mary. After her introduction, she will be featured in the rest of chapters 1 and 2 and mentioned one more time as Jesus' mother (Luke 8:19–21). Mary's name was not a revolutionary name; it was a common Jewish name, the name of one of her ancestors, Miriam, the sister of Moses and Aaron. However, it is the meaning of the name that sheds light on the story. Mary (Miriam) means *beloved*. Indeed, it is a fitting name for the mother of Jesus, who was beloved of God, who chose her from the moment of her conception in her mother's womb to be the mother of his Son. Her status of beloved is clearly seen in all her other names that attempt to capture its importance: Queen, Lady of the Rosary, Lady of Guadalupe, Immaculate Conception, Holy Mary, Holy Name, and Blessed Virgin Mary.

The LBVM(LL) invokes her as holy Mary; queen of angels, patriarchs, prophets, apostles, martyrs, confessors, virgins, all saints, and peace; queen conceived without original sin, and queen of the most holy rosary. The LBVMOCIBVM also elaborates on her name, calling her holy Mary; gentle lady, gracious lady, and our lady; queen of love, mercy, peace, angels, patriarchs and prophets, apostles and martyrs, confessors and virgins, and all saints; queen conceived without original sin; queen assumed into heaven, queen of all the earth, queen of heaven, and queen of the universe. It is fitting that Mary's name be honored. She, beloved, favored, and full of grace, like her ancestor Miriam, made her name a holy one by agreeing to conceive in her womb a Son, who was named Jesus, the Son of the Most High God. All this occurred by the overshadowing

---

The Common of the Blessed Virgin Mary, Gospel, Option 4; CMBVM: Lectionary: 2. The Blessed Virgin Mary and the Annunciation of the Lord, Gospel, Option A; CMBVM: Lectionary: 20. Holy Mary, the New Eve, Gospel, Option A; CMBVM: Lectionary: 21. The Holy Name of the Blessed Virgin Mary, Gospel; CMBVM: Lectionary: 22. Holy Mary, Handmaid of the Lord, Gospel; CMBVM: Lectionary: 23. The Blessed Virgin Mary, Temple of the Lord, Gospel; CMBVM: Lectionary: 27. The Blessed Virgin Mary, Image and Mother of the Church III, Gospel; CMBVM: Lectionary: 29. The Blessed Virgin Mary, Queen of All Creation, Gospel; CMBVM: Lectionary: 36. The Blessed Virgin Mary, Mother of Fairest Love, Gospel; CMBVM: Lectionary: 45. The Blessed Virgin Mary, Queen of Peace, Gospel.

power of the Holy Spirit, who made her name holy and the child in her womb holy. Thus, no matter how she is invoked, Mary's name is sacred.[28]

Journal/Meditation: What is the meaning of your name? How do you honor your name?

Prayer: Most High God, you named Mary of Nazareth beloved because you favored her with grace. Fill me with the Spirit that I always may be holy in your sight. Hear this prayer in the name of your Son, Jesus Christ, who is Lord forever and ever. Amen.

Beatitude[29]

Text: Luke 1:39–47

Scripture: "When Elizabeth heard Mary's greeting, the child leaped in her womb. And Elizabeth was filled with the Holy Spirit and exclaimed with a loud cry, 'Blessed are you among women, and blessed is the fruit of your womb.'" (Luke 1:41–42)

Reflection: In the nine-verse unique passage from Luke's Gospel that narrates Mary of Nazareth's visit with Elizabeth in the non-named, hill-country town of Judea, Elizabeth speaks three beatitudes. The first two, "Blessed are you among women, and blessed is the fruit of your womb" (Luke 1:42), form the second part of the first half of the "Hail, Mary," prayer. The first part of the first half of the "Hail, Mary," prayer comes from the angel Gabriel's greeting and declaration that Mary is full of grace (Luke 1:28). The third beatitude, ". . . [B]lessed is she who believed that there would be a fulfillment of what was spoken to her by the Lord" (Luke 1:45), praises Mary for her faith. Beatitudes are statements naming specific people blessed, that is, holy. They indicate perfect happiness and inner peace on earth as an indicator of what heavenly happiness will be like. Thus, in all three of her beatitudes Elizabeth declares Mary to

---

28. References: BYM, pars. 14, 18, 24–25, 96–98; CCC, pars. 485, 490, 494, 965, 973, 2617; DPPL, pars. 101, 197–202; MC, pars. 6, 8, 17, 26, 28, 37, 41–52, 54–55; RM, pars. 8–9, 13, 15, 27; RVM, pars. 1–43.

29. LM: 636B. Optional Memorial of the Most Holy Name of Mary, September 12, Gospel; LM: 690A. Feast of Our Lady of Guadalupe, December 12, Gospel, Second Option; LM: 712. The Common of the Blessed Virgin Mary, Gospel, Option 5; LM: 1002. The Blessed Virgin Mary, II. The Most Holy Name of Mary, Gospel; CMBVM: Lectionary: 19. Holy Mary, Mother of the Lord, Gospel; CMBVM: Lectionary: 34. The Blessed Virgin Mary, Cause of Our Joy, Gospel, Option A.

be the holiest and happiest of women with a holy and happy child in her womb because of her holy and happy faith.

The LBVM(LL) also emphasizes Mary's state of blessedness, invoking her as holy Mary, holy mother of God, and holy virgin of virgins. Likewise, the LBVMOCIBVM invokes her as holy Mary, holy mother of God, most honored of virgins, and mother of the Lord, along with gentle lady, gracious lady, and our lady. Mary is named holy in order to indicate that God chose her from the beginning of time to be the dwelling place for the incarnate Word. She continues to fulfill her mother's role as the gentle and gracious lady who intercedes with God on people's behalf, because she is full of grace, advocate of grace, and minister of holiness—states the LBVMOCIBVM. In naming Mary blessed or holy, as Gabriel named her full of grace, Elizabeth declares that she—in the words of the LBVM(LL)—is the mother of divine grace.[30]

Journal/Meditation: Besides the Blessed Virgin Mary, who among your relatives and friends serves as a mother of divine grace for you? Explain.

Prayer: LORD God, you declared Mary of Nazareth full of grace, and Elizabeth declared her to be blessed among women because you chose her to conceive and give birth to you Son, Jesus Christ. Grant me a share in Mary's faith that one day I may also come to share in her heavenly joy. Hear my prayer through Jesus Christ my Lord. Amen.

Song[31]

Text: Luke 1:39–56

Scripture: "... Mary said, 'My soul magnifies the Lord, and my spirit rejoices in God my Savior, for he has looked with favor on the lowliness of his servant. Surely, from now on all generations will call me blessed.'" (Luke 1:46–48)

Reflection: The author of Luke's Gospel incorporates a number of songs or canticles into his narrative (Luke 1:68–79; 2:14, 29–32; 19:38).

---

30. References: CCC, pars. 495, 506, 509, 773, 963, 971, 975, 2030, 2619; MC, pars. 7, 39; RM, pars. 12–14, 36; RVM, pars. 20, 33.

31. LM: 572. Feast of the Visitation of the Blessed Virgin Mary, May 31, Gospel; LM: 622. Solemnity of the Assumption of the Blessed Virgin Mary, August 15, Mass during the Day, Gospel; CMBVM: Lectionary: 3. The Visitation of the Blessed Virgin Mary, Gospel; CMBVM: Lectionary: 39. Holy Mary, Queen and Mother of Mercy II, Gospel; CMBVM: Lectionary: 44. The Blessed Virgin Mary, Health of the Sick, Gospel.

The first of these is found in Luke 1:46–55, commonly known as the *Magnificat*, Latin for "my soul magnifies," the first three words of the song in English. The author based the canticle on Hannah's song (1 Sam 2:1–10), which also praises God for looking with favor on the lowly and rescuing the poor. In a way, this song serves as a programmatic text, that is, a set of verses that serve as an outline for a section of the narrative. The child in Mary's womb, the Son of God, will show mercy to people by healing them; he will scatter the proud, challenge the powerful, lift up the lowly, and feed the hungry.

According to Luke's Gospel, the occasion for the singing of the song is Mary's visit to Elizabeth. After Elizabeth pronounces three beatitudes, Mary begins her canticle of praise of God's greatness for looking upon her and naming her blessed. The epitome of blessedness is found in the celebration of her assumption into heaven, even though this is not biblical; the LBVMOCIBVM invokes her as queen assumed into heaven. Twice in her canticle she praises God's mercy (Luke 1:50, 54), and so the LBVMOCIBVM invokes her as queen of mercy. And because Mary set out in haste to visit six-month-pregnant Elizabeth (Luke 1:26, 39), she is named health of the sick in the LBVM(LL). Her song invites the reader to rejoice in God's blessings.[32]

Journal/Meditation: What is your favorite Marian song? How does it prompt you to rejoice in God?

Prayer: My soul praises you, O LORD, and my spirit rejoices in you, O God, for the great things you have done for me. May your name be always hallowed for the mercy you show your people from one generation to the next. Hear this prayer in the name of your Son, Jesus Christ, who lives and reigns with you and the Holy Spirit, one God, forever and ever. Amen.

Abraham[33]

Text: Luke 1:46–48, 49–50, 53–54 or 1:46–48a, 48b–49, 50–51, 52–53, 54–55

---

32. References: BYM, pars. 31, 118; CCC, pars. 722, 971, 2619; MC, par. 18.

33. LM: 601. Optional Memorial of Our Lady of Mount Carmel, July 16, Responsorial Psalm; LM: 653. Memorial of Our Lady of the Rosary, October 7, Responsorial Psalm; LM: 680. Memorial of the Presentation of the Blessed Virgin Mary, November 21, Responsorial Psalm; LM: 709. The Common of the Blessed Virgin Mary, Responsorial Psalm, Option 5; LM: 1002. The Blessed Virgin Mary, II. The Most Holy Name

Scripture: "[The Mighty One] has helped his servant Israel, in remembrance of his mercy, according to the promise he made to our ancestors, to Abraham and to his descendants forever." (Luke 1:54–55)

Reflection: God's remembrance of his mercy is a source of hope, according to Mary's canticle in Luke's Gospel (1:54). The theme is found as early as chapter 8 in the HB (OT) book of Genesis; God remembers Noah and all the wild and domestic animals with him in the ark (Gen 8:1). And so he makes the wind to blow and the waters to subside in order to save all on the ark. God tells Noah that he will remember the covenant he made with the patriarch and every living creature when he sees the rainbow (Gen 9:15–16). Through the incarnation of the Most High's Son in the womb of the Blessed Virgin Mary, God is helping his servant Israel (Luke 1:54). God's remembrance of his mercy is also the source of trust in his promise made to Abraham and his descendants. That promise was to make of Abraham a great nation, to bless him, and make his name great (Gen 12:2). In Luke's second volume, the Acts of the Apostles, Peter references this point in a speech reminding his hearers that they are the descendants of the covenant that God gave to Abraham, in whom all the families of the earth were to be blessed (Acts 3:25). Jesus, a descendant of Abraham, has been sent to them, according to Peter, to bless them and turn them away from their wicked way (Acts 3:26). In his canticle, Zechariah, father of John the Baptist, summarizes this point, declaring, "[The Lord God of Israel] has shown the mercy promised to our ancestors, and has remembered his holy covenant, the oath that he swore to our ancestor Abraham, to grant us that we, being rescued from the hands of our enemies, might serve him without fear, in holiness and righteousness before him all our days" (Luke 1:72–75).

Mary's canticle gives rise to many of her titles in the LBVM(LL), especially holy Mary, cause of our joy, and queen of the most holy rosary. Likewise, in the LBVMOCIBVM, her canticle gives rise to the following invocations: holy Mary, handmaid of the Lord, champion of God's

---

of Mary, Responsorial Psalm; LM: 1002. The Blessed Virgin Mary, III. Our Lady, Queen of Apostles, Responsorial Psalm; CMBVM: Lectionary: 21. The Holy Name of the Blessed Virgin Mary, Responsorial Psalm; CMBVM: Lectionary: 22. Holy Mary, Handmaid of the Lord, Responsorial Psalm; CMBVM: Lectionary: 28. The Immaculate Heart of the Blessed Virgin Mary, Responsorial Psalm; CMBVM: Lectionary: 34. The Blessed Virgin Mary, Cause of Our Joy, Responsorial Psalm; CMBVM: Lectionary: 37. The Blessed Virgin Mary, Mother of Divine Hope, Responsorial Psalm; CMBVM: Lectionary: 39. Holy Mary, Queen and Mother of Mercy I, Responsorial Psalm; CMBVM: Lectionary: 43. Our Lady of Ransom, Responsorial Psalm.

people, and queen of mercy. No matter the invocation or the title, the joy and rejoicing with which the canticle begins are signs of God's blessing in giving the world a Savior to fulfill his promise made to Abraham. The lowly, the hungry, the poor, and the disenfranchised find hope in the virgin of Nazareth that they, like she, can be lifted up by the Mighty One, who never exhausts his mercy and never forgets the promise he made to Abraham and his descendants.[34]

Journal/Meditation: Which of the following invocations of the Blessed Virgin Mary do you like the best: holy Mary, cause of joy, queen of the most holy rosary, handmaid of the Lord, champion of God's people, and queen of mercy? How do you connect to that chosen invocation?

Prayer: Mighty One, you do great things for your people in remembrance of your mercy and according to the promise you made to Abraham and Sarah. Look with favor upon me and grant me deeper hope and trust in you. My spirit rejoices in you, Father, Son, and Holy Spirit, now and forever. Amen.

Genetrix[35]

Text: Luke 2:1–14

Scripture: "While [Mary and Joseph] were [in Bethlehem], the time came for her to deliver her child. And she gave birth to her firstborn son and wrapped him in bands of cloth, and laid him in a manger, because there was no place for them in the inn." (Luke 2:6–7)

Reflection: A genetrix is a biological mother. Mary is the biological mother of Jesus, the Son of God, who was born in Bethlehem—even though the couple lived in Nazareth. Only Luke's Gospel presents a census requiring those to be counted to return to the town in which they were born. Joseph and Mary—his fiancée (Luke 2:5)—travel to Bethlehem because he was descended from David (Luke 2:4). While they are in the registration process, Mary gives birth to her firstborn son and wraps him in bands of cloth before placing him in a manger. These two details are unique and important in Luke's Gospel. The bands of cloth is meant

---

34. References: BYM, pars. 13, 29–30, 32–33, 47; CCC, pars. 144, 489, 2619; DPPL, par. 205; MC, par. 8; RM, par. 14.

35. LM: 14. The Nativity of the Lord [Christmas], December 25, At the Mass during the Night, Gospel; LM: 712. The Common of the Blessed Virgin Mary, Gospel, Option 6; CMBVM: Lectionary: 5. The Blessed Virgin Mary, Mother of the Savior, Gospel.

to echo the end of the story; after Jesus is crucified and dies, his body is wrapped in a linen cloth before being placed in a tomb (Luke 23:53). And the detail about the newly-born Jesus being placed in a manger is meant to signal that he will be food for people (Luke 22:14–20). Once these important details are established, the author proceeds to narrate how the angel of the Lord appeared to poor shepherds and announced to them the good news of the Savior's birth; the signs given to them are the bands of cloth and the child in the manger (Luke 2:12)!

Thus, Mary is genetrix or mother of the Savior, the Messiah. The LBVM(LL) invokes her as both mother of Christ and mother of the Savior, while the LBVMOCIBVM invokes her as the holy mother of God, mother of Christ the King, and mother of the Lord. As mother, Mary nourishes her child at her breasts. She takes him home to Nazareth and cares for him. All the while in Luke's narratives, her motherhood is focused on Jesus, the Son of God. Mary's motherhood also reveals God's motherhood, especially since she is invoked in the LBVMOCIBVM as the holy mother of God. Since God is neither male nor female, he is both father and mother. With a father's love, the LORD overshadows Mary, and she conceives his Son through the power of the Holy Spirit. With a mother's love, God watches over his chosen daughter as she gives birth. Mary, as genetrix, reveals the beauty of the motherhood of God.[36]

Journal/Meditation: In what ways is God a mother to you?

Prayer: Father God, you conceived me in my mother's womb. Mother God, you brought me to birth, fed me at my mother's breasts, cared for me, and lavished your love upon me. Grant that I may be willing to reveal your tenderness to the world as did Mary, the mother of your Son, Jesus Christ, who is Lord forever and ever. Amen.

Treasure[37]

Text: Luke 2:15b–19

Scripture: ". . . Mary treasured all these words and pondered them in her heart." (Luke 2:19)

---

36. References: BYM, pars. 2–3, 8, 62–64, 71, 106, 109; CCC, pars. 495, 506, 509, 963, 971, 975, 2619; DPPL, pars. 107, 112; MC, pars. 5, 11, 14, 28, 32, 46, 56; RVM, pars. 10, 14, 33.

37. LM: 712. The Common of the Blessed Virgin Mary, Gospel, Option 7; CMBVM: Lectionary: 4. Holy Mary, Mother of God, Gospel; CMBVM: Lectionary: 24. The Blessed Virgin Mary, Seat of Wisdom, Gospel, Option B.

Reflection: The author of Luke's Gospel presents Mary's heart as a treasure chest (Luke 2:19, 52). She is a container for the words and events surrounding the birth, childhood, and ministry of Jesus. Twice Luke explains that she pondered all this in her heart, her treasure chest, where she remembered the events of his conception, the visit of the shepherds, and his words to her when she found him in the Temple. As only a mother could, she pondered them, not always knowing their meaning, but, nevertheless, reflecting upon what God was doing in her life. This resulted in discernment, the wisdom to see clearly what at first did not seem to be all that clear and to understand what God was asking of her.

Today, people refer to this as making memories. People make memories by taking cell phone photographs, which remain on the phone, or digital photographs, which remain on a computer or are often printed and arranged in albums. But many of the memories of a lifetime can only be saved in the treasure chest of the heart. By pondering the memory of love, one reaches the wisdom of the kinds of love. By pondering the memory of gifts received, one reaches the wisdom of the best gifts to give. By reflecting on the events of life, one reaches the wisdom of how to respond to life's situations. Collectively, such memories make a person wise. Wisdom means that a person can call forth from one's storehouse of memories the events of the past that have shaped one, taught the truths of living, and share these with others.[38]

Journal/Meditation: What memories of today's events in your treasure chest need to be discerned?

Prayer: All-knowing God, you never forget any of your people. Fill me with the Holy Spirit so that I may ponder and so discern your presence in my life. You are one God—Father, Son, and Holy Spirit—forever and ever. Amen.

Shepherds[39]

Text: Luke 2:15–20

Scripture: ". . . [The shepherds] went with haste and found Mary and Joseph, and the child lying in the manger." (Luke 2:16)

---

38. References: BYM, pars. 50, 141; RM, par. 20; RVM, par. 11.

39. LM: 15. The Nativity of the Lord [Christmas], December 25, At the Mass at Dawn, Gospel.

Reflection: Unique to Luke's Gospel is the narrative about the shepherds living in the fields around Bethlehem and keeping watch over their flocks when the angel of the Lord appears and gives them the good news about the Savior's birth. These poor Jewish shepherds living around David's city in Luke's Gospel are in contrast with the wealthy Gentile magi in Matthew's Gospel. In other words, Luke's shepherds inform the reader at Jesus' birth that later he will minister to the poor, the lowly, and the outcast. Furthermore, Luke uses them to emphasize an important theme both in his gospel and in his second volume, the Acts of the Apostles. That theme is hearing the word and doing it—telling what one hears and sees. Luke makes this clear when he narrates that, after finding Mary, Joseph, and Jesus, they make known what had been told them by the angel about the child. Then, in the last line of the above passage, the narrator states, "The shepherds returned [to the fields], glorifying and praising God for all they had heard and seen, as it had been told them" (Luke 2:20).

The Blessed Virgin Mary is another person who hears the word and does it by telling what she has heard and seen. She listens as the angel Gabriel tells her that God desires that she conceive Jesus in her womb, and she, God's servant, says yes to his will (Luke 1:26–38). Then, after hastening to Elizabeth, she praises God for all she hears and sees (Luke 1:46–55). Later in the narrative, the Lukan Jesus himself will declare that his true family are those who hear the word of God and do it (Luke 8:21). The shepherds living in the fields—the poor, the lowly, the outcast, the uneducated—are presented by Luke as models worthy of imitation.[40]

Journal/Meditation: In your life, whom do you recognize as a person who hears God's word and does it?

Prayer: Glory to you, O God, in the highest heaven, and on earth peace among those whom you favor! Grant me the spirit of the shepherd that I may hear your word and do it. Grant me the spirit of Mary that I may praise you for Jesus Christ, your Son, now and forever. Amen.

Circumcision[41]

Text: Luke 2:16–21

---

40. References: CCC, pars. 144, 494, 511, 967; DPPL, par. 106; RM, par. 16.
41. LM: 18. The Solemnity of Mary, the Holy Mother of God, January 1, Gospel.

Scripture: "After eight days had passed, it was time to circumcise the child; and he was called Jesus, the name given by the angel before he was conceived in the womb." (Luke 2:21)

Reflection: Circumcision is the removal of all or part of the male foreskin from the penis. As a religious ceremony, it is practiced by Jews and Moslems. Its religious origin begins with Abraham and God telling him that the sign of the covenant will be the circumcised flesh of his foreskin and every male among the people eight days after birth (Gen 17:9-14). Biblical culture presumes that the LORD is in charge of everything, even the conception of children. Furthermore, biblical culture understands that the male carries the seed, which he plants in the female through intercourse. Circumcision reminds God to open the female womb to receive the seed so that the couple can conceive a child. A woman who is declared barren is one whose womb the LORD did not remember to open when the man had intercourse with her.

Only the author of Luke's Gospel narrates the event of Jesus' circumcision on the eighth day of his birth. This is to illustrate one of the author's themes, namely, that Gentile Christianity emerges out of Judaism, or Judaism gives birth to Christianity. Clearly, Jesus is Jewish, born of Jewish parents and circumcised on the eighth day, but he—and Paul in Luke's second volume, the Acts of the Apostles—will be found primarily ministering to Gentiles. The eighth day of life is important in a culture which has not yet seen the invention of zero. Instead of beginning with nothing, the ancient system of counting began with one. Thus, the day of birth is the first day of life, and one week later is the eighth day (not seven), which represents fullness in God's presence. That is why this passage is proclaimed on the eighth day (or octave) of the Nativity of the Lord (Christmas), the Solemnity of Mary, the Holy Mother of God, so invoked in LBVM(LL) and in LBVMOCIBVM. On the eighth day the child was given his name.[42]

Journal/Reflection: In what ways do you think God is involved in the conception of children today?

Prayer: God of Abraham and Sarah and Joseph and Mary, you conceive and bring to birth your children Isaac and Jesus. As a sign of your presence, you decree that they be circumcised on the eighth day. Make me aware of your presence that brings me new life here and in your kingdom forever. Amen.

---

42. Reference: RM, par. 17.

Home[43]

Text: Luke 2:22, 39–40

Scripture: "When [Mary and Joseph] had finished everything required by the law of the Lord [in Jerusalem], they returned to Galilee, to their own town of Nazareth." (Luke 2:39)

Reflection: According to the HB (OT) book of Leviticus, a woman who conceives and bears a male child is ceremonially unclean for seven days, because on the eighth day her male child is circumcised. Then, her time of blood purification is thirty-three days, the sacred number three twice, indicating God's presence (Lev 12:2–4). Once the thirty-three days are past, she brings to the LORD a lamb for a burnt offering and a pigeon or a turtledove for a sin offering; after bringing these offerings and having them presented to the LORD by a priest, the woman is declared clean. However, if she cannot afford a sheep, she may substitute another pigeon or turtledove; thus, she brings two pigeons or turtledoves, one for a burnt offering and one for a sin offering (Lev 12:6–8). In ancient Israelite culture, the woman needed to be purified because she had participated in a dangerous mixture of life and death, namely the flow of blood at the birth of the child and the flow of blood which indicates her death. This crossing of boundaries between life and death requires ritual purification, after which Mary and Joseph return to their home in Nazareth.

Luke is not clear about where the family of Jesus, Mary, and Joseph live for forty-one days between Jesus' birth in Bethlehem and their trip to Jerusalem. Likewise, the author of Luke's Gospel is not clear whose home it is in Nazareth. Mary, the mother of Jesus, receives the message from Gabriel that she is to be the mother of the Savior in her home. In their home, Mary and Joseph raise Jesus, who grows, becomes strong, is filled with wisdom, and is favored by God (Luke 2:40). It is also presumed that it is from their Nazareth home that they travel to Jerusalem every year to celebrate Passover (Luke 2:41). However, in their home, the God of Israel chose to live in his incarnate form: Jesus. Their home essentially became a temple, a place of security, comfort, and rest.[44]

---

43. LM: 17. The Feast of the Holy Family of Jesus, Mary, and Joseph, Sunday within the Octave of the Nativity of the Lord [Christmas], or, if there is no Sunday, December 30, Gospel, Cycle B, Shorter Form; CMBVM: Lectionary: 8. Our Lady of Nazareth I, Gospel, Option A.

44. References: BYM, par. 14; CCC, par. 488; DPPL, pars. 107, 112; MC, par. 5; RM, pars. 1, 8, 17, 45.

Journal/Meditation: What does your home mean to you?

Prayer: God of Jerusalem, you chose to live among your people in your home in Jerusalem and to visit Mary in her home in Nazareth. Come and reside in my home. Give me security, comfort, and rest with the hope of living in your heavenly home forever and ever. Amen.

Simeon[45]

Text: Luke 2:22–32

Scripture: "... [T]he child's father and mother were amazed at what was being said about him. Then Simeon blessed them and said to his mother Mary, 'This child is destined for the falling and the rising of many in Israel, and to be a sign that will opposed so that the inner thoughts of many will be revealed—and a sword will pierce your own soul too.'" (Luke 2:33–35)

Reflection: At the time of Mary's purification in Jerusalem, the author of Luke's Gospel narrates the presence of a man named Simeon, whom he describes as righteous, devout, and guided by the Holy Spirit to the Temple. Luke is known for his theme of Spirit guidance (Luke 1:15, 35, 41; 2:25, 27). In other words, the author of this gospel presumes Pentecost before he narrates it in the Acts of the Apostles (2:1–1–13). Simeon, filled with the Holy Spirit, pronounces a paradoxical blessing, which serves as a foretelling of what the rest of the gospel will portray. The Spirit-child Jesus is destined by God to bring judgment and hope; upon God's initiative inner thoughts will be uncovered, and this will bring about suffering, even for the child's mother, Mary. Once Simeon has been guided by the Spirit and spoken the words provoked by the Spirit, he disappears from the narrative.

In Lukan understanding, everything is guided by the Holy Spirit. Just as in the HB (OT) God is portrayed as being in charge of everything from creation to birth control, so in the CB (NT) all the events that Luke narrates—from the announcement of the birth of John the Baptizer to his father, Zechariah, in the gospel, to Paul's imprisonment in the Acts of the Apostles—are guided by the Spirit. This is why before Jesus dies on the cross in Luke's Gospel he says, "Father, into your hands I commend my spirit" (Luke 23:46); he returns the Holy Spirit that conceived him in

---

45. LM: 524. The Feast of the Presentation of the Lord, February 2, Gospel, Shorter Form.

Mary's womb to the Father so that it can be poured out on the apostles at Pentecost. Simeon is one of several people who is guided by and filled with the Holy Spirit before Pentecost.[46]

Journal/Meditation: In what specific ways have you experienced the Holy Spirit guiding and filling you?

Prayer: God and Master, you may dismiss me, your servant, in peace, according to your word. My eyes have seen your salvation, which you have prepared in the presence of all peoples, a light for revelation to the Gentiles and for glory to your people Israel: Jesus Christ, who is Lord now and forever. Amen.

Anna[47]

Text: Luke 2:22–40

Scripture: "There was also a prophet, Anna . . . . She was of great age, having lived with her husband seven years after her marriage, then as a widow to the age of eighty-four. At that moment [after Simeon's words to Mary] she came, and began to praise God and to speak about the child to all who were looking for the redemption of Jerusalem." (Luke 2:36–37a, 38)

Reflection: Unique to Luke's Gospel is the character of Anna, a prophetess, a woman who interprets God's will by speaking about the child Jesus to those who were looking forward to the redemption of Jerusalem from Roman occupation. The author of Luke's Gospel often presents pairs of people in his orderly account; usual pairs consist of a man and woman. In the account of Joseph and Mary taking Jesus to Jerusalem for Mary's purification, Simeon is paired with Anna. Before this, Zechariah is paired with Elizabeth, and Mary is paired with Joseph. Throughout the rest of the gospel, the reader often encounters a story about a man paired with one about a woman.

Furthermore, women play a major role in Luke's Gospel. First, Mary is the recipient of the good news from the angel Gabriel that she will conceive and bear the Son of God. In her older years, Elizabeth conceives

---

46. References: DPPL, pars. 107, 120, 122–3, 136; MC, pars. 7, 20, 57; RM, par. 16; RVM, par. 20.

47. LM: 17. The Feast of the Holy Family of Jesus, Mary, and Joseph, Sunday within the Octave of the Nativity of the Lord [Christmas], or, if there is no Sunday, December 30, Gospel, Cycle B, Longer Form; LM: 524. The Feast of the Presentation of the Lord, February 2, Gospel, Longer Form.

and gives birth to John the Baptist. Women are portrayed in the role of disciples (Luke 8:2), are present at Jesus' crucifixion (Luke 23:27, 49) and burial (Luke 23:55), and discover Jesus' resurrection (Luke 24:5, 10). Anna lives seven complete years with her husband, who is presumed to have died, and then as a widow until she is eighty-four (eighty representing two lifetimes of forty each, and four representing the created order or the earth). Jesus raises the son of the widow of Nain (Luke 7:11)—a unique event in Luke's Gospel—tells a unique parable featuring a powerless widow who acts powerfully (Luke 18:1–5), and acknowledges a poor widow as an example of faith (Luke 21:1–4).

Journal/Meditation: What role have women played in your formation in faith?

Prayer: Eternal God, throughout time you have chosen women to speak your will to your people. Your prophetess Anna praised you for Mary's child. Hear my praise for the redemption you brought through your Son, Jesus Christ, who lives and reigns with you and the Holy Spirit, one God, forever and ever. Amen.

Praise[48]

Text: Luke 2:27–35

Scripture: "... [W]hen the parents brought in the child Jesus, to do for him what was customary under the law, Simeon took him in his arms and praised God . . . ." (Luke 2:27–28)

Reflection: The word *praise* can refer to worship and thanksgiving made to God or to an expression of great approval or admiration for someone. When the elderly, righteous, and devout man Simeon encounters Mary and Joseph in the Jerusalem Temple presenting their Son, he takes Jesus in his arms and combines both understandings of praise into one. He thanks God for not letting him see death before he had seen the Messiah. And he expresses his approval or admiration for the Spirit-child Jesus, Mary's Son, the salvation God prepared for all peoples.

Mary, the holy virgin of virgins, the most pure, most chaste, inviolate, undefiled, amiable, and admirable—according to the LBVM(LL)—and the most honored of virgins—according to the LBVMOCIBVM—submitted to the ritual of purification after childbirth, as specified in Torah

---

48. LM: 712. The Common of the Blessed Virgin Mary, Gospel, Option 8; CMBVM: Lectionary: 7. The Blessed Virgin Mary and the Presentation of the Lord, Gospel.

(Lev 12:1–8), and redeemed the Redeemer of the world (Exod 13:1–2, 11–12). This is why the LBVMOCIBVM invokes her as the helper of the Redeemer. This is why the Spirit-guided Simeon praises God with thanksgiving while expressing approval for the Lord's Messiah.[49]

Journal/Meditation: For what do you need to praise God today?

Prayer: All praise be to you, Father, for the presentation of your Son, Jesus Christ, to the world and for the guidance of the Holy Spirit. Deepen my awareness of your work in my life that I may never cease to worship you, Holy Trinity, forever and ever. Amen.

Sorrow[50]

Text: Luke 2:33–35

Scripture: "... Simeon ... said to [Jesus'] mother Mary, '... [A] sword will pierce your own soul....'" (Luke 2:34–35)

Reflection: Sorrow is a feeling of deep sadness caused by a loss or misfortune. Mary is honored on September 15, the day after the Feast of the Exaltation of the Holy Cross, as the Lady of Sorrows. She is given this title because, as the author of Luke's Gospel portrays Simeon telling her, her soul was pierced with the sword of Jesus' death on the cross. While it is only in John's Gospel where she stands near the cross, in Luke's Gospel her feeling of sorrow is predicted by Simeon at Jesus' presentation in the Jerusalem Temple. Thus, not only has the author given the end of the story, but he has tempted the reader to continue to read to see how this takes place.

Being human, Mary knew sorrow. As an unwed, pregnant, teenage girl, she had to feel sadness even though she had said yes to what the angel Gabriel had told her that God wanted her to do. She knew the sorrow of childbirth and maybe post-partum depression after listening to Simeon. Giving Mary the title of Lady of Sorrows indicates that she is able to sympathize with human loss or misfortune that results in the feeling of sorrow.[51]

---

49. References: BYM, pars. 36, 41, 44–46, 48–50; CCC, pars. 496, 498–9, 502, 505–7, 510; DPPL, pars. 107, 120, 122–3, 136; MC, pars. 7, 20, 57; RM, pars. 4, 16, 39; RVM, par. 20.

50. LM: 639. Memorial of Our Lady of Sorrows, September 15, Gospel, Second Option.

51. References: CCC, par. 964; DPPL, pars. 136, 145, 151; MC, pars. 7, 11; RM, par. 16; RVM, par. 10.

Journal/Meditation: Identify three to five great sorrows that you have experienced during your life? What helped you recover from the deep sadness?

Prayer: Holy Father, you granted the Blessed Virgin Mary a share in the sorrow predicted by your prophet Simeon. In times of deep sadness caused by loss or misfortune fill me with the Spirit of courage that you bestowed upon Mary as her Son hung dying on the cross. Hear me through the same Jesus Christ now and forever. Amen.

Spouse[52]

Text: Luke 2:41–51a

Scripture: "When [Jesus'] parents saw him they were astonished, and his mother said to him, 'Child, why have you treated us like this? Look, your father and I have been searching for you in great anxiety.'" (Luke 2:48)

Reflection: A spouse is someone's husband or wife. In its verb form, *to spouse* or *to espouse*, it means to marry another. While the author of Luke's Gospel presents Joseph as Jesus' legal father (Luke 2:27, 33, 41; 3:23b; 4:22b), there is nothing recorded in Luke's Gospel about the marriage of Joseph and Mary. In Luke's Gospel, Joseph is identified as the virgin's fiancée (Luke 1:27), as he is in Matthew's Gospel (1:18). However, Matthew refers to him as the husband of Mary (Matt 1:16, 19, 24), but he narrates no marriage ceremony between their engagement and espousal. The second-century apocryphal works—*The Proto-Gospel of James*[53] and *The Gospel of Pseudo-Matthew*[54]—present Joseph as Mary's guardian in order to guarantee her perpetual virginity.

The confusion over Joseph's status of spouse does not stop here. In Matthew's Gospel, Joseph is identified as the son of Jacob (Matt 1:16), but in Luke's Gospel, he is the son of Heli (Luke 3:23). He is not named at all in Mark's Gospel, and in John's Gospel, he is named only twice (John 1:45; 6:42). The name Joseph means "let him add" or "let him gather," a reference to CB (NT) Joseph's HB (OT) namesake identifying his function to save the world from famine. While he serves as an accessory character in

---

52. LM: 543. The Solemnity of St. Joseph, Spouse of the Blessed Virgin Mary, March 19, Gospel, Second Option.

53. Ehrman, *Other Gospels*, 24–36.

54. Ibid., 41–57.

Luke's Gospel—usually included in the word *parents*—present at Jesus' birth, circumcision, presentation, and finding in the Temple—he is not named, although he is identified as a carpenter (Matt 13:55). Joseph's purpose in Luke is to live up to the meaning of his name by joining or gathering with Mary and Jesus.[55]

Journal/Meditation: In what specific ways do you gather others together?

Prayer: LORD God, you made Joseph a just man and a spouse of the Blessed Virgin Mary to watch over your Son. Grant his unfailing protection of me as I seek to serve you faithfully. I ask this in the name of Jesus Christ, Son of Mary and Joseph, Lord forever and ever. Amen.

Boyhood[56]

Text: Luke 2:41–52

Scripture: "Now every year [Jesus'] parents [, Mary and Joseph,] went to Jerusalem for the festival of the Passover. And when he was twelve years old, they went up as usual for the festival." (Luke 2:41–42)

Reflection: Other than his birth and presentation in the Jerusalem Temple, this is the only story about Jesus' boyhood. Because there are no accounts of what he did until he was about thirty years old (Luke 3:23), the many apocryphal gospel writers saw this as an opportunity to fill in the missing years from when Jesus was twelve to thirty years old. Several elements of this unique Lukan narrative focus more on the particular themes of the author rather than narrating an historical boyhood story. The first obvious element is the mention of Passover, the annual celebration of the Hebrews' liberation from Egyptian slavery which included a pilgrimage to Jerusalem. In the Lukan narrative, Jesus will not return to Jerusalem for Passover until he goes there to die and be raised (Luke 19:28), although he has been headed there since Luke 9:51.

Jesus is twelve years old when he stays in Jerusalem after the Passover celebration is concluded and his parents, Mary and Joseph, have headed home to Nazareth. Twelve represents fullness; that is why there are twelve

---

55. References: CCC, pars. 488, 497; DPPL, pars. 218–23; MC, par. 5.

56. LM: 17. The Feast of the Holy Family of Jesus, Mary, and Joseph, Sunday within the Octave of the Nativity of the Lord [Christmas], or, if there is no Sunday, December 30, Gospel, Cycle C; LM: 712. The Common of the Blessed Virgin Mary, Gospel, Option 9; CMBVM: Lectionary 8. Our Lady of Nazareth I, Gospel, Option B; CMBVM: Lectionary: 10. Holy Mary, Disciple of the Lord, Gospel, Option A.

sons of Jacob, twelve tribes of Israel, and twelve apostles—the fullness of God's people. Jesus' act of sitting among the teachers in the Temple and asking them questions indicates his wisdom (Luke 2:40; 2:52) and points ahead to the conflict that will ensue (Luke 20:20–40). Another element of Luke's narrative is the seldom naming of Joseph, who is usually included with the use of the word *parents*. It is Jesus' mother who addresses him in the narrative and receives his answer about being in his Father's house (Luke 2:49), clearly indicating that he is the Son of God (Luke 1:32, 35). Finally, the unique narrative ends with Mary treasuring this event in her heart (Luke 2:19, 51) and a growth refrain (Luke 1:80; 2:40, 52). Thus, this unique boyhood story about Jesus being twelve years old is more of an opportunity for the author to present some of the major themes of his orderly account than it is to present an historical event in the life of Jesus.[57]

Journal/Meditation: What major theme in your adult life do you also find in your childhood, even if you were not aware of it when you were a child?

Prayer: Heavenly Father, your Son was presented to you in the Jerusalem Temple and came back twelve years later to teach there. Fill me with his wisdom and grant me increase in both divine and human favor now and forever. Amen.

Ponder[58]

Text: Luke 2:46–51

Scripture: "... [Jesus] went down [from Jerusalem] with [Mary and Joseph] and came to Nazareth, and was obedient to them. His mother treasured all these things in her heart." (Luke 2:51)

Reflection: When a person thinks about something very carefully over a period of time, he or she has pondered it. While such pondering is usually located in the heart of the physical body, it is more appropriately located in the mind. Careful, critical thinking yields maximum results. Sloppy thinking yields minimum results because it does not consider everything that is important to the issue. The author of Luke's Gospel presents the Blessed Virgin Mary as a person who engages in pondering.

---

57. References: MC, pars. 45–46; RM, pars. 17, 20; RVM, par. 20.

58. CMBVM: Lectionary 28. The Immaculate Heart of the Blessed Virgin Mary, Gospel, Option B.

After the birth of Jesus and the shepherds' visit, Mary ponders the events she has witnessed and the words that were spoken (Luke 1:19). Likewise, after finding her twelve-year-old son in the Temple and hearing his words—"Why were you searching for me? Did you not know that I must be in my Father's house?" (Luke 2:49)—she critically thinks about what she witnessed and what she heard.

With an immaculate heart, the Blessed Virgin Mary pondered the God-inspired events of her life. With an immaculate heart, she conceived the Son of God in her womb, being obedient to God like her Son become obedient to her and Joseph. Her immaculate heart led her to nourish Jesus' life with her own. And with the wonder of a disciple, she listened to and pondered Jesus' words, like she had done the same with his Father's, and observed her Son's actions, treasuring them in her heart. Mary is an example of how the myriad events kept in the heart need to be pondered in order to discern the presence of God in them.[59]

Journal/Meditation: What recent event have you pondered and found the presence of God?

Prayer: Father of Jesus, you graced his mother, Mary, with an immaculate heart in which she pondered your divine presence. Grant that I may hear your word, reflect upon it, and respond with obedience to it. I ask this in the name of your Son, who lives and reigns forever and ever. Amen.

Hearing/Doing[60]

Text: Luke 8:19–21

Scripture: "... [Jesus] was told, 'Your mother and your brothers are standing outside, wanting to see you.' But he said to them, 'My mother and my brothers are those who hear the word of God and do it.'" (Luke 8:20–21)

Reflection: One of Luke's sources for his orderly account is Mark's Gospel. A Markan narrative portraying Jesus rejecting his family (Mark 3:31–35) is transformed by the author of Luke's Gospel into a statement of a favorite theme. When the mother and brothers of Jesus come to him,

---

59. References: BYM, par. 137; CCC, pars. 490–2, 508; RM, par. 20; RVM, pars. 10–11.

60. CMBVM: Lectionary 17. Our Lady of the Cenacle, Gospel, Option A.

they cannot reach him because of the crowd—not because he refuses to come out to them as Mark states it. For Luke this presents the occasion for Jesus to voice the author's theme: hearing and doing the word of God. This theme is first presented in the narrative about Zechariah, the father of John the Baptist, who heard God's word through the angel Gabriel but did not do it (Luke 1:8–20). He is contrasted with Mary, who also heard God's word through the angel Gabriel and did it (Luke 1:26–38); with Elizabeth, who heard God's word and did it (Luke 1:57–63); with the shepherds who heard God's word and did it (Luke 2:8–18); and with Simeon and Anna, who heard God's word and did it (Luke 2:25–38).

The author of Luke's Gospel weaves the theme of hearing God's word and doing it into his material about John the Baptist (Luke 3:2) and Jesus (Luke 4:1–12, 14–30), who has heard God's word so well that he can quote it to the devil. In Capernaum, a demon hears God's word through Jesus and comes out of a man (Luke 4:31–37). Simon hears Jesus' word about where to fish and does it (Luke 5:1–11), as does a paralyzed man (Luke 5:17–26), a tax collector named Levi (Luke 5:27–28), and a man with a withered right hand (Luke 6:6–11). There are many other accounts of people hearing God's word through Jesus and doing it. Thus, by the time the reader gets to Luke 8:19–21, he or she has read about it over and over again, even though this is the first time that it is stated explicitly.[61]

Journal/Meditation: When have you most recently heard the word of God and done it?

Prayer: LORD God, you give people the ability to hear your word and to do it. Grant that I may follow the example of the Blessed Virgin Mary, who heard and obeyed the voice of the Spirit, who with you and your Son, Jesus Christ, are one God forever and ever. Amen.

Listening[62]

Text: Luke 10:38–42

Scripture: "[Martha] had a sister named Mary, who sat at the Lord's feet and listened to what he was saying." (Luke 10:39)

---

61. References: BYM, pars. 54, 72–74, 76–77; CCC, pars. 144, 494, 511, 967; RM, par. 20.

62. CMBVM: Lectionary 24. The Blessed Virgin Mary, Seat of Wisdom, Gospel, Option C.

Reflection: The person who is wise sits at Jesus' feet and listens to his word. In Luke's unique narrative about Jesus entering a certain village and being welcomed by Martha into the home she shared with her sister, Mary, the Lukan Jesus declares, "Mary has chosen the better part, which will not be taken away from her" (Luke 10:42b). Mary takes the position of a disciple—sitting at Jesus' feet—after Jesus had named blessed those who listen (Luke 10:24). Martha is distracted with the tasks of ancient hospitality, but the Lukan Jesus trumps that obligation with listening to his words. Thus, being a disciple who sits at Jesus' feet and listens to his words trumps hospitality. Mary is identified as the wise woman.

John's Gospel also contains a story about a Martha and Mary, who are sisters of Lazarus (John 11:1–12:8). While the context is different, the portrayal of the sisters remains similar. Martha professes faith in Jesus (John 11:21–27) only later to doubt him (John 11:39b–40). Mary kneels at Jesus' feet and professes faith in him (John 11:32). The two sisters are present again six days before Passover and Martha is serving dinner (John 12:1–2). Again, assuming the position of a disciple, Mary takes a pound of costly perfume and anoints Jesus feet and wipes them with her hair (John 12:3). As he identified Mary's wisdom in Luke's Gospel, the Johannine Jesus does the same, declaring: "She bought [the perfume] so that she might keep it for the day of my burial" (John 12:7b). Thus, once again, Mary is identified as the wise woman because she listens to Jesus. And so is Jesus' mother, Mary, a wise woman, who hears the word of God and keeps it.[63]

Journal/Meditation: In what specific ways do you display your discipleship?

Prayer: God of wisdom, your Son, Jesus Christ, declared wise those who sit at his feet and listen to his word. Grant me this better part that I, like the Blessed Virgin Mary, may hear your truth and come to a deeper knowledge of your love. Hear my prayer through the same Christ my Lord. Amen.

Blessedness[64]

Text: Luke 11:27–28

---

63. References: BYM, pars. 54, 72–74, 76–77; MC, pars. 5, 25, 57; RM, par 20.

64. LM: 563A. Optional Memorial of Our Lady of Fatima, May 13, Gospel; LM: 613. Optional Memorial of the Dedication of the Basilica of St. Mary Major, August

Scripture: "... [A] woman in the crowd raised her voice and said to [Jesus], 'Blessed is the womb that bore you and the breasts that nursed you!'" (Luke 11:27).

Reflection: An unnamed woman in a crowd listening to Jesus shouts a beatitude about his mother. She declares blessed the womb that conceived him and the breasts at which he nursed. The woman, unique to Luke's Gospel, identifies Mary as one who has received a divine favor. Elizabeth had already declared Mary to be blessed among women, and the fruit in her womb to be blessed (Luke 1:42). The unnamed woman now acknowledges not only her blessed womb, but her blessed breasts as having received God's favor. Mary is praised for the grace that God bestowed upon her in naming her the mother of his Son. However, the Lukan Jesus, reiterating a favorite theme of the author of this gospel while not degrading the blessedness of his mother, points toward a greater blessedness for anyone: hearing the word of God and obeying or doing it (Luke 11:28).

The Lukan Jesus had already presented this theme (Luke 8:21), and Luke illustrated it with Mary (Luke 1:26–38), Elizabeth (Luke 1:57–63), shepherds (Luke 2:8–18), and Simeon and Anna (Luke 2:25–38) in the first two chapters of the gospel. Also, he wove it into John the Baptist (Luke 3:2) and Jesus himself (Luke 4:1–12, 14–30). Luke even gave examples of it to be sure that the reader grasped it (Luke 4:31–37; 5:1–11, 17–28; 6:6–11). Because Luke likes portraying Mary as the first Christian, that is, a disciple of her Son, she becomes the best example of how to hear the word and obey it. As a follower of Jesus, it is what makes her a pillar of faith. She believes. She trusts God. She remains faithful. Her blessedness—of womb and breasts—is attested by the unnamed woman in a crowd.[65]

Journal/Meditation: In what ways are you blessed or favored by God?

Prayer: Father, you made the Blessed Virgin Mary, mother of your Son, blessed, so that she might serve your people as an example of one

---

5, Gospel; LM: 621. Solemnity of the Assumption of the Blessed Virgin Mary, August 15, At the Vigil Mass, Gospel; LM: 712. The Common of the Blessed Virgin Mary, Gospel, Option 10; CMBVM: Lectionary 28. The Immaculate Heart of the Blessed Virgin Mary, Gospel, Option A; CMBVM: Lectionary: 35. The Blessed Virgin Mary, Pillar of Faith, Gospel.

65. References: BYM, pars. 51, 78, 126; CCC, pars. 273, 494, 506, 964, 967–8, 973; DPPL, par. 174; MC, pars. 11, 30, 35; RM, pars. 8, 20, 41; RVM, pars. 10, 15, 33.

who hears your word and obeys it. Grant, through her intercession, that I may be steadfast in faith and one day counted among those who are called blessed in the kingdom where you live with Jesus Christ and the Holy Spirit forever and ever. Amen.

Suffering[66]

Text: Luke 24:44–53

Scripture: "[Jesus said to his disciples], 'Thus it is written that the Messiah is to suffer and to rise from the dead on the third day . . . .'" (Luke 24:46)

Reflection: The Lukan theme of a suffering Messiah is woven throughout the author's orderly account. It begins with Simeon's words to Mary about a sword piercing her own soul (Luke 1:35). Jesus tells his disciples that the Son of Man must undergo great suffering, be rejected by the authorities, be killed, and rise on the third day (Luke 9:22). He predicts his suffering and death several more times (Luke 9:43–45; 12:50; 13:33; 17:25; 18:31–33; 22:15). The suffering-Messiah theme reaches a crescendo in the post-resurrection stories. Two men in Jesus' empty tomb remind the women of the theme (Luke 24:6–7). Jesus in disguise reminds two travelers to Emmaus, who have already mentioned the suffering-Messiah theme (Luke 24:19b–20), of the theme (Luke 24:26), and the eleven disciples in Jerusalem (Luke 24:46). Thus, the sword that pierced his mother's soul is identified as his death.

Jesus suffers and dies according to God's plan in Luke's Gospel. Suffering is best understood as experiencing that which is unfavorable; for Jesus it is physical, and it is deliberately inflicted upon him as it contributes to the unfolding of God's plan for the salvation of the world. For the author of Luke's Gospel, suffering represents the world's brokenness in which Jesus participates and which he redeems through his death and resurrection. Using the prophet Isaiah's suffering servant poems (Isa 42:1–7; 49:1–6; 50:4–9a; 52:13–53:12) as his basis, Luke portrays Jesus' suffering bringing about God's promise of restoration and salvation for his people. Mary, his mother, shares in his suffering, as Simeon's words to

---

66. CMBVM: Lectionary: 17. Our Lady of the Cenacle, Gospel, Option B; CMBVM: Lectionary: Appendix, Gospel, Option 21 (Optional Gospel in Mass 17).

her make clear, and just as he entered into glory through his resurrection, so has she through her assumption.[67]

Journal/Meditation: In what specific ways has your suffering been a part of God's plan of salvation?

Prayer: LORD God, I see your servant, Jesus, exalted and lifted high in resurrection after his suffering and death on the cross. By his wounds I have been healed. Help me to understand that it is through my good suffering that you continue to accomplish your plan of redemption through Christ my Lord. Amen.

JOHN'S GOSPEL

Word[68]

Text: Longer Form: John 1:1–18; Shorter Form: John 1:1–5, 9–14

Scripture: ". . . [T]he Word became flesh and lived among us, and we have seen his glory, the glory as of a father's only son, full of grace and truth. From his fullness we have all received, grace upon grace." (John 1:14, 16)

Reflection: Only John's Gospel begins at the beginning with the existence of the Word that was with God and was God (John 1:1). Only in John's Gospel does the Word enter into history by becoming flesh in the person of Jesus of Nazareth. Only in John's Gospel does the Word reveal the Father's glory, being his only Son and filled with grace and truth. The only Son of God enables people to see the God who cannot be seen (John 1:18)! This is but the first of many paradoxes—contradictory statements—from which deep truth is revealed in the opening verses of the Fourth Gospel.

The first paradox is presented in the first verse of the first chapter. The Word reveals a paradoxical relationship. It is with God, that is, distinct from God, and it is God, that is, it shares the divine identity. The second paradox presents the Word as being the source of all things, yet nothing created knows him (John 1:3, 10–11). The third paradox presents the world as the stage for the becoming flesh of the Word, the Light, yet it is also the place of darkness (John 1:5). The next paradox presumes that the Word is Jewish, and he is rejected by his own people (John 1:11).

---

67. References: CCC, pars. 965, 2617.

68. LM: 16. The Nativity of the Lord [Christmas], December 25, At the Mass during the Day, Gospel; LM: 19. Second Sunday after Christmas, Gospel.

Believers in the Word have been born into it through the intercourse of their parents; however, believing in the Word they are reborn as children of God with human flesh having nothing to do with it (John 1:12–13). The final paradox is the Word becoming flesh; God the Father sends God the Son in the flesh to make God known to those who are in the flesh. The God who forbids images of himself (Exod 20:4–6; Deut 5:8-10) makes one: Jesus, Son of Mary.[69]

Journal/Meditation: Which paradox gets most of your attention? What deep truth does it reveal to you?

Prayer: Father, in the beginning was the Word, and the Word was with you, and the Word was you. In the fullness of time, the Word became flesh and lived on the earth. Grant me deeper faith in him that I may be counted among the children of God and see your glory, the glory of Jesus Christ, and the glory of the Holy Spirit forever and ever. Amen.

Providence[70]

Text: John 2:1-11

Scripture: "On the third day there was a wedding in Cana of Galilee, and the mother of Jesus was there. When the wine gave out, the mother of Jesus said to him, 'They have no wine.' His mother said to the servants. 'Do whatever he tells you.'" (John 2:1, 3, 5)

Reflection: Providence is the wisdom, care, and guidance provided by God. In the case of the mother of Jesus, it is God's grace, counsel, hope, mercy, and help mediated through the Blessed Virgin Mary and illustrated in the unique Johannine account of the wedding at Cana. In biblical literature, God is the power that sustains and guides the universe

---

69. References: DPPL, pars. 195–6; MC, par. 37; RM, pars. 1, 4, 11, 24, 38–9; RVM, par. 24.

70. LM: 531. Optional Memorial of Our Lady of Lourdes, February 11, Gospel; LM: 712. The Common of the Blessed Virgin Mary, Gospel, Option 11; CMBVM: Lectionary: 9. Our Lady of Cana, Gospel; CMBVM: Lectionary: 20. Holy Mary, the New Eve, Gospel, Option B; CMBVM: Lectionary: 26. The Blessed Virgin Mary, Image and Mother of the Church II, Gospel; CMBVM: Lectionary: 30. The Blessed Virgin Mary, Mother and Mediatrix of Grace, Gospel; CMBVM: Lectionary: 33. The Blessed Virgin Mary, Mother of Good Counsel, Gospel; CMBVM: Lectionary: 37. The Blessed Virgin Mary, Mother of Divine Hope, Gospel; CMBVM: Lectionary: 39. Holy Mary, Queen and Mother of Mercy I, Gospel; CMBVM: Lectionary: 40. The Blessed Virgin Mary, Mother of Divine Providence, Gospel; CMBVM: Lectionary: 42. The Blessed Virgin Mary, Help of Christians, Gospel.

and human destiny; God provides for the future. As the mother of divine providence, the mother of Jesus—who is never named in John's Gospel—illustrates God's care by pointing out the lack of wine at the wedding to Jesus and then telling the servants to do whatever her Son told them to do. In the beauty of the incarnation, Mary gave birth to the One who insured a future for the universe. Jesus referred to that future as the kingdom of God.

The mother of Jesus illustrates the trust required to see the future brought about by God. Even though the hour of Jesus' suffering, death, and glorification had not yet arrived, God—in the person of Jesus—took care of his people. The reader was told this from the opening notice about it being the third day; three indicates the presence of God. Furthermore, there is no bride at this wedding because it begins the union of people and God in the person of Jesus. The six stone water jars confirm this fact; six is an incomplete number. The reader must continue through John's Gospel to find the seventh jar of wine (John 19:29)—seven indicates completeness—and the second appearance of the mother of Jesus (John 19:25–27), the completion of the wedding (John 19:30), and Jesus' resurrection on the third day (John 20:1). The marriage covenant, sealed in Jesus' blood and witnessed by his mother, provides all the trust in God's wisdom, care, and guidance that is needed for the future.[71]

Journal/Meditation: In what ways have you experienced God's wisdom, care, and guidance that provided for your future?

Prayer: Provident God, through the death and resurrection of your Son, you established your new covenant with people. Fill me with the trust of the mother of Jesus that I may come to share in the eternal wedding feast of the kingdom, where you live and reign, Father, Son, and Holy Spirit, one God, forever and ever. Amen.

Darkness[72]

Text: John 3:1-6

Scripture: "Now there was a Pharisee named Nicodemus, a leader of the Jews. He came to Jesus by night . . . ." (John 3:1–2)

---

71. References: BYM, pars. 20, 34–36, 138; CCC, pars. 773, 2618-9; DPPL, par. 106; MC, pars. 18, 33, 57; RM, pars. 21–22, 45; RVM, pars. 14, 16, 121.

72. CMBVM: Lectionary: 16. Holy Mary, Fountain of Light and Life, Gospel, Option B.

Reflection: When the author of John's Gospel first introduces his unique character named Nicodemus, he states that this leader of the Jews comes to Jesus during the night. Nicodemus comes in the darkness to discuss the meaning of born-again life with Jesus. As the author of the Fourth Gospel often does, he portrays Jesus speaking with a double entendre, that is, a word or phrase that can have two or more meanings. The Johannine Jesus tells Nicodemus about being born of water and the Spirit or born above into eternal life, indicating baptism. Nicodemus understands being born as the attempt to crawl back into his mother's womb and emerge from there a second time. Nicodemus, a teacher who should be in the light, is in darkness. However, in the course of John's Gospel he will come to understand gradually (John 7:50–51), and then he will emerge into the light, making a unique appearance at the burial of Jesus (John 19:39–40).

The mother of Jesus shines brightly in contrast to Nicodemus's initial darkness. Born into the light, she was graced by God from the first moment of her conception in the womb of her mother, Anne. She was filled with the light of the Holy Spirit to understand what God was asking of her when Gabriel announced the incarnation to her. And she gave birth to the light of the world (John 8:12; 9:5; 12:46) so that the darkness would not overcome it (John 1:5; 12:35). Thus, she is like an overflowing fountain of light which bestows eternal life on all who believe in her Son, Jesus.

Journal/Meditation: When have you, like Nicodemus, emerged from darkness into light?

Prayer: Almighty Father, through water and the Spirit, you give new birth to your children on this earth. Every day draw me from darkness into light through the life-giving grace of your Son, Jesus Christ, born of the Blessed Virgin Mary, until I reach eternal life forever and ever. Amen.

Booths[73]

Text: John 7:37-39a

Scripture: "On the last day of the festival [of Booths], the great day, while Jesus was standing there, he cried out, 'Let anyone who is thirsty come to me, and let the one who believes in me drink.'" (John 7:37–38a)

---

73. CMBVM: Lectionary: 31. The Blessed Virgin Mary, Fountain of Salvation II, Gospel.

Reflection: The Jewish festival of Booths, also known as Tabernacles or Sukkoth, is a major Jewish festival, one of three pilgrimage festivals, held in the autumn (September or October), to commemorate the sheltering of the Israelites in the wilderness. While they spent forty years in the desert, they lived in booths or tents. This yearly remembrance often features shelters built by families using branches and inhabited to commemorate their living in booths or tents during the harvest when grains and fruits were gathered. The festival lasts for eight days; the last day is the occasion for the Johannine Jesus to invite anyone who thirsts to come to him and anyone who believes in him to come and drink. As he does elsewhere in the Fourth Gospel, the Johannine Jesus replaces all Jewish festivals with himself. In this case, he becomes the booth in which believers live.

The Blessed Virgin Mary is honored as the fountain of salvation because she gave birth to Jesus, who declared himself to be the fountain of salvation. Furthermore, many shrines dedicated to Mary feature a spring of water used by people on pilgrimage for healing. Serving as a type of booth, the womb of the Blessed Virgin Mary sheltered the incarnate Word, who then pitched his booth or tabernacle in the flesh on earth (John 1:14). Since the water from the rock (Num 20:2–13) was also commemorated at the Festival of Booths, Isaiah's future blessings (Isa 44:3; 55:1) underlie Jesus' words and the author's note about the water being a reference to the Spirit who would flow from Jesus, Son of Mary, like a fountain for thirsty believers.

Journal/Meditation: What waters flowing from Jesus have you tasted?

Prayer: Father, through the cooperation of the Blessed Virgin Mary, you unsealed the fountain of salvation, your Son, Jesus Christ. Grant that I may always drink from this stream and bring forth a rich harvest of the fruits of the Holy Spirit forever and ever. Amen.

Prophecy[74]

Text: John 11:45–52

Scripture: "... Caiaphas, who was high priest ..., said to [the chief priests and Pharisees] ... , 'You do not understand that it is better for you to have one man die for the people than to have the whole nation

---

74. CMBVM: Lectionary: 38. Holy Mary, Mother of Unity, Gospel, Option A.

destroyed.' He did not say this on his own, but being high priest that year he prophesied that Jesus was about to die for the nation, and not for the nation only, but to gather into one the dispersed children of God." (John 11:49-52)

Reflection: After Jesus raises Lazarus, brother of Martha and Mary, from the dead, many Jews believed in him, but some ran to the Pharisees with the message that something needed to be done about the sign-performing Jesus; otherwise, all would believe in him. The Johannine author presents the wisdom of Caiaphas, high priest, by having him tell them that it is better for one man to die for the people rather than for the whole nation of Israel to be eliminated by the Romans because of the deeds of Jesus (John 18:14). The narrator explains that Caiaphas was prophesying, even though he did not know that he was doing so! The narrator relates Caiaphas's prediction about Jesus' dying not just to save Israel, but as a means to gather into one all the dispersed children of God, thus forming a unity between people and God.

The Blessed Virgin Mary is invoked as the untarnished image of the church, splendor of the church, queen of all the earth, and queen of the universe in the LBVMOCIBVM to stress her role as mother in bringing together all God's children. First of all, she is the source of unity for the divine and human natures of Jesus; in her womb occurs the incarnation. Second of all, the Johannine author imagines Jesus, her Son, being in a wedding between people and God, represented by Jesus, which is finished on the cross. Third of all, Jesus prays that all may be one in the same way as he and the Father are one. In her role as mother of the church, the Blessed Virgin Mary assists in gathering into one the dispersed children of God whom Jesus, the bridegroom, chose for his bride.[75]

Journal/Meditation: How does the Blessed Virgin Mary serve as the mother of the church for you?

Prayer: Father of my Lord Jesus Christ, you desire that all your scattered children be gathered into one. Through the intercession of the mother of your Son, grant that people everywhere may come to your crucified and risen Christ, who lives with you and the Holy Spirit, one God, forever and ever. Amen.

---

75. References: BYM, pars. 10, 36, 61, 101; CCC, pars. 503, 773, 963, 975, 2617; MC, par 26.

Representative[76]

Text: John 12:44–50

Scripture: Jesus cried aloud, "I have come as light into the world, so that everyone who believes in me should not remain in the darkness. What I speak, therefore, I speak just as the Father has told me." (John 12:46, 50)

Reflection: A representative is somebody who speaks for another. In John's Gospel, Jesus presents himself as God's representative. He is sent into the world by God to speak for God. He makes this very clear in John's Gospel when he declares that anyone who believes in him believes not in him but in God who sent him (John 12:44). Likewise, anyone who sees him sees the Father who sent him (John 12:45). He, the representative of God's light, removes believers from the world's darkness. Jesus does not function as judge; God is the judge. The Johannine Jesus' words are not his; they represent the Father, who has commanded him what to say to engender eternal life in those who believe in and see him.

The Blessed Virgin Mary not only conceived the Light and gave birth to the Light, but she followed the Light. In the words of the Johannine Jesus, she walked while she had the light so that the darkness did not overtake her (John 12:35). She saw her Son as God's representative. She recognized his words as those which God desired him to speak. Mary recognized that belief in Jesus was belief in the Father, who had sent Jesus into her womb. In accepting God's will, she had come into God's Light and into the Light of the One who declared himself to be the Light of the world. And that Light was eternal life (John 14:6a). According to John's Gospel, no one can go to the Father to enjoy eternal life except through Jesus (John 14:6b).

Journal/Meditation: From what darkness of the world has Jesus led you to God's light?

Prayer: Father, your Light became flesh in the womb of the Blessed Virgin Mary in order to be your representative and lead many out of the world's darkness. Accomplish in me what you worked in her that I may be led into eternal life by Jesus Christ, who is Lord forever and ever. Amen.

---

76. CMBVM: Lectionary: 16. Holy Mary, Fountain of Light and Life, Gospel, Option A.

Comfort[77]

Text: John 14:15–21, 25–27

Scripture: Jesus said to Philip, "... [T]he Advocate, the Holy Spirit, whom the Father will send in my name, will teach you everything, and remind you of all that I have said to you. Do not let your hearts be troubled, and do not let them be afraid." (John 14:26, 27c)

Reflection: In John's Gospel, chapter 14 begins a four-chapter insert (John 14:1—17:26) of Jesus' direct address, discourse, or monologue. That it was inserted at a date later than the original gospel is clearly seen by the smooth transition from John 13:36–38 to John18:1. The insert begins with Jesus stating, "Do not let your hearts be troubled" (John 14:1), and the first section of it ends with the same words (John 14:27c). Troubled hearts need comfort, and that is exactly what the Johannine Jesus promises. He tells Philip that he will ask the Father to give another Advocate to be with him forever (John 14:16). This Advocate, also called the Spirit of truth (John 14:17), will live in believers. The Advocate, who is also called the Paraclete, the Comforter, and Helper, will serve as a foster-parent to those who may feel like they have been orphaned: Jesus' followers. However, the Advocate, also called the Holy Spirit (John 14:26), will teach believers everything they need to know because he takes the place of Jesus once Jesus has died and been raised. The temporary presence of the Incarnate Word gives way to the permanent presence of the Advocate.

The Blessed Virgin Mary is invoked as comforter of the afflicted in the LBVM(LL), while the LBVMOCIBVM invokes her as the advocate of grace and champion of God's people. God is portrayed as comforter of his people (Isa 12:1; 40:1). Jesus is presented as the incarnate comforter of people. He sends the Spirit, the Advocate, to continue to comfort people. Paul declares that the Father of the Lord Jesus Christ is the "God of all consolation, who consoles ... in all ... affliction, so that [people] may be able to console those who are in any affliction with the consolation with which [they themselves] are consoled by God" (2 Cor 1:3–4). Paul continues his reflection on sharing consolation (2 Cor 1:5–7). Mary is the mother of consolation because she gave birth to Jesus, God's supreme

---

77. CMBVM: Lectionary: 41. The Blessed Virgin Mary, Mother of Consolation, Gospel, Option B.

consolation, who asked the Father to send the Comforter (Advocate, Paraclete, Helper) to continue to console the world.[78]

Journal/Meditation: What consolation have you received from the Father, the Son, and/or the Holy Spirit?

Prayer: Your Son, born of the Blessed Virgin Mary, requested that you send the Advocate, Father, that the world might continue to experience your consolation after Jesus' death and resurrection. Fill me with the Holy Spirit's comfort that I may share it with all my sisters and brothers in Christ Jesus forever and ever. Amen.

Delight[79]

Text: John 15:9–12

Scripture: Jesus said, "I have said these things to you so that my joy may be in you, and that your joy may be complete." (John 15:11)

Reflection: The word *delight* means great joy and pleasure. Somebody or something brings or gives somebody great joy and pleasure. Following his analogy about being the true vine, his Father being the vinegrower, and all his followers being the branches, the Johannine Jesus applies the analogy by exhorting his listeners to abide in his love as he abides in his Father's love. This abiding in love brings delight or great joy to the listeners, Jesus, and God. Furthermore, Jesus tells his listeners to love one another just as he has loved them and as God loves him. In this way, all share in delightful love that brings great joy and pleasure.

The LBVM(LL) invokes Mary as the cause of joy, and the LBVMOCIBVM invokes her as the joy of Israel. She is the cause of joy because she is responsible for bringing Jesus into the world. She is the joy of Israel because the good news of great joy of the Messiah's birth is delivered to his own people first. In other words, because Mary cooperated with God she became the cause of great joy and delight for the whole world. Her Son, in turn, brought delight to his disciples after his resurrection (John 20:20) and ascension (Luke 24:52) after having taught them to

---

78. References: CCC, par. 969; MC, pars. 14, 22, 26–27, 57; RM, pars. 7–10, 24, 39–40; RVM, pars. 23, 25.

79. CMBVM: Lectionary: 34. The Blessed Virgin Mary, Cause of Our Joy, Gospel, Option B.

take delight in loving one another in imitation of the delight the Father and Son takes in abiding in each other's love.[80]

Journal/Meditation: In what have you most recently taken delight? What great joy did it give you? How was God present to you?

Prayer: Joyful God, you shared your joy with the world through the birth of your only-begotten Son, born of the Blessed Virgin Mary, the cause of joy, the joy of Israel. Fill me with the same joy that I may delight in praising you, Father, Son, and Holy Spirit, one God, forever and ever. Amen.

One[81]

Text: John 17:20–26

Scripture: Jesus prayed, "As you, Father, are in me and I am in you, may [those you have given me] also be in us, so that the world may believe that you have sent me. The glory that you have given me I have given them, so that they may be one, as we are one, I in them and you in me, that they may become completely one, so that the world may know that you have sent me . . . ." (John 17:21b–23)

Reflection: The last chapter (John 17:1–26) of the insert in John's Gospel (14:1–17:26) is a prayer for unity said by Jesus and addressed to the Father. In the prayer, Jesus asks that all believers—then present and future—may be one. Their unity will reflect the oneness of the Father and the Son. Moreover, the unity of believers will be united to the unity of Father and Son. Such a display of union should be enough for the world to believe that the Father sent Jesus. The Son has shared the glory he has with the Father before creation with his followers so that all may be completely one: Jesus in them and God in Jesus, and, thus, God in them. In the final petition of his prayer, Jesus asks the Father that those he has given Jesus may be in glory with them, furthering the uniformity Jesus desires through the mutual love of God, Jesus, and Jesus' followers.

Earlier, Jesus, using the metaphor of sheep, had reminded his listeners that he had other sheep that did not belong to the fold, and that he would bring them along with all the others. "So, there will be one flock, one shepherd" (John 10:16). The Blessed Virgin Mary represents unity as the Word and flesh of Jesus united in her womb. She also represents unity

---

80. References: BYM, par. 22; RM, par. 44.

81. CMBVM: Lectionary: 38. Holy Mary, Mother of Unity, Gospel, Option B.

as the mother of the church, often referred to as the bride of Christ. Just as Jesus gathered the scattered children of God (John 11:52), Mary, his mother, continues to gather together into one with Christ, and, thus, with the Father, all people.[82]

Journal/Meditation: What has been your most recent experience of human unity? How did you experience the oneness of the Father, the Son, and the Holy Spirit?

Prayer: Righteous Father, the world does not know you, but I know you, and I know that you sent Jesus into the world to gather into one all your scattered children. Through the intercession of the Blessed Virgin Mary, gather together all the families of nations in the love you share with your Son and the Holy Spirit forever and ever. Amen.

Church[83]

Text: John 19:25–27

Scripture: ". . . [S]tanding near the cross of Jesus [was] his mother . . . . When Jesus saw his mother and the disciple whom he loved standing beside her, he said to his mother, 'Woman, here is you son.'" (John 19:25b–26)

Reflection: In popular imagination and in iconography, Mary is depicted standing at the foot of the cross of her crucified Son. However, this event is recorded only in John's Gospel, and the author does not name her as Mary. The author of Mark's Gospel refers to her as Jesus' mother (3:31) and calls her Mary (6:3), and that is the last the reader hears about her. The author of Matthew's Gospel refers to her as the mother of Jesus

---

82. References: BYM, par. 116; CCC, pars. 503, 507, 773, 963, 967, 972, 2619; RM, pars. 1, 38–39.

83. LM: 639. Memorial of Our Lady of Sorrows, Gospel, First Option; LM: 712. The Common of the Blessed Virgin Mary, Gospel, Option 12; LM: 1002. The Blessed Virgin Mary, I. The Blessed Virgin Mary, Mother of the Church, Gospel; LM: 1002. The Blessed Virgin Mary, III. Our Lady, Queen of Apostles, Gospel, Second Option; CMBVM: Lectionary: 11. The Blessed Virgin Mary at the Foot of the Cross I, Gospel; CMBVM: Lectionary: 12. The Blessed Virgin Mary at the Foot of the Cross II, Gospel; CMBVM: Lectionary: 13. The Commending of the Blessed Virgin Mary, Gospel; CMBVM: Lectionary: 14. The Blessed Virgin Mary, Mother of Reconciliation, Gospel; CMBVM: Lectionary: 18. The Blessed Virgin Mary, Queen of Apostles, Gospel; CMBVM: Lectionary: 25. The Blessed Virgin Mary, Image and Mother of the Church I, Gospel; CMBVM: Lectionary: 32. The Blessed Virgin Mary, Mother and Teacher in the Spirit, Gospel, Option B; CMBVM: Lectionary: 43. Our Lady of Ransom, Gospel.

(13:55) and as Mary in the same verse, and that is the last the reader hears about her. The author of Luke's Gospel calls her mother for the last time at Luke 8:19 and Mary for the last time at Luke 2:34, and never mentions her again. The author of John's Gospel names others standing near the cross (John 19:25b), but there are two who have no name: the mother of Jesus and the disciple whom he loved (John 19:26).

The mother of Jesus is a sign of the church, people, being married to Jesus. Her first and only other appearance occurs at the wedding at Cana (John 2:1–11), where there is no bride, but where the wedding between people and God (in the person of Jesus) begins. Her appearance at the cross is the other bookend to the marriage story. Jesus' final words, "It is finished" (John 19:30), means the wedding is over; Jesus, the bridegroom, has completed the wedding with his church, represented by his mother, the bride, who is entrusted to the care of the disciple Jesus loved. The beloved disciple is a sign of those entrusted with the members of the church. He makes only three appearances (John 13:33, 19:26–27; 20:1–10) in one of the original blocks of John's Gospel before 14:1–17:26 was inserted between13:38 and 18:1. The three appearances of the disciple Jesus loved—like the three appearances of Nicodemus (John 3:1–21; 7:50–51; 19:39)—signal the divine presence.[84]

Journal/Meditation: In what specific ways has the church been a mother for you?

Prayer: Father, at the cross your Son, Jesus, entrusted his mother to the disciple whom he loved and the beloved disciple to his mother, thus sealing the marriage covenant between you and all people. Keep me faithful to this new covenant that I may one day share in the eternal wedding banquet with you, Father, your Son, Jesus Christ, and the Holy Spirit forever and ever. Amen.

Blood[85]

Text: John 19:25–34

Scripture: ". . . [O]ne of the soldiers pierced [Jesus'] side with a spear, and at once blood and water came out." (John 19:34)

---

84. References: BYM, pars. 5, 113–4, 117; CCC, pars. 507, 773, 963, 967, 972, 975, 2619; RM, pars. 5–6, 47; RVM, par. 15.

85. LM: 572A. Memorial of the Blessed Virgin Mary, Mother of the Church, Monday after Pentecost, Gospel.

Reflection: With a unique scene of a soldier piercing the side of the dead Jesus on the cross and blood and water coming out the author of John's Gospel portrays Jesus as a type of new man. In the second story of creation, the LORD God causes a deep sleep to fall upon the man, and from the man's side the LORD extracts a rib and builds it into a woman (Gen 2:21–22). Thus from the man's side there comes the life of woman. The author of John's Gospel is developing that image further by his portrayal of blood and water coming out of the side of Jesus, whom the author portrays as a new man. This new man gives birth to the church, and since Jesus is the Son of Mary, she is considered to be the mother of the church, according to the LBVM(LL).

Throughout John's Gospel, water plays a significant role as a sign representing the church. Water is first mentioned in association with John the Baptist (John 1:26, 31, 33; 3:23) where it reveals the Incarnate Word. Next, water becomes wine (John 2:6, 7, 9; 4:46), which looks like blood, which must be drunk in order to have eternal life (John 6:53–56). Nicodemus learns that no one can enter God's kingdom without being born of water and Spirit (John 3:5), while the Samaritan woman learns that she must drink of living water (John 4:7, 10-15, 28; 7:37-38), which heals (John 5:7) and cleanses (John 13:5). The significance of water and blood (signs of baptism and eucharist) reaches a crescendo in John's Gospel with the soldier piercing the side of the new man (who is in the deep sleep of death) and blood and water coming out, that is, giving birth to the church.[86]

Journal/Meditation: What does blood signify for you? What does water signify for you?

Prayer: Father of mercy, out of the side of your dead Son on the cross you brought forth the life of the church through blood and water. Grant that through the intercession of Jesus' mother, Mary, your church may continue in fruitfulness, giving birth to many children and nourishing them with the blood of Christ forever and ever. Amen.

---

86. References: BYM, pars. 20, 38, 70, 130; MC, pars. 11, 16, 19, 21, 28, 35; RM, pars. 27–30, 42–44.

Lamb[87]

Text: John 19:25–37

Scripture: "Since it was the day of Preparation, the Jews did not want the bodies [of Jesus and two others] left on the cross during the sabbath, especially because that sabbath was a day of great solemnity." (John 19:31a)

Reflection: In John's Gospel, John the Baptist introduces Jesus two times by naming him the lamb of God (John 1:29, 35). The Johannine Jesus makes three trips to Jerusalem to celebrate Passover ([1] 2:13, 23; [2] 6:4; [3] 11:55; 12:1; 13:1; 18:28, 39a), the yearly Jewish commemoration of the escape from Egyptian slavery. The Johannine author wants the reader to be aware that "it was the day of Preparation for Passover, and it was about noon" (John 19:14a) when Pilate hands over Jesus to be crucified. At noon the Temple priests began slaughtering the Passover lambs in the Temple; they collected their blood and splashed it upon the altar. Before he dies, Jesus is offered a sponge full of wine on a branch of hyssop, just like the first Passover lamb's blood is smeared on the doorposts and lintels of Hebrew homes (Exod 12:22). The Johannine author continues to build his case that Jesus is the new Passover lamb by noting the fulfillment of a HB (OT) passage that states none of the Passover lamb's bones should be broken (Exod 12:46; Num 9:12), just like Jesus' legs are not broken because he is already dead.

In John's Gospel, Jesus does not eat the Passover meal with his disciples as he does in the Synoptic Gospels (Mark, Matthew, Luke). He dies on the day when the Jews prepare to celebrate Passover by taking the lamb to the Temple to be slaughtered and, then, preparing it to be eaten at sunset. Furthermore, unique to John's Gospel is the presentation of Passover and Sabbath falling on the same day, Saturday, that year, making that Passover a very solemn celebration. Thus, Jesus dies on Friday before sunset at the same time as the Passover lambs are being slaughtered in the Temple. This makes him, Son of Mary and Son of God, in Johannine thought the new, sacrificed Passover lamb (1 Cor 5:7b), whose blood saves people, just like the blood of the first Passover lamb saves the Hebrews from death and slavery (Exod 12:12–13). John the Baptist prepared for this understanding when he saw Jesus coming toward him

---

87. CMBVM: Lectionary: 31. The Blessed Virgin Mary, Fountain of Salvation I, Gospel.

and declared, "Here is the Lamb of God who takes away the sin of the world" (John 1:29)!

Journal/Meditation: From what has the Lamb of God saved you?

Prayer: Father, carrying his cross by himself and dying on it your Son united people to you in a new covenant of blood. Grant me a share among those redeemed by the blood of the new Passover Lamb, Jesus Christ, who lives and reigns with you and the Holy Spirit forever and ever. Amen.

ACTS OF THE APOSTLES

Witness[88]

Text: Acts 1:6–14

Scripture: Jesus said to the apostles, ". . . [Y]ou will receive power when the Holy Spirit has come upon you; and you will be my witnesses in Jerusalem, in all Judea and Samaria, and to the ends of the earth." (Acts 1:8)

Reflection: A witness is somebody who sees or hears something that happens and gives evidence about it. The word *witness* comes from the Greek word for *martyr*, somebody who witnesses to his or her faith to the point of being willing to die for what he or she believes to be the truth. In the Acts of the Apostles, written by the same person who wrote Luke's Gospel, the author presents the pre-ascended Jesus instructing his eleven apostles about the power they will receive from the Holy Spirit to be his witnesses in Jerusalem, Judea, Samaria, and the ends of the earth. In effect, this is the geographical outline for the rest of the Acts of the Apostles. After receiving the Spirit, the apostles witness to Jesus in Jerusalem (Acts 2:1–8:1), Judea and Samaria (Acts 8:2–15:35), and, under the leadership of Paul, take the witness to the ends of the earth, Rome (Acts 15:36–28:31).

The Blessed Virgin Mary, the mother of Jesus, is a witness. She heard the angel Gabriel deliver God's message to her, and she witnessed the birth of Jesus. In giving birth to her Son, she shed her blood. Simeon told her that a sword would pierce her soul, later identified as Jesus' crucifixion and death. The strength that saw her through his martyrdom was the Holy Spirit, who had overshadowed her from the moment she had

---

88. CMBVM: Lectionary: 17. Our Lady of the Cenacle, First Reading.

conceived Jesus in her womb. Joining with the apostles, she awaited the fullness of strength that the Spirit bestows so that witnessing could continue in Jerusalem, in Judea, in Samaria, and to the ends of the earth.[89]

Journal/Meditation: How are you a witness?

Prayer: Holy Father, you raised Jesus from the dead. Before he ascended to you, he instructed his followers to wait for your gift of the Holy Spirit to strengthen them in bearing witness to his death and resurrection. Make me an effective witness of Christ, risen and ascended, now and forever. Amen.

Prayer[90]

Text: Acts 1:12–14

Scripture: "All [eleven apostles in the room upstairs] were constantly devoting themselves to prayer, together with certain women, including Mary the mother of Jesus, as well as his brothers." (Acts 1:14)

Reflection: Contrary to the usually understood definition of prayer—people telling God what to do—is the biblical understanding that prayer is listening to God tell people what they need to do. God prays in human beings, revealing to them in the depths of their hearts and minds what course of action they need to take, what kind of life they need to live. This understanding of private prayer requires quiet, disengagement from all electronic gadgets, and the easing of one's resistance to be told what to do. Even when engaging in community prayer, people must still themselves in order to hear God speak to them through each other. The unity engendered through saying prayers, singing hymns, and sitting with others quietly imitates the prayer of Jesus' apostles and his mother and brothers after his ascension and before the descent of the Holy Spirit.

The apostles, some women, Mary, and Jesus' brothers gather in community prayer in an upstairs room in which they are staying in Jerusalem. They are united in waiting for the gift of the Holy Spirit according to

---

89. References: BYM, pars. 79, 115; DPPL, pars. 155–6; MC, pars. 11, 18, 26, 28, 57; RM, pars. 24, 26, 40; RVM, pars. 12, 14.

90. LM: 572A. Memorial of the Blessed Virgin Mary, Mother of the Church, Monday after Pentecost, First Reading, Second Option; LM: 653. Memorial of Our Lady of the Rosary, October 7, First Reading; LM: 708. The Common of the Blessed Virgin Mary, First Reading, Option 1; LM: 1002. The Blessed Virgin Mary, I. The Blessed Virgin Mary, Mother of the Church, First Reading, Second Option; CMBVM: Lectionary: 26. The Blessed Virgin Mary, Image and Mother of the Church II, First Reading.

Jesus' instructions. All await the power of the Holy Spirit that will enable them to be witnesses to Jesus from Jerusalem to the ends of the earth (Acts 1:8). The LBVMOCIBVM invokes the Blessed Virgin Mary as the untarnished image of the church and the splendor of the church. In other words, she represents what the total church should look like in community prayer and in individual prayer. The stance taken is that of waiting for God to act instead of telling God what he needs to do.[91]

Journal/Meditation: In what ways have you experienced God praying in you?

Prayer: Heavenly Father, you once gathered the apostles, some women, Mary, and Jesus' brothers in prayer awaiting the gift of the Holy Spirit. Grant that I learn from them how to listen for your word in my heart and mind and through my brothers and sisters in the church. Come dwell in me as Father, Son, and Holy Spirit, one God, forever and ever Amen.

Spirit[92]

Text: Acts 1:12–14; 2:1–4

Scripture: "All of [the apostles] were filled with the Holy Spirit and began to speak in other languages, as the Spirit gave them ability." (Acts 2:4)

Reflection: In popular imagination and iconography, the twelve apostles are pictured gathered six on either side of the Blessed Virgin Mary while drops of fire hover over all their heads. While that is a good depiction of Pentecost, it is not the one presented in the Acts of the Apostles. The Acts, written by the same person who authored Luke's Gospel, presents eleven apostles with some women, Mary, and Jesus' brothers gathered in prayer in an upstairs room (Acts 1:12–14). After this, Peter gives a speech to about two hundred twenty people in which he directs them to nominate two men to take the place of Judas, who died in a field. After all pray for God's guidance, lots are cast, and Matthias becomes apostle number twelve (Acts 1:15–26). Now that the twelve apostles are reconstituted Pentecost can occur.

---

91. References: BYM, pars. 79, 115; CCC, pars. 965, 2617; DPPL, pars. 155–6; MC, pars. 11, 18, 26, 28, 57; RM, pars. 24, 26, 40; RVM, pars. 12, 14.

92. CMBVM: Lectionary: 18. The Blessed Virgin Mary, Queen of Apostles, First Reading; CMBVM: Lectionary: 33. The Blessed Virgin Mary, Mother of Good Counsel, First Reading, Option B.

The author depicts the twelve gathered together in one place, where all hear the sound of a violent wind (1 Kgs 19:11b), see divided tongues of fire rest on them (Exod 19:18), and speak in various languages, reversing the chaos of Babel with order (Gen 11:7). In other words, this is a theophanic experience, a manifestation of God. And it follows the use of one of the author's favorite phrases: "filled with the Holy Spirit" (Luke 1:15, 41b, 67; Acts 2:4). Even though Mary is often depicted with the apostles for this theophany, the Holy Spirit had already come upon her when she conceived Jesus in her womb (Luke 1:35). Nevertheless, the image endures as the LBVM(LL) lauds her as queen of apostles, and the LBVMOCIBVM invokes her as the queen of apostles and martyrs. She, who gave birth to the Spirit-child Jesus, is also invoked in the LBVMOCIBVM as the glory of the Holy Spirit.[93]

Journal/Meditation: What image do you use to depict the Holy Spirit?

Prayer: You make your presence known, LORD God, with wind and fire. Grant that I may recognize you in the daily events of my life and be guided by your Holy Spirit, who fills me with the new life of the resurrection of Jesus Christ, your Son, Lord forever and ever. Amen.

Repent[94]

Text: Acts 2:14a, 36–40a, 41–42

Scripture: Peter said to his fellow Israelites, "Repent, and be baptized every one of you in the name of Jesus Christ so that your sins may be forgiven, and you will receive the gift of the Holy Spirit." (Acts 2:38)

Reflection: The way to have access to the light and life of Jesus Christ, born of the Blessed Virgin Mary and raised from the dead by God, is to repent, according to Peter in the Acts of the Apostles. The verb *to repent* means to recognize the wrong one has done and be sorry about it. The word also means to change one's behavior. Biblically, a person who changes his or her mind and then changes his or her behavior repents. Thus it is that Peter tells his fellow Israelites to repent of the wrong they did in having Jesus crucified (Acts 2:23) because God has raised Jesus from the dead and made him both Lord and Messiah (Acts 2:36). As a

---

93. References: CCC, pars. 497, 721–2; MC, pars 5, 11, 22, 26–27; RM, pars. 9, 41; RVM, par. 23.

94. CMBVM: Lectionary: 16. Holy Mary, Fountain of Light and Life, First Reading.

sign that they recognize the wrong they did, are sorry about it, and are changing their behavior, Peter tells them to be baptized, and they will receive the gift of the Holy Spirit.

Such repentance was accomplished by God in the Blessed Virgin Mary from the moment she was conceived in her mother's womb. Because she was wrapped in grace, she did no wrong and was ever-ready to fulfill God's will of conceiving in her womb and giving birth to the light and life of the One who had already enveloped her in light and life. In the words of the LBVMOCIBVM, this made her, the queen conceived without original sin, a minister of holiness. Furthermore, what God accomplished in the Blessed Virgin Mary, he continues to work in the church through the fountain of baptism and the gift of the Holy Spirit for those who repent.[95]

Journal/Meditation: Of what have you most recently repented? What change in your behavior did you make?

Prayer: Lord, through the apostle Peter, you call all people to repent. With the gift of the Holy Spirit move me to acknowledge my sin, be sorry, and change my behavior in the hope of sharing in the light and life of your Son, Jesus Christ, who lives and reigns with you and the Holy Spirit, one God, forever and ever. Amen.

Raised[96]

Text: Acts 13:16–17, 22–25

Scripture: In the synagogue in Antioch in Pisidia, Paul addresses the Israelites and other God-fearers, saying: "Of [David's] posterity God has brought to Israel a Savior, Jesus, as he promised." (Acts 13:23)

Reflection: The author of the Acts of the Apostles is the same man who wrote Luke's Gospel. One of the ways the two books are connected is through their characters. In Luke 4:14–30, Jesus delivers his first speech after the prophet Isaiah is read. Likewise, after the law and the prophets are read in the synagogue in Antioch, Paul stands up and begins his speech in which he presents a short summary of Israelite history (Acts 13:13–52). Furthermore, the author connects Jesus, "a Savior, who is the

---

95. References: BYM, pars. 52, 56; CCC, pars. 488, 490, 511; MC, pars. 14, 22, 57; RM, pars. 7–10, 24, 39, 41.

96. LM: 13. Solemnity of the Nativity of the Lord [Christmas], December 25, At the Vigil Mass, Second Reading.

Messiah, the Lord" (Luke 2:11) announced to the Jewish shepherds by the angel of the Lord, and the "Leader and Savior" (Acts 5:31) proclaimed by Peter to the council, to Paul's speech about God's promise to Israel of a Savior (Acts 13:23).

Of particular importance is Paul's linking of Jesus to King David (Acts 13:22). Luke has already linked Jesus to David by indicating that Mary, his mother, is engaged to a man named Joseph of the house of David (Luke 1:27), and by setting his birth in Bethlehem, the city of David's birth, because Joseph was descended from the house and family of David (Luke 2:4). Furthermore, Zechariah, father of John the Baptist, declares that the God of Israel has raised up a mighty savior in the house of David (Luke 1:69; 3:31), and the blind man in Jericho calls to Jesus, Son of David, desiring to be cured (Luke 18:38–39). Finally, the Lukan crowd hails Jesus as the king who comes in the name of the Lord when he enters Jerusalem (Luke 19:38). By linking Jesus, born of Mary, to David in Paul's speech, Luke hopes to bring both Jews and other God-fearers (Acts 13:16b) to accept the message, the good news, of salvation that they have received about the Savior promised by God: Jesus, whom their leaders had crucified in Jerusalem and God raised from the dead (Acts 13:26–41).[97]

Journal/Meditation: Why is it important to proclaim the resurrection of Christ on Christmas Eve?

Prayer: Father, the apostle Paul delivered the good news that what you promised to your people you fulfilled by raising Jesus, your Son, from the dead. Give me the courage to proclaim this message of salvation to the ends of the earth now and forever. Amen.

ROMANS

Faith[98]

Text: Romans 4:13, 16–18, 22

Scripture: ". . . [T]he promise that he would inherit the world did not come to Abraham or to his descendants through the law but through the righteousness of faith." (Rom 4:13)

---

97. References: BYM, pars. 23, 27; RM, par. 15.

98. LM: 543. Solemnity of St. Joseph, Spouse of the Blessed Virgin Mary, March 19, Second Reading.

Reflection: In the HB (OT) book of Genesis, the LORD appears to Abram (later named Abraham) in a vision and promises him that he will have an heir and that his descendants will be as numerous as the stars in the sky (Gen 15:1–5). Then, the narrator states that Abram "believed the LORD; and the LORD reckoned it to him as righteousness" (Gen 15:6). This becomes the basis for Paul's statement in his Letter to the Romans that salvation is not based on adherence to Torah, since the Law came after Abraham. According to Paul, salvation depends on faith and not on keeping Torah. Because Abraham was as good as dead without a descendant, God gave life to the good-as-dead man by calling into existence a descendant, Isaac—because Abraham believed God's promise (Rom 4:17). This is how, according to Paul, Abraham's faith was reckoned to him as righteousness (Rom 4:22). In other words, God's promise to Abraham is given by God as a gift, grace (Rom 4:16), and it is received in faith by Abraham, making him righteous, that is, in a healthy relationship of trust with God.

For Paul, Abraham's righteous living through faith (Hab 2:4) becomes the model both for Jews and Gentiles who believe in the same God who raised Jesus from the dead (Rom 4:24). The absolute trust that Abraham placed in the LORD—the trust that God declared righteous—now enables both Jews and Gentiles—Paul's way of saying everyone—to be justified by faith (Rom 5:1) and to be declared righteous by God (Rom 3:24) by proclaiming that God raised the crucified Jesus from the dead—once again giving life to the dead. Joseph, whom the author of Matthew's Gospel declares to be a righteous man (Matt 1:19), breaks Torah by taking Mary, mother of Jesus, as his spouse, believing the words of the angel of the Lord (a code phrase for God). Joseph does the right thing, trusting the divine words delivered by the angel, even though it means breaking the Law. Like Abraham before him, according to Paul, his faith is credited to him as righteousness. He lives in a healthy relationship with God.[99]

Journal/Meditation: Do you live by faith, absolute trust in the God who raises the dead to life, or do you live by works, presuming that you have to earn salvation through what you do or don't do? Explain.

Prayer: God of Abraham and Joseph, you give life where people presume there is death. Fill me with the grace of the Holy Spirit that I may boldly proclaim that you raised Jesus from the dead and reckon my faith as righteousness. Hear me through the same Jesus Christ, your Son

---

99. References: BYM, pars. 13, 28–30, 32–33, 47, 142; CCC, pars. 273, 488, 497, 506, 967; DPPL, par. 101; RM, par. 14.

and Mary's Son, who lives and reigns with you and the Holy Spirit, one God, forever and ever. Amen.

Eve[100]

Text: Romans 5:12, 17–19

Scripture: ". . . [J]ust as by the one man's disobedience the many were made sinners, so by the one man's obedience the many will be made righteous." (Rom 5:19)

Reflection: In his Letter to the Romans, Paul presents a parallel between the old man and the new man. The old man is Adam, who brings sin and death into the world (Gen 3:6, 19; 4:25; Rom 5:12), and the new man is Jesus Christ, through whom God conquered sin and death (Rom 5:15). By faith, trust, that God raised the new man from the dead, people accept God's new offer of abundant grace (Rom 5:15), righteousness, and life (Rom 5:17). Paul summarizes his new man-old man parallel by writing that the first man's trespass led to condemnation to death for all, but the new man's righteousness leads to justification and life for all (Rom 5:18). If the old man's disobedience was commuted to all, making all sinners, the new man's obedience is commuted to all, making them righteous, that is, enjoying a healthy relationship with God.

If the old man-new man parallel works for Jesus Christ, then the old woman-new woman parallel can work for Eve and Mary. In the book of Genesis, the old woman, whom the man names Eve (Gen 3:20), takes the fruit from the forbidden tree of the knowledge of good and evil and eats it in disobedience to God (Gen 2:17). Luke's Gospel presents Mary as the new woman, who hears God's words from the angel Gabriel about conceiving and giving birth to God's Son, and she obeys God (Luke 1:26–38). Thus, what Paul writes about the old man-new man parallel can be said of the old woman-new woman parallel. The first woman's trespass led to condemnation to death for all, but the new woman's righteousness leads to new life for all. If the old woman's disobedience was commuted to all, making all sinners, the new woman's obedience is a model of how to have a healthy relationship with God for all. Through Mary, God has lavished

---

100. LM: 710. The Common of the Blessed Virgin Mary, Second Reading, First Option; CMBVM: Lectionary: 20. Holy Mary, the New Eve, First Reading, Option B; CMBVM: Lectionary: Appendix, First Reading, Option 9 (Optional First Reading in Mass 20).

grace and righteousness in Christ Jesus upon the world, making it a new creation.[101]

Journal/Meditation: What other comparisons and contrasts can you draw from the parallel of Adam and Jesus Christ? from Eve and Mary?

Prayer: LORD God, the first man and the first woman disobeyed you and brought death into the world. The new man, Jesus Christ, and the new Eve, his mother, brought life into the world. Overwhelm me with your grace that I may follow Jesus Christ to the kingdom, where he lives with his mother now and forever. Amen.

Predestined[102]

Text: Romans 8:28–30

Scripture: "... [T]hose whom [God] predestined he also called; and those whom he called he also justified; and those whom he justified he also glorified." (Rom 8:30)

Reflection: The verb *to predestine* means to decide in advance what is going to happen. According to Paul in his Letter to the Romans, God foreordained from the beginning events that have occurred. It is important to note here that Paul is not writing about the doctrine known as predestination in which God decided at the beginning of time who would go to heaven and who would not after death. Paul's understanding of God's foreknowledge is that it exists before time begins. Once creation has occurred, in all things God works for good (Rom 8:28). Those who love God and cooperate with him accomplish his purpose (Rom 8:28) because they are connected to him through the Spirit (Rom 8:26–27). Because God knows everything from the beginning, Paul presents God's plan as Paul sees it in the middle of the first century CE. According to Paul, God has predestined those he foreknew to be conformed to the image of his Son, so that the Son could be the firstborn of a large family comprised of all who believe that God raised Jesus from the dead. Total predestination removes human free will and turns people into puppets. God gives those

---

101. References: BYM, pars. 13–15, 40–41, 55; CCC, pars. 504–5; RM, pars. 9, 37, 47.

102. LM: 636. The Feast of the Nativity of the Blessed Virgin Mary, September 8, First Reading, Second Option; LM: 710. The Common of the Blessed Virgin Mary, Second Reading, Second Option; CMBVM: Lectionary: Appendix, First Reading, Option 10.

he predestined a choice. He calls them, and if they respond, he justifies them in a healthy relationship with him, and he glorifies those who willingly cooperate with him. People have the free will to accept or reject being a part of God's larger purpose.

When applying Paul's words to the Blessed Virgin Mary, it is easy to understand that by a singular grace God preserved her from the moment of her conception in the womb of her mother, Anne, from the original sin of Adam and Eve. He did not let their disobedience be commuted to her, because he planned for her to be the mother of his Son. This did not erase her free will; she remained free to reject his offer to conceive Jesus in her virgin womb and give birth to the only-begotten Son of God. In other words, she freely cooperated with God. She was called, and, once she responded, she was justified, declared to be in a healthy relationship with her Creator. Once she was justified, at the end of her life God glorified her by raising her sinless body from the dead, just like he raised the sinless body of her Son from the dead.[103]

Journal/Meditation: For what has God predestined you? For what part in God's larger purpose did he foreknow you?

Prayer: In all things you work for good, LORD God, according to your foreknown purpose. Guide me with the Holy Spirit so that I may readily answer your call, be justified, and be glorified as I am conformed to the image of your Son, Jesus Christ, who is Lord forever and ever. Amen.

Love[104]

Text: Romans 8:31b–39

Scripture: ". . . I am convinced that neither death, nor life, nor angels, nor rulers, nor things present, nor things to come, nor powers, nor height, nor depth, nor anything else in all creation, will be able to separate us from the love of God in Christ Jesus our Lord." (Rom 8:38–39)

Reflection: In his Letter to the Romans, Paul uses the Greek word *agape*—meaning self-sacrificial love—to indicate what God did in Christ for people. It is important to remember that the doctrine about Jesus

---

103. References: BYM, pars. 19, 53, 55; CCC, pars. 488, 490, 511; MC, par. 56; RM, pars. 7, 9.

104. CMBVM: Lectionary: 11. The Blessed Virgin Mary at the Foot of the Cross I, First Reading, Option A.

Christ being one-hundred percent divine and one-hundred percent human had not yet been formulated when Paul wrote to the Romans. Paul presumes that Jesus is a man called and anointed by God, just like the kings of Israel and Judah were called, anointed (*messiahed, christed*), and named sons of God. Jesus' call by God is confirmed by God raising him from the dead. Thus, looking backward from Christ's resurrection, Paul reflects on the self-sacrificial love of God demonstrated by his giving up Jesus to death on a cross (Rom 8:32). Those who believe that God raised Jesus from the dead, the elect, have been justified by God through their faith, and so they have nothing to fear (Rom 8:33). Likewise, they have no fear of condemnation because Christ (meaning *anointed*) Jesus, who sits at God's right hand, intercedes for them (Rom 8:34). Therefore, there is nothing—there is no threat from heaven or on earth—that can separate believers from the self-sacrificial love of God in Christ Jesus; they have conquered everything through God, who has displayed self-sacrificial love in Christ Jesus (Rom 8:35–37). This agapic love is so strong, according to Paul, that absolutely nothing can separate people from the love of God in Christ Jesus (Rom 8:38–39).

When applied to the Blessed Virgin Mary, uniquely depicted standing by Jesus' cross before he dies in John's Gospel (19:25) along with the beloved disciple (John 19:26), she is shown as sharing in the sacrifice of God's own Son, the one he gave up for all. Not only does Jesus' death display God's self-sacrificial love, but the presence of the disciple whom Jesus loved at the cross confirms it. Before he dies, the Son of God entrusts his mother to the care of the beloved disciple and the latter to the love of the former. They form the communion of love that is so strong that nothing, even Jesus' death, can separate them from the love of God in Christ Jesus, whom God raised from the dead.[105]

Journal/Meditation: In what ways has God revealed his self-sacrificial love to you?

Prayer: Almighty God, you did not withhold your own Son from death but gave him up as a demonstration of your self-sacrificial love for people which also led you to raise him to new life. Grant that nothing separates me from your love in Christ Jesus, who sits at your right hand and intercedes for me now and forever. Amen.

---

105. References: BYM, pars. 37, 115; CCC, par. 2618; MC, pars. 7, 11, 20; RM, pars. 23–24, 43–45; RVM, pars. 7, 10.

Hospitality[106]

Text: Romans 12:9–16a

Scripture: "Let love be genuine; hate what is evil, hold fast to what is good; love one another with mutual affection; outdo one another in showing honor. . . . [E]xtend hospitality to strangers." (Rom 12:9–10, 13b)

Reflection: In his Letter to the Romans, Paul provides a list of moral advice which attempts to sketch a profile of sincere behavior tempered by genuine concern for others (Rom 12:9–21). He begins presenting his outline with words about genuine, self-sacrificial love; he tells the Romans that it should be genuine. Likewise, he tells them that they should love one another self-sacrificially, expressing to each other their shared feelings and attempting to outdo one another in honoring each other. Also on the list is the apostle's advice that the Romans extend hospitality to strangers.

Paul believes that genuine love springs from deep inside a person, demonstrated best by God's love shown in Jesus' death and resurrection. Mutual love cannot be forced; it flows out of sincere concern for others and their needs. Of course, this is nothing other than hospitality, welcoming others into one's inner circle, in which are found security and honor. When one person visits another and feels the love and honor being given to him or her—like Mary experienced Elizabeth's welcome, love, honor, and hospitality—God is there. Indeed, anytime people create an environment of freedom in which everyone experiences genuine, self-sacrificial, mutual love, honor, and hospitality, God is there.

Journal/Meditation: When did you last experience genuine love, honor, and hospitality and discover the presence of God?

Prayer: God of hospitality, you offered genuine love to all people in the person of your Son, Jesus Christ. Help me to love others sincerely as he did and bestow honor upon them through hospitality. Hear this prayer through the same Jesus Christ my Lord. Amen.

---

106. LM: 572. Feast of the Visitation of the Blessed Virgin Mary, May 31, First Reading, Second Option; CMBVM: Lectionary: Appendix, First Reading, Option 11.

1 CORINTHIANS

All[107]

Text: 1 Corinthians 15:20-26

Scripture: ". . . [A]ll will be made alive in Christ. But each in his own order: Christ the first fruits, then at his coming those who belong to Christ." (1 Cor 15:22-23)

Reflection: A person cannot invoke Mary as queen of all creation—or as queen of all the earth, of heaven, and of the universe, as does the LBVMOCIBVM—unless one understands the evolutionary character of theology, and in particular Mariology. Beginning with Paul's list of the order in which all will be alive, namely, Christ, then those who belong to him, the reader moves to the next stage of theological development, namely, the doctrine that Jesus Christ is one-hundred percent divine and one-hundred percent human. Once this is established, then it must be true that Jesus' mother must be sinless, that is, preserved from original sin by a singular act of God, in order to give birth to the Son of God. And if she is without sin, then she, like him, had to be raised from the dead by God and welcomed into heaven.

Once Christ is elevated to the status of king and Mary is declared to be the mother of Christ the king, mother of the Lord, and holy mother of God in the LBVMOCIBVM, she is elevated to the status of queen of all creation, including angels, patriarchs, prophets, apostles, martyrs, confessors, virgins, and all saints in the LBVMOCIBVM. In other words, Mary is queen of all creation because Christ is king, and she is his mother and belongs to him. The metaphor breaks down when one understands the queen is usually the wife of the king, whereas in Mariology, the mother of the king is declared to be the queen mother. In the LBVM(LL) Mary is also invoked as the holy mother of God and Christ and queen of angels, patriarchs, prophets, apostles, martyrs, confessors, virgins, and all saints. She is the first to be made alive in Christ after Christ, the first fruits of the resurrection.[108]

Journal/Meditation: What are the implications of invoking Mary as the Mother of God? as Queen of all Creation?

107. CMBVM: Lectionary: 29. The Blessed Virgin Mary, Queen of All Creation, First Reading, Option C; CMBVM: Lectionary: Appendix, First reading, Option 12 (Optional First Reading in Mass 29).

108. References: BYM, pars. 57-60, 104, 110-1; CCC, pars. 966, 969, 972, 974; DPPL, pars. 180-1; MC, pars. 6, 45; RM, pars. 40-41, 50; RVM, par 23.

Prayer: Father, by raising your Son from death, you made him the first fruits of the resurrection. By preserving his mother from original sin, you made her follow him into heaven. Grant that through the intercession of the queen mother that I may be counted among those who belong to Christ when he comes in glory. Amen.

Harvest[109]

Text: 1 Corinthians 15:20–27

Scripture: ". . . Christ has been raised from the dead, the first fruits of those who have died. For since death came through a human being, the resurrection of the dead has also come through a human being; for as all die in Adam, so all will be made alive in Christ." (1 Cor 15:20–22)

Reflection: In his First Letter to the Corinthians, Paul refers to Christ's resurrection as the first fruits, the initial results of the harvest, of the dead. In other words, Jesus' resurrection is a prelude to the raising of the dead at the end of time. The full harvest of all those who have died and will die is yet to come. Using one of his favorite parallels, the apostle reminds the Corinthians that death came through Adam, a human being, and so the resurrection of the dead comes through Christ, a human being. Death remains as the last enemy to be destroyed by Christ when he comes and God subjects everything to Christ, and he hands all things over to God so that "God may be all in all" (1 Cor 15:28).

Mary, the mother of Jesus, has already followed Christ. Because of her special place in the plan of salvation, she was preserved from sin. God chose to raise her from the dead, so that she already has been harvested and shares in eternal life. For Mary, just as for Jesus, God has destroyed death. Along with her Son, Mary represents hope for all to be harvested at the end of time. As Paul makes clear, the whole human race is subject to death because of Adam, but through Christ, the whole human race can share in resurrection. Christ's resurrection and Mary's assumption—making her the second to be raised from the dead—are presented as validations of God's promise for the complete harvest that is yet to come.[110]

---

109. LM: 622. Solemnity of the Assumption of the Blessed Virgin Mary, August 15, At the Mass during the Day, Second Reading.

110. References: BYM, pars. 57–60, 104, 110–1; CCC, pars. 966, 969, 972, 974; DPPL, pars. 180–1; MC, pars. 6, 45; RM, pars. 40–41, 50; RVM, par. 23.

Journal/Meditation: How do you experience resurrection now? How is Mary a sign of hope for you?

Prayer: Ever-living God, once death came through Adam, you brought the resurrection of the dead through Christ, your Son, and granted his mother, the Blessed Virgin Mary, the privilege of sharing in it. Mold me into the image of Jesus that, when he comes, I may be among those harvested to risen life forever and ever. Amen.

Imperishability[111]

Text: 1 Corinthians 15:54–57

Scripture: "When this perishable body puts on imperishability, and this mortal body puts on immortality, then the saying that is written will be fulfilled: 'Death has been swallowed up in victory.'" (1 Cor 15:54)

Reflection: In his First Letter to the Corinthians, Paul quotes the prophet Isaiah's words about what will take place in Jerusalem on Mount Zion, namely, the LORD of hosts "will swallow up death forever" (Isa 25:8a). Because Paul thinks that he will still be alive when Christ returns in glory, he tells the Corinthians that even though he and they will be alive and escape death, they will be changed, just as the dead will be raised and changed (1 Cor 15:51–52). The transformation is required so that the perishable body puts on imperishability, that is, death is swallowed up in the victory of Christ's resurrection over death! Through the resurrection of Jesus, God has turned what was perishable into what is imperishable, and he has made it possible for every human being to be transformed into what is imperishable. Death has been defeated, swallowed up in victory, by God.

The transformation from the perishable to the imperishable for the Blessed Virgin Mary is referred to as her assumption. Since she was the mother of Jesus, God's only-begotten Son, and since she was preserved from the stain of sin, she, like Jesus, was raised by God to eternal life. She was the first, after Christ, to experience resurrection, to be transformed from the perishable body to an imperishable one. In other words, her mortal body was given immortality. She was spared the decay of the tomb because from her own body, graced by her Creator, she gave birth to the

---

111. LM: 621. Solemnity of the Assumption of the Blessed Virgin Mary, August 15, At the Vigil Mass, Second Reading; CMBVM: Lectionary: Appendix, First Reading, Option 13.

author of all life. Her transformation from the perishable to the imperishable represents the hope that death will be swallowed in the victory of resurrection for all who follow Christ.[112]

Journal/Meditation: How do you experience perishability and mortality? How do those experiences lead you to hope for imperishability and immortality?

Prayer: Imperishable and immortal God, by raising Jesus from the dead you swallowed death in victory and granted his mother, Mary, a share in that same victory. When I am overcome with the perishable and mortal things of life, give me the hope of sharing new life with you, your Son, and the Holy Spirit forever and ever. Amen.

2 CORINTHIANS

Mercies[113]

Text: 2 Corinthians 1:3–7

Scripture: "Blessed be the God and Father of our Lord Jesus Christ, the Father of mercies and the God of all consolation, who consoles us in all our affliction, so that we may be able to console those who are in any affliction with the consolation with which we ourselves are consoled by God." (2 Cor 1:3–4)

Reflection: Mercy is the compassionate kindness or forgiveness shown to an offender or to somebody a person has power over. Simply put, someone in power offers kindness or forgiveness to someone over whom he or she has power, like an employer over an employee. In his Second Letter to the Corinthians, Paul begins a prayer of blessing by identifying God as the Father of mercies, that is, as the God who does not deal with people as they deserve to be treated: sinners deserving punishment. To the contrary, according to Paul, God consoles people in any distress so that they are able to console others in any adversity with the same consolation they have received from God. Once mercy is received, a person has an obligation to share it with others in the same way that God bestows mercy on him or her. Furthermore, God is not the God of mercy

---

112. References: BYM, pars. 57–60, 104, 110–1; CCC, pars. 966, 969, 972, 974; DPPL, pars. 180–1; MC, pars. 6, 45; RM, pars. 40–41, 50; RVM, par. 23.

113. CMBVM: Lectionary: 41. The Blessed Virgin Mary, Mother of Consolation, First Reading, Option B.

for Paul, but the God of mercies; often and frequently he has consoled and continues to console people in distress.

Paul also identifies God as the Father of Jesus Christ. Because he was preaching the gospel of Christ, Paul writes that he was sharing in the abundant sufferings of Christ, who repeatedly showed him mercy (2 Cor 1:5). Furthermore, the apostle notes that any distress and any consolation serves as an example for the Corinthians of how they should patiently participate in suffering and consolation while remaining unshaken in faith. The Blessed Virgin Mary is invoked as the queen of mercy in the LBVMOCIBVM and as comforter of the afflicted in the LBVM(LL), because through her, God sent his Son to be the incarnate mercy and comforter for all people. Through her intercession, Mary, who received God's mercy when he raised Jesus from the dead, continues to share that consolation with others in any adversity. In other words, the mercy she has received is passed on to others in the same way that God bestowed it on her.[114]

Journal/Meditation: In what specific ways have you experienced the mercies of God?

Prayer: Blessed are you, God and Father of Jesus Christ, the Father of mercies, and the God of all consolation. As you consoled the Blessed Virgin Mary with the resurrection of her Son, console me in all my afflictions and grant that I may console others with the same mercies you have given to me. I pray in the name of Christ Jesus my Lord. Amen.

Reconciliation[115]

Text: 2 Corinthians 5:17–21

Scripture: ". . . [W]e are ambassadors for Christ, since God is making his appeal through us; we entreat you on behalf of Christ, be reconciled to God." (2 Cor 5:20)

Reflection: Reconciliation is the result of ending a conflict and/or renewing a friendly relationship between two disputing parties. In his Second Letter to the Corinthians, Paul begins with the new order brought by Christ, through whom God started over with a new creation (2 Cor

---

114. References: CCC, par. 969; MC, pars. 5, 11, 57; RM, pars. 41, 43–44; RVM, par. 25.

115. CMBVM: Lectionary: 14. The Blessed Virgin Mary, Mother of Reconciliation, First Reading.

5:17). The apostle declares that not only did God do this through Christ, but the ensuing reconciliation between God and people has resulted in Paul's ministry of reconciliation (2 Cor 5:18). Whatever conflict existed between God and people before Christ has now ended. This message, according to Paul, has been entrusted to him for the Gentiles; he is an ambassador, an official envoy or representative, for Christ, through whom God is making his appeal that people accept the free gift of righteousness through faith that he is offering them. Paul begs his readers on behalf of Christ to be reconciled to God (2 Cor 5:20). Then, he reminds them that Jesus became human so that people made new by his death and resurrection might be declared in a healthy relationship with God again.

Jesus became human through the womb of his mother, the Blessed Virgin Mary. She herself, by a singular act of God's grace, was reconciled to God before he reconciled the world to himself. She became a new creation before God made everything new in Christ. Whatever conflict existed between God and people was ended by God when he established a friendly relationship with her. The sign of her righteousness was her willing cooperation with God in conceiving and giving birth to his Son. Since it was through his Son that God reconciled the world to himself, Mary is hailed as the mother of reconciliation. Thus, before Paul declared himself an ambassador of God's message of reconciliation, the Blessed Virgin Mary was the living embodiment of reconciliation.[116]

Journal/Meditation: In what reconciliation, that is, in what end of a conflict between you and God, have you participated?

Prayer: God of reconciliation, through Christ Jesus, you brought to an end all conflict between you and people and established a new creation in your Son. Like the Blessed Virgin Mary and Paul, make me an ambassador for Christ so that your appeal will be heard in the world. Grant this through the same Jesus Christ my Lord. Amen.

GALATIANS

Adoption[117]

Text: Galatians 4:4–7

---

116. References: BYM, pars. 10, 18, 21, 56, 102, 110–1; DPPL, pars. 101–2, 174; MC, pars. 3, 11, 56; RM, pars. 3, 10, 41.

117. LM: 18. Solemnity of Mary, the Holy Mother of God, January 1, Second Reading; LM: 636B. Optional Memorial of the Most Holy Name of Mary, September 12,

Scripture: "... [W]hen the fullness of time had come, God sent his Son, born of a woman, born under the law, in order to redeem those who were under the law, so that we might receive adoption as children." (Gal 4:4–5)

Reflection: Paul, a Pharisee well-trained in the six hundred thirteen precepts of Torah, emphasizes Jesus' humanity and Jewish origin. Jesus was born of a woman which indicates that he was a human being, that is, he became flesh in the womb of his mother, Mary. He was born under the law which indicates that he was Jewish. He was subject to the terms of the covenant God made with Abraham and ratified by Moses on Mount Sinai (Horeb). His mission, as interpreted by Paul, was to deliver the Jews from the six hundred thirteen precepts of Torah, which in the apostle's thought failed in their attempt to restore unity between God and people. According to Paul, while the Torah came from God, it ultimately failed to restore people's relationship with God; that is quite a statement for a Pharisee to make!

Jesus, when the fullness of time had come, redeemed, that is, restored, the relationship between God and people that the first man and woman had destroyed. He made all people adopted children of God. They are no longer slaves of Torah, but children and heirs of what God accomplished through Christ Jesus. Thus, the time of Torah has passed. In the fullness of time, God chose Mary to be the mother of Jesus, God's Son and God. Thus, both the LBVM(LL) and the LBVMOCIBVM invoke her as holy Mary and holy mother of God. She was adopted by God to give to the world Jesus Christ, who did for it what the Torah was unable to do.[118]

Journal/Meditation: What are the benefits of your adoptive relationship with God?

Prayer: When the fullness of time had come, Abba, Father, you sent your Son, born of the Blessed Virgin Mary, born under the law, in order to redeem those who were under the law, so that all might receive adoption as your children. Send your Spirit into my heart to prompt my praise for making me an heir of eternal life through Christ Jesus. Amen.

First Reading; LM: 710. The Common of the Blessed Virgin Mary, Second Reading, Third Option; LM: 1002. The Blessed Virgin Mary, II. The Most Holy Name of Mary, First Reading, First Option; CMBVM: Lectionary: 4. Holy Mary, Mother of God, First Reading; CMBVM: Lectionary: 8. Our Lady of Nazareth I, First Reading.

118. References: BYM, par. 12; CCC, pars. 488, 490, 492, 495, 509, 511, 963, 971, 975, 2519; DPPL, par. 249; RM, pars. 1, 38, 44, 47.

EPHESIANS

Chosen[119]

Text: Ephesians 1:3–6, 11–12 or 1:3–6, 15–18

Scripture: "... [God] chose us in Christ before the foundation of the world to be holy and blameless before him in love." (Eph 1:4)

Reflection: The second-generation Pauline author of the Letter to the Ephesians writes about God choosing people in Christ before the foundation of the world. The author tells his readers that they were picked by God, preferred before all others. He is contrasting the chosen status of his Gentile readers to that claimed by the Jews, who according to the HB (OT) were selected by God to play a unique role in world history. Now, God has picked both Jews and Gentiles to be blameless before him in self-sacrificial love (Eph 1:4). This was their destiny: to be God's adopted children through Christ Jesus and receive the inheritance of eternal life (Eph 1:5, 11). Seeing God's will so accomplished in Christ praises God's glorious grace that he freely bestowed on people in his beloved Son (Eph 1:6, 12).

Mary, the mother of Jesus, is counted among those chosen by God. From the moment that she was conceived in her mother's womb, God picked her for his own special purpose from the creation of the world. He preserved her from sin so that she might conceive the Christ in her womb. Mary's immaculate conception is a one-time only event before the foundation of the world, but God's choosing of all people—Jews and Gentiles—continues today. God wills that all people live in self-sacrificial love in response to the rich grace that God has lavished on people through the death and resurrection of Christ (Eph 1:7). Mary shares in God's purpose, and her Son, Jesus, shares in engendering the adoption of all people as children of God. With Mary all God's adopted children praise him for the righteousness he has given freely in Christ Jesus.[120]

---

119. LM: 19. Second Sunday after Christmas, Second Reading; LM: 689. Solemnity of the Immaculate Conception of the Blessed Virgin Mary, December 8, Second Reading; LM: 710. The Common of the Blessed Virgin Mary, Fourth Option; LM: 1002. The Blessed Virgin Mary, II. The Most Holy Name of Mary, First Reading, Second Option; CMBVM: Lectionary: 20. Holy Mary, the New Eve, First Reading, Option B; CMBVM: Lectionary: Appendix, First Reading, Option 14 (Optional First Reading in Mass 20).

120. References: BYM, pars. 10, 18, 21, 56, 102, 110–1; DPPL, pars. 101–2, 174; MC, pars. 3, 11, 56; RM, pars. 3, 10, 41.

Journal/Meditation: How have you been chosen to respond to God's grace?

Prayer: Blessed are you, God and Father of Jesus Christ. You have blessed me in Christ with every spiritual blessing and chosen me in Christ before the foundation of the world to be holy and blameless before you in love. Hear my prayer of praise for adopting me as your child and for the grace you continue to bestow upon me through Jesus Christ, your Son. Amen.

Gift[121]

Text: Ephesians 2:4–10

Scripture: ". . . God, who is rich in mercy, out of the great love with which he loved us even when we were dead through our trespasses, made us alive together with Christ—by grace you have been saved—and raised us up with him in the heavenly places in Christ Jesus." (Eph 2:4–6)

Reflection: God, according to the second-generation Pauline author of the Letter to the Ephesians, has always offered grace to people. The gift of the divine self to his creation represents God making the first move to establish a relationship with people. God offers the undeserved, merciful gift of grace to people because they are not able to respond without it. Then, God waits for a response to this offer of self-sacrificial love. Even though people may look like they are dead because of their sins, God brings them to life with Christ when they accept his merciful gift. This is not a work that people can do in order to earn salvation or boast (Eph 2:9); it is a free gift to which people respond with good works in Christ Jesus.

Christ Jesus was born of Mary, upon whom God bestowed the immeasurable riches of his grace by preserving her from any trespasses from the moment of her conception. In her immaculate womb, God's mercy became flesh, and Mary became the queen mother of mercy, according to the LBVMIOCIBVM. Mary experienced God's merciful gift in a special way. The remarks of the author of the Letter to the Ephesians are appropriately applied to the Blessed Virgin Mary, ". . . [B]y grace you have been saved through faith, and this is not your own doing; it is the

---

121. CMBVM: Lectionary: 39. Holy Mary, Queen and Mother of Mercy II, First Reading.

gift of God" (Eph 2:8). In other words, God created Mary and prepared her beforehand with his unmerited gift of grace.[122]

Journal/Meditation: What gifts of grace has God given you?

Prayer: God, you are rich in mercy and love and make people alive in your Son. Fill me with your gifts of grace and faith that I may do the good works that you have created me to do in Christ Jesus forever and ever. Amen.

Epiphany[123]

Text: Ephesians 3:2–3a, 5–6

Scripture: ". . . [T]he Gentiles have become fellow heirs, members of the same body, and sharers in the promise in Christ Jesus through the gospel." (Eph 3:6)

Reflection: An epiphany can be a manifestation of a divine being or a sudden intuitive leap of understanding especially through an ordinary occurrence. On the Solemnity of the Epiphany of the Lord both understandings of the word are employed. The former refers to Jesus' manifestation to the magi Gentiles in Matthew's Gospel (Matt 2:1–12). The latter refers to what the second-generation Pauline author of the Letter to the Ephesians refers to as a revelation (Eph 3:3), which had not become known to former generations as it now has to apostles and prophets by the Spirit (Eph 3:5). The earth-shaking insight is that the Gentiles are now co-heirs, members of the same body, and sharers in the promise in Christ Jesus through the preaching of the gospel (Eph 3:6). Indeed, for Jewish readers, who considered themselves the only chosen people of God, this would be considered quite an epiphany!

The vehicle for this epiphany is the Jewish, Blessed Virgin Mary, the mother of Jewish Jesus. From a Jewish perspective, the people of the world were divided into two groups: Jews and Gentiles. The Jews were God's chosen people. Everyone else was Gentile. The author of Ephesians is following the insight of his mentor, Paul, who in his Letter to the Romans spends several chapters working to a similar understanding (Rom 9:1–11:36). According to the author of Ephesians, in Christ Jesus the

---

122. References: CCC, pars. 411, 493, 508, 766, 967; MC, pars. 14, 22, 57; RM, pars. 7–10, 24, 39.

123. LM: 20. Solemnity of the Epiphany of the Lord, January 6 (in the United States, the Sunday after January 1), Second Reading.

Gentiles, who were once far off, have been brought near by the blood of Christ (Eph 2:13). In his flesh, born of the Virgin Mary, Jesus made both groups of Jews and Gentiles into one and broke down the wall dividing them from each other so that he could create a new, single humanity in himself in place of the previous two (Eph 2:14). Thus, this is the sudden understanding of the author of the Letter to the Ephesians: Jews and Gentiles belong together.[124]

Journal/Meditation: What moments of insight have been epiphanies to you recently?

Prayer: Father, you made known your mystery by revelation to people that you had chosen all people—Jews and Gentiles—to be heirs, members of the same body, and sharers in the promise in Christ Jesus, your Son, through the gospel. With the guidance of your Spirit fill me with insights concerning him born of the Blessed Virgin Mary for the salvation of the world forever. Amen.

COLOSSIANS

Completing[125]

Text: Colossians 1:21–24

Scripture: "I am now rejoicing in my sufferings for your sake, and in my flesh I am completing what is lacking in Christ's afflictions for the sake of his body, that is, the church." (Col 1:24)

Reflection: The Letter to the Colossians is a second-generation Pauline composition; the author knew Paul's basic theology, but needed to update it for the next generation of believers. After repeating a typical Pauline understanding about God having reconciled everyone to himself through the blood of Jesus' cross (Col 1:23), the Colossians are exhorted to continue steadfast in faith in order to maintain their holiness, blamelessness, and irreproachability (Col 1:22–23). Furthermore, they are told not to shift in the hope that the gospel promises (Col 1:23). The author reminds the readers that this gospel was the one Paul served (Col 1:23). A new element is now added to Pauline thought; there is a certain amount of suffering that is necessary before the expected end can arrive (Col

---

124. References: DPPL, pars. 106, 118; MC, par. 5.

125. CMBVM: Lectionary: 11. The Blessed Virgin Mary at the Foot of the Cross I, First Reading, Option B; CMBVM: Lectionary: Appendix, First Reading, Option 15 (Optional First Reading in Mass 11).

1:24). That is why the author states that he is completing what is lacking in Christ's afflictions for the sake of his body, that is, the church (Col 1:24). Thus, any suffering brings the end sooner.

The author of the Letter to the Colossians adds a new element to Paul's body-of-Christ theology. He equates the body of Christ with the church (Col 1:18, 24); this is not in keeping with Pauline thought which states that everyone who believes that Jesus died and God raised him from the dead is a member of his body (Rom 12:3–8; 1 Cor 12:12–31). Colossians limits the body of the Christ to the church which is evidence that it is post-Pauline in origin near the end of the first century. Nevertheless, all who belong to the body, the church, participate in its suffering, and that suffering brings the end closer. Since the Blessed Virgin Mary is the first member of the body of Christ, the church, she, too, rejoices in her sufferings, completing what is lacking in the body of Christ's afflictions.[126]

Journal/Meditation: Which of your sufferings have completed further what is lacking in Christ's afflictions for the sake of his body, the church?

Prayer: Almighty God, all things hold together in your beloved Son, Jesus Christ, head of the body, the church. Accept my sufferings as an offering to completing what is lacking in the body, and, through your Spirit, help me to recognize you even in my afflictions. Grant that I may rejoice in you now and forever. Amen.

Clothes II[127]

Text: Longer Form: Colossians 3:12–21; Shorter Form: Colossians 3:12–17 or 3:14–15, 17, 23–24

Scripture: "As God's chosen ones, holy and beloved, clothe yourselves with compassion, kindness, humility, meekness, and patience. Above all, clothe yourselves with love, which binds everything together in perfect harmony." (Col 3:12, 14)

---

126. References: BYM, pars. 5, 20, 38, 70, 113–4, 117, 130; CCC, par. 964; MC, pars. 11, 16, 19, 21, 28, 35; RM, pars. 5, 6, 27–30, 42, 44; RVM, par. 15.

127. LM: 17. Feast of the Holy Family of Jesus, Mary, and Joseph, Sunday within the Octave of the Nativity of the Lord [Christmas], or, if there is no Sunday, December 30, Second Reading, Cycle A; LM: 559. Optional Memorial of St. Joseph the Worker, May 1, First Reading, Second Option; CMBVM: Lectionary: 8. Our Lady of Nazareth II, First Reading, Shorter Form.

Reflection: Besides the clothes in which one dresses, there are clothes of virtues, according to the author of the Letter to the Colossians. These virtue-clothes are invisible, yet they visibly manifest who one is deep down inside. Compassion, the ability to feel another's pain and sympathize with him or her, is one of those invisible items of clothing. Another virtue is kindness, assistance offered another that is unrequested and unsolicited. Humility, a third invisible item of clothing, is not self-degradation, but a healthy understanding of who one is in terms of strengths and weaknesses. Meekness-clothing recognizes the equality of human dignity of every person. And patience, the ability to wait, completes one's wardrobe of virtues. However, the best piece of clothing is love; self-sacrificial love between people binds them together in perfect harmony, like that of a symphony orchestra.

Mary of Nazareth dressed herself in compassion, kindness, humility, meekness, patience, and love. She not only wore these invisible virtues, but she also made them visible in her life with Jesus and Joseph in Nazareth. Self-sacrificial love both covered and activated all the virtues. She had already manifested sacrificial love when agreeing to conceive and give birth to Jesus, God's only-begotten Son. She continued to reveal them by nurturing her Son and showing him to put them on and wear them. Through his life and teaching, he demonstrated that he was wearing compassion, kindness, humility, meekness, and patience. And he not only taught about sacrificial love, he manifested its power to bind everything together in perfect harmony through his death on the cross and his resurrection from the dead.[128]

Journal/Meditation: Besides physical clothes, what other types of virtue-clothes do you wear and manifest every day?

Prayer: Heavenly Father, you have made me one of your chosen ones, holy and beloved. Clothe me in compassion, kindness, humility, meekness, patience, and love. Let the peace of Christ rule my heart and the word of Christ dwell in me richly now and forever. Amen.

---

128. References: CCC, pars. 273, 506, 967; RM, pars. 43–44.

1 TIMOTHY

Mediator[129]

Text: 1 Timothy 2:5–8

Scripture: ". . . [T]here is one God; there is also one mediator between God and humankind, Christ Jesus, himself human, who gave himself a ransom for all—this was attested at the right time." (1 Tim 2:5–6)

Reflection: In the early Christian creed preserved in the First Letter to Timothy, people profess that there is one God. This belief is nothing new; it comes directly from daily Jewish prayer: "Hear, O Israel: The LORD is our God, the LORD alone" (Deut 6:4). However, the next part of the declaration of faith is new. Jesus is identified as the one mediator between God and people. Jesus, Son of God and Son of Mary, fulfilled the role of go-between, the one who occupied the intermediate place between God and people. He bore divinity to bring God to people, and he bore humanity in order to bring people to God. This was accomplished by his death on the cross, an instrument which itself reached upwards toward God and downwards to people. On the cross Jesus gave himself as a ransom, a payment, for all.

The Blessed Virgin Mary is presented as the mother of unity because in her womb the divinity and humanity of Jesus became one. She stands as an image of what the union of God and people can be. Jesus not only spoke about unity; he enacted it by calling people to follow him. By stretching out his arms on the cross, he reached out to gather all God's scattered children into one so that never again would God and people be separated. Then, he sealed this unity with the gift of the Holy Spirit, who engenders unity from the diversity of God's children. This ever-present challenge of unity is attested every time the Profession of Faith or the Apostles' Creed is said. One of its earliest forms is found in the First Letter to Timothy.[130]

Journal/Meditation: How do you foster unity? Is unity one of the elements in your personal creed?

Prayer: One God, you sent one mediator between you and people, Jesus Christ, himself divine and human, to ransom all your people. In

---

129. CMBVM: Lectionary: 38. Holy Mary, Mother of Unity, First Reading, Option B.

130. References: BYM, par. 6; CCC, par. 970; MC, pars. 6, 32; RM, pars. 1, 22, 38–39; RVM, par. 16.

the womb of his mother, the Blessed Virgin Mary, divinity and humanity became one. Send the Holy Spirit to bring all people together in Christ now and forever. Amen.

TITUS

Grace[131]

Text: Titus 2:11–14

Scripture: "... [T]he grace of God has appeared, bringing salvation to all." (Titus 2:11)

Reflection: Grace is God's invisible life that the Holy One shares with people, and they, in turn, share it with each other. Grace is what God offers to people in order to begin a relationship, because people are unable to respond to God unless the Mighty One gives them the ability to do so. Grace is the LORD's generosity offered to people as a free gift; it is a favor that God gives. Grace is participation in divine life—it is supernatural—and, as such, it is sanctifying—making people holy; it is deifying—making people divine; it is habitual—it fosters a permanent relationship of cooperation with God; it is actual—activating the ongoing growth of a person in the Holy Spirit. And according to the Letter to Titus, grace appeared, took flesh, in the person of Jesus, whose manifestation in glory is still awaited (Titus 2:13).

The LBVM(LL) invokes the Blessed Virgin Mary as the mother of divine grace, and the LBVMOCIBVM invokes her as full of grace and advocate of grace. As a treasure house of grace, Mary conceives Jesus in her womb and gives birth to him, and grace appears in the world. God's invisible life is made visible in Jesus of Nazareth. God offered himself as grace to Mary, and she, who was full of grace, accepted his relationship, cooperating with his generous offer and participating in divine life. God's sanctifying grace made holy the Virgin of Nazareth and activated her ongoing growth with the Holy Spirit until she was deified—raised from the dead and assumed into heaven, where she, too, awaits her Son's manifestation in glory while serving as an advocate of grace for all.[132]

---

131. LM: 14. Solemnity of the Nativity of the Lord [Christmas], December 25, At the Mass during the Night, Second Reading.

132. References: CCC, pars. 490, 493, 968, 969, 2617; MC, pars. 14, 22, 57; RM, pars. 7–10, 24, 39.

Journal/Meditation: In what specific ways have you experienced God's grace?

Prayer: Great God and Savior, your grace appeared bringing salvation to all in the birth of your Son, Jesus, born of the Blessed Virgin Mary. Grant that I may live my life with self-control, being upright and godly, while I wait for the blessed hope and the manifestation of the glory of Jesus Christ, who is Lord forever and ever. Amen.

Rebirth[133]

Text: Titus 3:4–7

Scripture: "[God our Savior appeared and] saved us … through the water of rebirth and renewal by the Holy Spirit." (Titus 3:6)

Reflection: The Letter to Titus reflects the author's knowledge of Pauline thought near the end of the first century CE. This is easily seen in his statement about God saving people "not because of any works of righteousness that [they] had done, but according to his mercy" (Titus 3:5). However, the author non-Pauline-like presumes that Jesus is God, stating that salvation is the result of the goodness and loving kindness of God the Savior's appearance (Titus 3:4)—which is why this passage is read on Christmas at dawn. While Paul understands that Jesus is the Son of God, just like the kings of Judah and Israel were anointed sons of God on the day of their coronation, Paul does not presume that Jesus is God; Christ's resurrection declares him to be Son of God (Rom 1:4). The theological development of Jesus as God does not occur until the end of the first century CE and is not worked out until the fourth century CE.

Furthermore, the emphasis in Titus is on baptism, that is, "the water of rebirth and renewal by the Holy Spirit" (Titus 3:5). Paul's emphasis is on baptism into the death of Christ and being buried with him by baptism into death (Rom 6:3–4) in order to be raised to new life with him now. The apostle never uses the word rebirth or renewal; this further emphasizes the non-Pauline authorship of the Letter to Titus. Titus's focus is on the rebirth and renewal by the Spirit that occurs on the other side of death and creates people anew. This is why Titus declares that the Spirit has been poured out richly in Jesus Christ, the Savior, so that people

---

133. LM: 15. Solemnity of the Nativity of the Lord [Christmas], December 25, At the Mass at Dawn, Second Reading.

become heirs according to their hope of eternal life (Titus 3:6–7). Thus, the celebration of the appearance (birth) of Jesus, who was conceived by the power of the Holy Spirit, is simultaneously a celebration of rebirth and renewal in the hope of eternal life on the other side of death.

Journal/Meditation: What rebirth and renewal occur in you through your celebration of Christmas?

Prayer: God my Savior, your goodness and loving kindness appeared in the person of Jesus Christ because of your mercy. Continue to pour on me the Holy Spirit that rebirth and renewal will bring me to eternal life where you are one God—Father, Son, and Holy Spirit—forever and ever. Amen.

HEBREWS

Glory[134]

Text: Hebrews 1:1–6

Scripture: "Long ago God spoke to our ancestors in many and various ways by the prophets, but in these last days he has spoken to us by a Son, whom he appointed heir of all things, through whom he also created the worlds. He is the reflection of God's glory and the exact imprint of God's very being, and he sustains all things by his powerful word." (Heb 1:1–3a)

Reflection: The opening verses of the Letter to the Hebrews read on Christmas Day echo the prologue that begins John's Gospel (1:1–5). God has been speaking to people in the past; of particular note are the prophets, who listened to the LORD and shared and recorded his words for the benefit of Hebrews, Israelites, and Jews. In the "last days" of Hebrews—near the end of the first century CE—the author declares that God has spoken a Son, who is pre-existent with God, the vehicle for creation, the heir of all things, and the one who keeps everything in existence. Because Jesus himself is not created, he is eternal with God while enjoying a Father-Son relationship as noted in the quotation from the royal coronation Psalm 2:7: "[The LORD] said to me, 'You are my son; today I have begotten you.'" When the kings of Israel and Judah were anointed, they were declared to be sons of God. The author of Hebrews declares that Jesus is the Son of God from eternity.

[134]. LM: 16. Solemnity of the Nativity of the Lord [Christmas], December 25, At the Mass during the Day, Second Reading.

Furthermore, Hebrews declares that the Son is the reflection of God's glory (Heb 1:3). Glory refers to God's presence, manifested in the past in cloud, smoke, fire, lightning, thunder, etc. Now, according to Hebrews, Jesus, the Son, reflects God's glorious light and presence. The invisible LORD, who in the past manifested his presence in various natural phenomena, has now chosen to make his invisible divinity visible in a person: Jesus, "the exact imprint of God's very being" (Heb 1:3), that is, the visible image of God's essence. Although the LORD's invisible essence cannot be seen by people, it becomes available to the senses through the birth of Jesus, Mary's Son, spoken by God. Therefore, according to the author of Hebrews, readers must pay greater attention to what they have heard, so that they do not drift away from it (Heb 2:1).

Journal/Meditation: What has God said to you through Jesus, his Son?

Prayer: Long ago, O God, your spoke through the prophets. Now, you have spoken through a Son, the reflection of your glory and the exact imprint of your very being. Open my ears to listen intently to your words, Father, that I may one day see the glory you share with Jesus Christ and the Holy Spirit, one God, forever and ever. Amen.

Flesh and Blood[135]

Text: Hebrews 2:14–18

Scripture: "Since . . . the children share flesh and blood, [Jesus] himself likewise shared the same things, so that through death he might destroy the one who has the power of death, that is, the devil . . . ." (Heb 2:14)

Reflection: On the Feast of the Presentation of the Lord—the only biblical text presenting this account, found in Luke's Gospel (2:22–40)—the passage from the Letter to the Hebrews recognizes that Jesus shared the flesh and blood of humankind; he received that flesh and blood from Mary, his mother. Hebrews makes clear that because Jesus was a man of flesh of blood, he died in order to destroy death. That is the basic gospel paradox; by dying Jesus freed those who all their lives were held as slaves in fear of death (Heb 2:15). His purpose was not to help angels, but the descendants of Abraham (Heb 2:16), that is, everyone. In other words, Jesus came in human form to experience human life, to know of what

---

135. LM: 524. Feast of the Presentation of the Lord, February 2, Second Reading.

mercy consists and how it is needed by people; to be a faithful high priest by offering himself as a sacrifice to God; and to atone for the sins of all people. Being of flesh and blood, Jesus was tested by human suffering so that he could understand it and show compassion to the descendants of Abraham. All this is why Hebrews declares that he had to become flesh and blood.

Standing behind Hebrews' basic gospel paradox are the words from the OT (A) book of Wisdom: ". . . God created us for incorruption, and made us in the image of his own eternity, but through the devil's envy death entered the world, and those who belong to his company experience it" (Wis 2:23–24). By his own life and death, Jesus restored people to the image of God's eternity, often referred to as eternal life. By being one with humankind in flesh and blood and all else, Jesus is the ideal mediator with God. He entered the temple not made with human hands—the womb of his mother—and he was presented in the Temple made with human hands in Jerusalem.

Journal/Meditation: How does being flesh and blood enable you to sympathize with others?

Prayer: Eternal God, through the flesh and blood of your Son, Jesus, you destroyed death and restored people to the image of your eternity. Through the intercession of the Blessed Virgin Mary, send your Spirit to fill me with eternal life now and forever and ever. Amen.

Obedience[136]

Text: Hebrews 5:7–9

Scripture: "Although [Jesus] was a Son, he learned obedience through what he suffered." (Heb 5:8)

Reflection: After presenting the Son's eternal existence with the Father (Heb 1:1–14), the unknown author of the Letter to the Hebrews focuses on his humanity. As a man, Jesus reverently submitted himself to his Father's will, learning obedience through what he suffered all the way to the cross (Heb 5:7). To be submissive to the command of another person is hard enough in a modern world of personal freedom, religious independence, and psychological individuality. Hebrews contends that it

---

136. LM: 639. Memorial of Our Lady of Sorrows, September 15, First Reading; CMBVM: Lectionary: 12. The Blessed Virgin Mary at the Foot of the Cross II, First Reading, Option C; CMBVM: Lectionary: Appendix, First Reading, Option 16 (Optional First Reading in Mass 12).

was through his human suffering that Jesus became perfect. Thus, while obedience carries negative connotations today, it deserves positive reflection. The attempt to provoke this positive contemplation is the reason the passage is chosen for the Memorial of Our Lady of Sorrows.

Mary, the mother of Jesus, another human being, knew suffering resulting from obedience to God that perfected her. Her unwed, pregnant status in her world brought her suffering. She knew the suffering of childbirth, the suffering of raising a child, and the suffering associated with watching her Son die on the cross. But like her Son, Mary learned obedience to God's word through suffering. To call her Our Lady of Sorrows is to bestow a title upon her which declares that she is able to sympathize with human suffering, the result of obedience to God. The type of suffering resulting in obedience is the bending of the human will to the divine will. Instead of attempting to find a way around it, Mary embraced suffering and its accompanying obedience in imitation of her Son, who, though divine, was made humanly perfect through his reverent submission to God.[137]

Journal/Meditation: In what specific ways have you learned obedience to God through your human suffering?

Prayer: Father, I offer prayers and supplications with loud cries and tears to you in the hope that you will save me from death because of my reverent submission to you. Guide me with the Holy Spirit that I may know your will and do it in the hope of sharing the perfection of your Son, Jesus Christ, now and forever. Amen.

Discern[138]

Text: Hebrews 10:4–10

Scripture: ". . . [I]t is by God's will that we have been sanctified through the offering of the body of Jesus Christ once for all." (Heb 10:10)

Reflection: The unknown author of the Letter to the Hebrews argues that it is impossible for the blood of goats and bulls to take away sins (Heb 10:4). While the author of the HB (OT) book of Leviticus would disagree (Lev 16:11–15), the CB (NT) Letter to the Hebrews is intent upon proving that Jesus establishes a new covenant in his blood once for

---

137. References: CCC, pars. 144, 494, 511, 967; DPPL, par. 101; MC, pars. 26, 57.

138. LM: 545. Solemnity of the Annunciation of the Lord, March 25, Second Reading.

all. In order to do this, the author of Hebrews puts some of the words of Psalm 40 on Jesus' lips to announce the new covenant. Psalm 40 is a song about trusting in the LORD's steadfast love and faithfulness. It is in that context that the author declares that sacrifice and offering, burnt offering and sin offering are not what God desires (Ps 40:6). God wants the whole self; that is why the psalmist states, "Then I said, 'Here I am; in the scroll of the book it is written of me I delight to do your will, O my God; your law is within my heart" (Ps 40:7–8). In other words, according to the psalmist, God wants the total person to do his will obediently. Jesus becomes the model of how to discern God's will, according to Hebrews.

The author of Hebrews argues that the LORD's desire for offerings made according to Torah (Lev 16:11–15) is abolished by Jesus coming to do God's will obediently (Heb 10:8–9). Hebrews considers the law to be a shadow of the good things that were to come and not the true form of reality (Heb 10:1). By so doing he is able to declare that Jesus was the good that came, that he is the true form of reality, and that he replaced Torah's requirement for sin offerings with his suffering obedience to God; he made a single sacrifice for sins (Heb 10:12). He gave himself totally to the LORD in discerned trust. It was God's will that the body of Jesus be offered on the altar of the cross once for all (Heb 10:10). Thus, through Jesus, Son of Mary, God announces a new covenant with Jesus as its mediator (Heb 9:15).

Journal/Meditation: What do you understand the announcement of the new covenant to mean? How do you discern God's will for your life?

Prayer: LORD God, I have discerned that sacrifices and offerings you do not desire, but you have prepared a body for me to do your will. Continue to sanctify me through the offering of the body of Jesus once for all. He lives and reigns with you and the Holy Spirit, one God, forever and ever Amen.

Assurance[139]

Text: Hebrews 11:8, 11–12, 17–19

---

139. LM: 17. Feast of the Holy Family of Jesus, Mary, and Joseph, Sunday within the Octave of the Nativity of the Lord [Christmas], or, if there is no Sunday, December 30, Second Reading, Cycle B.

Scripture: "By faith [Abraham] received power of procreation, even though he was too old—and Sarah herself was barren—because he considered him faithful who had promised." (Heb 11:12)

Reflection: Chapter 11 of the Letter to the Hebrews is a reflection on the faith of Abraham, Moses, and others with the given definition of faith: ". . . [F]aith is the assurance of things hope for, the conviction of things not seen" (Heb 11:1). Basically, faith means acceptance of God's assuring word about what one hopes; it is being convinced that God is faithful even though at the present moment the hope is not realized or seen. Abraham is presented as one who modeled this definition of faith, first of all setting out from his home and not knowing where he was going (Heb 11:8). He also illustrates faith when he believed that God would raise up descendants for him even though he and Sarah were past their childbearing ages. Once Isaac is born, Abraham trusts that God will still provide him with descendants even though he has been instructed to offer Isaac as a holocaust (Heb 11:17–19).

The conclusion is that God is faithful to those who have faith in his promises. Abraham so embodies Hebrews's definition of faith that the author states Abraham "considered the fact that God is able even to raise someone from the dead—and figuratively speaking, he did receive [Isaac] back" (Heb 11:19). In other words, Abraham is steadfast in God's assurance of Abraham's hoped-for and promised descendants; he is convinced of things not seen but promised by God. Even when faced with death—either because of his and Sarah's age or because of the offering of Isaac—Abraham remains steadfast. The patriarch is presented as a model of faith for Jesus, Mary, and Joseph on the Feast of the Holy Family.[140]

Journal/Meditation: Who is a model of faith for you?

Prayer: O God, you instilled in Abraham and Sarah the assurance of a son even though both of them were past their childbearing years. Like Abraham and Sarah, keep me faithful to your promises, give me the conviction of things not seen, and make me alive in hope for resurrection from the dead through Jesus Christ my Lord. Amen.

---

140. References: BYM, pars. 13, 29–30, 32–33, 134; CCC, pars. 144, 489, 2619; DPPL, pars. 107, 112; MC, par. 5; RM, par. 14.

1 JOHN

Children[141]

Text: 1 John 3:1-2, 21-24

Scripture: "See what love the Father has given us, that we should be called children of God; and that is what we are. Beloved, we are God's children now; what we will be has not yet been revealed." (John 3:1a, 2a)

Reflection: Young human beings between birth and puberty are called children. They are sons and daughters of human parents. In the reflection found in the First Letter of John, the author tells his readers that all of them are children of God; this means that they enjoy a relationship with God that acknowledges him as Father and them as children. This is the same status that John presents for Jesus, God's Son, who relates to him as a Father. According to John, this status is due to God's self-sacrificial love. The Father-Son divine relationship is a metaphor based on the father-son and mother-daughter human relationship. The metaphor enables the writer to compare the human father-son relationship to the divine Father-Son relationship, knowing all that while the metaphor limps. It cannot adequately capture the divine dynamics of Jesus' relationship to God, whom he called Father. In other words, while something is revealed about the Father-Son relationship, there is also something that remains hidden about it.

But there is more. God's self-sacrificial love identified in the Father sending the Son and identified in naming people children of God possesses a hidden dimension, as noted above. What people will be has not been revealed. All they can know is that when the fullness of the relationship is revealed that they will be like God, seeing God as he is (1 John 3:2b). In other words, there is more to come. In the meantime, God's children love one another (1 John 3:11). By participating in God's self-sacrificial love through self-sacrificial love for one another, and by believing in the name of God's Son, Jesus Christ, they abide in God and God abides in them (1 John 3:23-24). In other words, self-sacrificial love binds together God, his Son, and all his children now. Such love is but a prelude to being totally like God and seeing him as he is.

---

141. LM: 17. Feast of the Holy Family of Jesus, Mary, and Joseph, Sunday within the Octave of the Nativity of the Lord [Christmas], or, if there is no Sunday, December 30, Second Reading, Cycle C.

Journal/Meditation: How is the Holy Family of Jesus, Mary, and Joseph a model of self-sacrificial love for you?

Prayer: God of love, through the birth of Jesus Christ, you demonstrated your love and made me one of your children. Keep me faithful to your Son's command to love that I may one day see you as you are: Father, Son, and Holy Spirit abiding in love as one God forever and ever. Amen.

BOOK OF REVELATION

Presence[142]

Text: Revelation 11:19a; 12:1–6a, 10ab

Scripture: ". . . God's temple in heaven was opened, and the ark of his covenant was seen within his temple. A great portent appeared in heaven: a woman clothed with the sun, with the moon under her feet, and on her head a crown of twelve stars." (Rev 11:19a; 12:1)

Reflection: Verse 19 of chapter 11 of the CB (NT) Book of Revelation ends the second story in the work which takes place in heaven and portrays John of Patmos as a heavenly traveler. Verse 1 of chapter 12 begins the last story in the book which takes place on earth and portrays John as a seer or prophet. The temple in heaven is described like the one built by Solomon in Jerusalem with the ark containing the tablets of the Law in the Holy of Holies. Above the ark cherubim held aloft their wings, which formed a throne for God. Thus, the Temple contained God's presence. The womb of the Blessed Virgin Mary is like the Holy of Holies because God came to live there in the person of Jesus. The incarnation, the becoming flesh of God, turned Mary's womb into an ark containing God's presence.

The sign appearing in the heaven of a woman clothed with the sun, with the moon under her feet, and on her head a crown of twelve stars is a reminder of the HB (OT) Joseph, twelfth son of Jacob, who had a dream in which the sun and the moon and eleven stars bowed down to him. Just as Joseph's dream foretold that one day he would save from famine his father, mother, and eleven brothers, so the woman represents God's people, who gave the Messiah to the world to save people; of course, she

---

142. LM: 622. Solemnity of the Assumption of the Blessed Virgin Mary, August 15, Mass during the Day, First Reading; LM: 690A. Feast of Our Lady of Guadalupe, December 12, First Reading, Second Option; LM: 708. The Common of the Blessed Virgin Mary, First Reading, Option 2.

also represents Mary, who "gave birth to a son, a male child, who is to rule all the nations" (Rev. 12:5). To echo Revelation's images, the LBVM(LL) invokes Mary as a vessel of honor, a singular vessel of devotion, and the ark of the covenant. The LBVMOCIBVM invokes her as the woman clothed with the sun and the woman crowned with stars. However, Mary is not the only person to represent God's presence; every human being is a dwelling place for God.[143]

Journal/Meditation: In what ways are you a dwelling place for God?

Prayer: God of heaven, you made your dwelling place on earth in the Jerusalem Temple, seated upon the throne of the ark of the covenant. In the fullness of time, you chose the Blessed Virgin Mary to be the mother of your Son, who came to dwell in her. Make me a worthy dwelling place for your Spirit forever and ever. Amen.

Michael[144]

Text: Revelation 12:1–3, 7-12ab, 17

Scripture: ". . . [W]ar broke out in heaven; Michael and his angels fought against the dragon. The dragon and his angels fought back, but they were defeated, and there was no longer any place for them in heaven." (Rev 12:7–8)

Reflection: According to the HB (OT) book of Daniel, Michael is "the great prince, the protector of [the Jewish] people" (Dan 12:1). This is why he makes an appearance in the CB (NT) Book of Revelation. He is the heavenly counterpart to the earthly Jewish people. Because Michael means *who is like God?* or *who can compare with God?* he is the defender of God's people, or better, he represents God helping his people. This is one of the greatest messages of both Judaism and Christianity: God never abandons people. Once God enters into a covenant relationship with them, God never gives up on people. The Holy One continuously seeks them, reconciles them, and invites them into his kingdom. The author of the Book of Revelation portrays God in the person of Michael fighting a heavenly war against the dragon, identified as the Devil, Satan, and the

---

143. References: BYM, pars. 25–27; DPPL, par. 102; MC, pars. 6, 26, 56; RM, pars. 3, 11.

144. CMBVM: Lectionary: 42. The Blessed Virgin Mary, Help of Christians, First Reading, Option A.

deceiver of the whole world (Rev 12:9), and defeating him. Thus, God comes to the aid of his people.

The greatest sign of God's help shown to people is Jesus, born of the Virgin Mary. He is the incarnate presence of God, the Lamb once slain who lives forever (Rev 5:6), according to the Book of Revelation. Jesus is the fulfillment of God's promise never to abandon his people. Because Mary gave birth to the Son of God, the One who never ceases to help his followers, she is invoked as the help of Christians in the LBVM(LL) and the champion of God's people in the LBVMOCIBVM. Anyone who faithfully follows her Son can be assured of her help along with the help of God and Christ.

Journal/Meditation: In what specific way most recently have you experienced God helping you?

Prayer: Heavenly Father, salvation, the power of your kingdom, and the authority of your Messiah have come. Michael has conquered with the blood of the Lamb. Through the intercession of the Blessed Virgin Mary, grant me your assistance in any need that I may rejoice in you now and forever. Amen.

Bride[145]

Text: Revelation 21:1-5a

Scripture: "... I [, John of Patmos,] saw a new heaven and a new earth; for the first heaven and the first earth had passed away, and the sea was no more. And I saw the holy city, the new Jerusalem, coming down out of heaven from God, prepared as a bride adorned for her husband." (Rev 21:1–2)

Reflection: A bride is a woman who is about to marry or one who has just married. The image of the bride is used as a metaphor by the author of the CB (NT) Book of Revelation to describe the holy city, the new Jerusalem, the people of God, God's bride. God has joined himself

---

145. LM: 613. Optional Memorial of the Dedication of the Basilica of St. Mary Major, August 5, First Reading; LM: 708. The Common of the Blessed Virgin Mary, First Reading, Option 3; CMBVM: Lectionary: 15. The Blessed Virgin Mary and the Resurrection of the Lord, First Reading; CMBVM: Lectionary: 20. Holy Mary, the New Eve, First Reading, Option A; CMBVM: Lectionary: 23. The Blessed Virgin Mary, Temple of the Lord, First Reading, Option B; CMBVM: Lectionary: 27. The Blessed Virgin Mary, Image and Mother of the Church III, First Reading; CMBVM: Lectionary: 46. The Blessed Virgin Mary, Gate of Heaven, First Reading, Option A.

to his bride in a covenant of self-sacrificial love through the death and resurrection of his Son. Jesus' death and resurrection renew the covenant (marriage) vows and seal God and people in a new covenant. These bridal people participate in the new creation in which the chaos, represented by the sea, no longer exists. They are adorned in the new garment they receive when baptized and prepared to meet their husband, God.

The Blessed Virgin Mary, mother of Jesus, is a type of church, since God married her from the first moment of her conception by overwhelming her with grace. When she was about to be joined to Joseph, her fiancé, God stole her from him, and, through the overshadowing of the Holy Spirit, placed the life of his only-begotten Son in her womb. Her willingness to do the will of God along with her faithfulness makes her a model of what the church, the entire people of God, should strive to be. As a model of faithfulness, those who follow Mary's Son can learn from her how to keep the marriage vows between them and God.[146]

Journal/Meditation: As a member of the church and a bride of God, how do you maintain faithfulness to your marriage vows (baptismal promises)?

Prayer: God of the new earth, through the death and resurrection of your Son, you made the members of the church your bride, united to you through an unbreakable bond of love. Keep me faithful to my promises that I may share in the new heaven, where you live and reign with Jesus Christ and the Holy Spirit, one God, forever and ever. Amen.

---

146. References: BYM, pars. 36, 61; CCC, par. 773; MC, pars. 8, 26.

Appendices

1 THE LITANY OF THE BLESSED VIRGIN MARY (LITANY OF LORETO)[1]

    Lord, have mercy.
    Christ, have mercy.
    Lord, have mercy.
    Christ, hear us.
    Christ, graciously hear us.
    God the Father of Heaven, have mercy on us.
    God the Son, Redeemer of the world, have mercy on us.
    God the Holy Spirit, have mercy on us.
    Holy Trinity, One God, have mercy on us.
    Holy Mary, pray for us.
    Holy Mother of God, pray for us.
    Holy Virgin of virgins, pray for us.
    Mother of Christ, pray for us.
    Mother of divine grace, pray for us.
    Mother most pure, pray for us.
    Mother most chaste, pray for us.
    Mother inviolate, pray for us.
    Mother undefiled, pray for us.
    Mother most amiable, pray for us.
    Mother most admirable, pray for us.
    Mother of good counsel, pray for us.
    Mother of our Creator, pray for us.
    Mother of our Savior, pray for us.

---

1. Weller, *Roman Ritual*, 445–450.

Mother of the Church, pray for us.[2]
Virgin most prudent, pray for us.
Virgin most venerable, pray for us.
Virgin most renowned, pray for us.
Virgin most powerful, pray for us.
Virgin most merciful, pray for us.
Virgin most faithful, pray for us.
Mirror of justice, pray for us.
Seat of wisdom, pray for us.
Cause of our joy, pray for us.
Spiritual vessel, pray for us.
Vessel of honor, pray for us.
Singular vessel of devotion, pray for us.
Mystical rose, pray for us.
Tower of David, pray for us.
Tower of ivory, pray for us.
House of gold, pray for us.
Ark of the covenant, pray for us.
Gate of heaven, pray for us.
Morning star, pray for us.
Health of the sick, pray for us.
Refuge of sinners, pray for us.
Comforter of the afflicted, pray for us.
Help of Christians, pray for us.
Queen of Angels, pray for us.
Queen of Patriarchs, pray for us
Queen of Prophets, pray for us.
Queen of Apostles, pray for us.
Queen of Martyrs, pray for us.
Queen of Confessors, pray for us.
Queen of Virgins, pray for us.
Queen of all Saints, pray for us.
Queen conceived without original sin, pray for us.
Queen of the most holy Rosary, pray for us.
Queen of Peace, pray for us.

2. Inserted by Pope St. John Paul II in 1980.

Lamb of God, who takes away the sins of the world, spare us, O Lord.
Lamb of God, who takes away the sins of the world, graciously hear us, O Lord.
Lamb of God, who takes away the sins of the world, have mercy on us.

Pray for us, O holy Mother of God.
That we may be made worthy of the promises of Christ.
Let us pray.
Grant, we beseech you, O Lord God, that we, your servants, may enjoy lasting health of mind and body, and by the glorious intercession of the Blessed Mary, ever Virgin, be delivered from present sorrow and enter into the joy of eternal happiness. Through Christ our Lord. Amen.

The above versicle, response, and prayer appear in a slightly different form in The Roman Ritual for the Seasons of Lent and Ordinary Time:
Pray for us, God's holy mother.
That we may be made worthy of Christ's promise.
Let us pray.
Grant us, your servants, O Lord God, we implore, the joy of continual health in body and mind, and by the glorious intercession of Blessed Mary ever Virgin, free us from present sadness, and establish us in everlasting gladness. Through Christ our Lord. Amen.

During the Season of Advent, the following versicle, response, and prayer are given in The Roman Ritual:
The angel of the Lord declared unto Mary.
And she conceived of the Holy Spirit.
Let us pray.
O God, you did will that at the message of the angel your Word should take flesh in the womb of the Blessed Virgin Mary. So grant that we your humble suppliants, who believe her to be God's mother indeed, may have her as an advocate at your heavenly throne. Through the selfsame Christ our Lord. Amen.

During the Season of Christmas, the following versicle, response, and prayer are given in The Roman Ritual:
After childbirth you did remain a virgin inviolate.
Mother of God, make intercession for us.

Let us pray.

O God, who through the fruitful virginity of Blessed Mary did ensure eternal salvation to the human race, grant, we pray you, that we may experience the intercessory power of her through whom we have been privileged to receive the author of life, Jesus Christ, your Son, our Lord. Amen.

During the Season of Easter, the following versicle, response, and prayer are given in The Roman Ritual:

Be glad and be joyful, O Virgin Mary, Alleluia!

For the Lord is risen verily, Alleluia!

Let us pray.

O God, who through the resurrection of your Son, Christ Jesus, our Lord, did deign to bring joy into the world, grant, we implore you, that through his Virgin Mother, Mary, we may take possession of the bliss of life never ending. Through the same Christ our Lord. Amen.

2 LITANY OF THE BLESSED VIRGIN MARY IN THE "ORDER OF CROWNING AN IMAGE OF THE BLESSED VIRGIN MARY"[3]

Lord, have mercy. Lord, have mercy.
Christ, have mercy. Christ, have mercy.
Lord, have mercy. Lord, have mercy.
God our Father in heaven, have mercy on us.
God the Son, Redeemer of the world, have mercy on us.
God the Holy Spirit, have mercy on us.
Holy Trinity, one God, have mercy on us.
Holy Mary, pray for us.
Holy Mother of God, pray for us.
Most honored of virgins, pray for us.
Chosen daughter of the Father, pray for us.
Mother of Christ the King, pray for us.
Glory of the Holy Spirit, pray for us.
Virgin daughter of Zion, pray for us.
Virgin poor and humble, pray for us.
Virgin gentle and obedient, pray for us.
Handmaid of the Lord, pray for us.
Mother of the Lord, pray for us.
Helper of the Redeemer, pray for us.
Full of grace, pray for us.
Fountain of beauty, pray for us.
Model of virtue, pray for us.
Finest fruit of the redemption, pray for us.
Perfect disciple of Christ, pray for us.
Untarnished image of the Church, pray for us.
Woman transformed, pray for us.
Woman clothed with the sun, pray for us.
Woman crowned with stars, pray for us.
Gentle Lady, pray for us.
Gracious Lady, pray for us.
Our Lady, pray for us.

3. "Crowning," par. 41.

Joy of Israel, pray for us.
Splendor of the Church, pray for us.
Pride of the human race, pray for us.
Advocate of grace, pray for us.
Minister of holiness, pray for us.
Champion of God's people, pray for us.
Queen of love, pray for us.
Queen of mercy, pray for us.
Queen of peace, pray for us.
Queen of angels, pray for us.
Queen of patriarchs and prophets, pray for us.
Queen of apostles and martyrs, pray for us.
Queen of confessors and virgins, pray for us.
Queen of all saints, pray for us.
Queen conceived without original sin, pray for us.
Queen assumed into heaven, pray for us.
Queen of all the earth, pray for us.
Queen of heaven, pray for us.
Queen of the universe, pray for us.
Lamb of God, you take away the sins of the world, spare us, O Lord.
Lamb of God, you take away the sins of the world, hear us, O Lord.
Lamb of God, you take away the sins of the world, have mercy on us.

Pray for us, O glorious Mother of the Lord.
That we may become worthy of the promises of Christ.

God of mercy, listen to the prayers of your servants who have honored your handmaid Mary as mother and queen. Grant that by your grace we may serve you and our neighbor on earth and be welcomed into your eternal kingdom. We ask this through Christ our Lord. Amen.

3 LIST OF MARIAN CELEBRATIONS DURING THE LITURGICAL YEAR AND SCRIPTURE TEXTS ASSIGNED FOR EACH[4]

Here are listed according to Lectionary number the Marian celebrations throughout the liturgical year with the Scripture texts assigned for each. To find the reflection associated with each biblical text, merely look for the text in this book, which presents it in biblical-book order. For example, to find the reflection associated with the first reading for the Solemnity of Mary, the Holy Mother of God, on January 1, go to chapter 1, skip the selections from Genesis, Exodus, and Leviticus, and the entries for Numbers can be located.

The order for each set of Scripture texts is First Reading, Responsorial Psalm, Second Reading—when there is one—and Gospel. When there are options for the First Reading, Responsorial Psalm, Second Reading, or Gospel, (First Option) and (Second Option) precede the various notations following the order given above. For example, LM 543. The Solemnity of St. Joseph, Spouse of the Blessed Virgin Mary, has a (First Option) and a (Second Option) for the Gospel. Also, there are often longer and shorter forms of a text.

> LM 13. Solemnity of the Nativity of the Lord [Christmas], December 25, At the Vigil Mass: Isaiah 62:1–5; Psalm 89:4–5, 16–17, 27, 29; Acts 13:16–17, 22–25; (Longer Form) Matthew 1:1–25 or (Shorter Form) Matthew 1:18–25

> LM 14: Solemnity of the Nativity of the Lord [Christmas], December 25, At the Mass during the Night: Isaiah 9:1–6; Psalm 96:1–2, 2–3, 11–12, 13; Titus 2:11–14; Luke 2:1–14

> LM 15: Solemnity of the Nativity of the Lord [Christmas], December 25, At the Mass at Dawn: Isaiah 62:11–12; Psalm 97:1, 6, 11–12; Titus 3:4–7; Luke 2:15–20

> LM 16: Solemnity of the Nativity of the Lord [Christmas], December 25, At the Mass during the Day: Isaiah 52:7–10; Psalm 98:1, 2–3, 3–4, 5–6; Hebrews 1:1–6; (Longer Form) John 1:1–18 or (Shorter Form) John 1:1–5, 9–14

---

4. Found in the Lectionary for Mass: Volumes I, II, and III.

LM 17: Feast of the Holy Family of Jesus, Mary, and Joseph, Sunday within the Octave of the Nativity of the Lord [Christmas], or, if there is no Sunday, December 30, Cycle A: Sirach 3:2–7, 12–14; Psalm 128:1–2, 3, 4–5; (Longer Form) Colossians 3:12–21 or (Shorter Form) Colossians 3:12–17; Matthew 2:13–15, 19–23

LM 17: Feast of the Holy Family of Jesus, Mary, and Joseph, Sunday within the Octave of the Nativity of the Lord [Christmas], or, if there is no Sunday, December 30, Cycle B: Genesis 15:1–6, 21:1–3; Psalm 105:1–2, 3–4, 5–6, 8–9; Hebrews 11:8, 11–12, 17–19; (Longer Form) Luke 2:22–40 or (Shorter Form) Luke 2:22, 39–40

LM 17: Feast of the Holy Family of Jesus, Mary, and Joseph, Sunday within the Octave of the Nativity of the Lord [Christmas], or, if there is no Sunday, December 30, Cycle C: 1 Samuel 1:20–22, 24–28; Psalm 84:2–3, 5–6, 9–10; 1 John 3:1–2, 21–24; Luke 2:41–52

LM 18: Solemnity of Mary, the Holy Mother of God, January 1: Numbers 6:22–27; Psalm 67:2–3, 5, 6, 8; Galatians 4:4–7; Luke 2:16–21

LM 19: Second Sunday after the Nativity [Christmas]: Sirach 24:1–2, 8–12; Psalm 147:12–13, 14–15, 19–20; Ephesians 1:3–6, 15–18; (Longer Form) John 1:1–18 or (Shorter Form) John 1:1–5, 9–14[5]

LM 20: The Solemnity of the Epiphany of the Lord, Sunday between January 2 and January 8 in the United States or January 6: Isaiah 60:1–6; Psalm 72:1–2, 7–8, 10–11, 12–13; Ephesians 3:2–3a, 5–6; Matthew 2:1–12

LM 524: Feast of the Presentation of the Lord, February 2: Malachi 3:1–4; Psalm 24:7, 8, 9, 10; Hebrews 2:14–18; (Longer Form) Luke 2:22–40 or (Shorter Form) Luke 2:22–32

---

5. In the United States, the Second Sunday after the Nativity [Christmas] is replaced with the Solemnity of the Epiphany of the Lord on the Sunday between January 2 and January 8. In other countries, the Sunday after January 1 is the Second Sunday after the Nativity [Christmas], and the Solemnity of the Epiphany of the Lord is celebrated on January 6.

APPENDICES

LM 531: Optional Memorial of Our lady of Lourdes, February 11: Isaiah 66:10–14c; Judith 13:18bcde, 19; John 2:1–11 or CBVM, LM: 707–712[6]

LM 543: Solemnity of St. Joseph, Spouse of the Blessed Virgin Mary, March 19: 2 Samuel 7:4–5a, 12–14a, 16; Psalm 89:2–3, 4–5, 27 and 29; Romans 4:13, 16–18, 22; (First Option) Matthew 1:16, 18–21, 24a or (Second Option) Luke 2:41–51a

LM 545: Solemnity of the Annunciation of the Lord, March 25: Isaiah 7:10–14; 8:10; Psalm 40:7–8a, 8b–9, 10, 11; Hebrews 10:4–10; Luke 1:26–38

LM 559: Optional Memorial of St. Joseph the Worker, May 1: (First Option) Genesis 1:26—2:3 or (Second Option) Colossians 3:14–15, 17, 23–24; Psalm 90:2, 3–4, 12–13, 14 and 16; Matthew 13:54–58

LM 563A: Optional Memorial of Our Lady of Fatima, May 13: Isaiah 61:9–11; Psalm 45:11–12, 14–15, 16–17; Luke 11:27–28[7] or CBVM, LM: 701–712[8]

LM 572: Feast of the Visitation of the Blessed Virgin Mary, May 31: (First Option) Zephaniah 3:14–18a or (Second Option) Romans 12:9–16; Isaiah 12:2–3, 4bcd, 5–6; Luke 1:39–56

LM 572A: Memorial of the Blessed Virgin Mary, Mother of the Church, Monday after Pentecost: (First Option) Genesis 3:9–15, 20 or (Second Option) Acts 1:12–14; Psalm 87:1–2, 3 and 5, 6–7; John 19:25–34[9]

LM 573: Memorial of the Immaculate Heart of the Blessed Virgin Mary, Saturday following the Second Sunday after Pentecost: Isaiah 61:9–11; 1 Samuel 2:1, 4–5, 6–7, 8abcd; Luke 2:41–51 or CBVM, LM: 707–710[10]

---

6. See Appendix 4.
7. Found in the Lectionary for Mass: Supplement.
8. See Appendix 4.
9. Found at http://www.usccb.org/about/divine-worship/liturgical-calendar/mother-of-the-church.cfm; cf. "Pope Francis," 9–10.
10. See Appendix 4.

LM 601: Optional Memorial of Our Lady of Mount Carmel, July 16: Zechariah 2:14–17; Luke 1:46–47, 48–49, 50–51, 52–53, 54–55; Matthew 12:46–50 or CBVM, LM: 707–710[11]

LM 606: Memorial of Saints Joachim and Anne, Parents of the Blessed Virgin Mary, July 26: Sirach 44:1, 10–15; Psalm 132:11, 13–14, 17–18; Matthew 13:16–17

LM 613: Optional Memorial of the Dedication of the Basilica of St. Mary Major, August 5: Revelation 21:1–5a; Judith 13:18, 19, 20; Luke 11:27–28 or CBMV, LM: 707–710[12]

LM 621: Solemnity of the Assumption of the Blessed Virgin Mary, August 15, At the Vigil Mass: 1 Chronicles 15:3–4, 15–16; 16:1–2; Psalm 132:6–7, 9–10, 13–14; 1 Corinthians 15:54b–57; Luke 11:27–28

LM 622: Solemnity of the Assumption of the Blessed Virgin Mary, August 15, At the Mass during the Day: Revelation 11:19a; 12:1–6a, 10ab; Psalm 45:10, 11, 12, 16; 1 Corinthians 15:20–27; Luke 1:39–56

LM 627: Memorial of the Queenship of the Blessed Virgin Mary, August 22: Isaiah 9:1–6; Psalm 113:1–2, 3–4, 5–6, 7–8; Luke 1:26–38 or CBVM, LM: 707–712[13]

LM 636: Feast of the Nativity of the Blessed Virgin Mary, September 8: (First Option) Micah 5:1–4a or (Second Option) Romans 8:28–30; Psalm 13:6ab, 6c; (Longer Form) Matthew 1:1–16, 18–23 or (Shorter Form) Matthew 1:18–23

LM 636B: Optional Memorial of the Most Holy Name of Mary, September 12: Galatians 4:4–7; Luke 1:46–47, 48–49, 50–51, 52–53, 54–55; Luke 1:39–47[14] or CBVM, LM: 707–712[15]

---

11. Ibid.
12. Ibid.
13. Ibid.
14. Found in the Lectionary for Mass: Supplement.
15. See Appendix 4.

LM 639: Memorial of Our Lady of Sorrows, September 15: Hebrews 5:7–9; Psalm 31:2 and 3b, 3cd–4, 5–6, 15–16, 20; (First Option) John 19:25–27 or (Second Option) Luke 2:33–35

LM 653: Memorial of Our Lady of the Rosary, October 7: Acts 1:12–14; Luke 1:46–47, 48–49, 50–51, 52–53, 54–55; Luke 1:26–38 or CBVM, LM: 707–712[16]

LM 680: Memorial of the Presentation of the Blessed Virgin Mary, November 21: Zechariah 2:14–17; Luke 1:46–47, 48–49, 50–51, 52–53, 54–55; Matthew 12:46–50 or CBVM, LM: 707–712[17]

LM 689: The Solemnity of the Immaculate Conception of the Blessed Virgin Mary, December 8: Genesis 3:9–15, 20; Psalm 98:1, 2–3ab, 3cd–4; Ephesians 1:3–6, 11–12; Luke 1:26–38

LM 690A: Feast of Our Lady of Guadalupe, December 12: (First Option) Zechariah 2:14–17 or (Second Option) Revelation 11:19a; 12:1–6a, 10ab; Judith 13:18bcde, 19; (First Option) Luke 1:26–38 or (Second Option) Luke 1:39–47 or CBVM, LM: 707–712[18]

---

16. Ibid.
17. Ibid.
18. Ibid.

4 THE COMMON OF THE BLESSED VIRGIN MARY[19] AND VOTIVE MASSES OF THE BLESSED VIRGIN MARY

When no biblical texts are specified for a Marian celebration or when texts are only suggested, Scripture texts are chosen from the following. Here are listed the optional Scripture texts according to Lectionary number. To find the reflection associated with each biblical text, merely look for the text in this book, which presents it in biblical-book order. For example, to find the reflection associated with the first reading, option 5, from Proverbs 8:22–31, go to chapter 1, skip the selections from Genesis through Psalms, and the entries for Proverbs can be located.

LM 707: Reading I from the Old Testament

  Option 1: Genesis 3:9–15, 20
  Option 2: Genesis 12:1–7
  Option 3: 2 Samuel 7:1–5, 8b–11, 16
  Option 4: 1 Chronicles 15:3–4, 15–16; 16:1–2
  Option 5: Proverbs 8:22–31
  Option 6: Sirach 24:1–4, 8–12, 18–21
  Option 7: Isaiah 7:10–14; 8:10
  Option 8: Isaiah 9:1–6
  Option 9: Isaiah 61:9–11
  Option 10: Micah 5:1–4a
  Option 11: Zechariah 2:14–17

LM 708: Reading I from the New Testament during the Season of Easter

  Option 1: Acts 1:12–14
  Option 2: Revelation 11:19a; 12:1–6a, 10ab
  Option 3: Revelation 21:1–5a

LM 709: Responsorial Psalm

  Option 1: 1 Samuel 2:1, 4–5, 6–7, 8abcd
  Option 2: Judith 13:18bcde, 19
  Option 3: Psalm 45:11–12, 14–15, 16–17
  Option 4: Psalm 113:1b–2, 3–4, 5–6, 7
  Option 5: Luke 1:46–47, 48–49, 50–51, 52–53, 54–55

---

19. Found in Lectionary for Mass: Volumes II, III, and IV.

LM 710: Reading II from the New Testament

> First Option: Romans 5:12, 17–19
> Second Option: Romans 8:28–30
> Third Option: Galatians 4:4–7
> Fourth Option: Ephesians 1:3–6, 11–12

LM 712: Gospel

> Option 1: (Longer Form) Matthew 1:1–16, 18–23 or (Shorter Form) Matthew 1:18–23
> Option 2: Matthew 2:13–15, 19–23
> Option 3: Matthew 12:46–50
> Option 4: Luke 1:26–38.
> Option 5: Luke 1:39–47
> Option 6: Luke 2:1–14
> Option 7: Luke 2:15b–19
> Option 8: Luke 2:27–35
> Option 9: Luke 2:41–52
> Option 10: Luke 11:27–28
> Option 11: John 2:1–11
> Option 12: John 19:25–27

LM 1002: Votive Masses: 10. The Blessed Virgin Mary

I. The Blessed Virgin Mary, Mother of the Church: (First Option) Genesis 3:9–15, 20 or (Second Option) Acts 1:12–14; Judith 13:18bcde, 19; John 19:25–27[20]

II. The Most Holy Name of Mary: (First Option) Galatians 4:4–7 or (Second Option) Ephesians 1:3–6, 11–12; Luke 1:46–47, 48–49, 50–51, 52–53, 54–55; Luke 1:39–47[21]

III. Our Lady, Queen of Apostles: Acts 1:12–14; Luke 1:46–47, 48–49, 50–51, 52–53, 54–55; (First Option) Matthew 12:46–50 or (Second Option) John 19:25–27[22]

---

20. Found in Lectionary for Mass: Volume IV.
21. Ibid.
22. Found in the Lectionary for Mass: Supplement.

5 COLLECTION OF MASSES OF THE BLESSED VIRGIN MARY AND SCRIPTURE TEXTS ASSIGNED FOR EACH

Here are listed according to the Collection of Masses of the Blessed Virgin Mary: Lectionary the number of the Mass with the Scripture texts assigned for each. To find the reflection associated with each biblical text, merely look for the text in this book, which presents it in biblical-book order. For example, to find the reflection associated with the First Reading, Option A, for CMBVM: Lectionary 1. The Blessed Virgin Mary, Chosen Daughter of Israel, go to chapter 1, and look for the selections from Genesis.

When the CMBVM: Lectionary presents an optional First Reading from the Appendix, it simultaneously presents an optional Responsorial Psalm from the Appendix, because every First Reading in the Appendix has a Responsorial Psalm that accompanies it. Thus, in this list of biblical texts the number of the Responsorial Psalm is derived from the number of the First Reading, which it accompanies in the Appendix. For example, the Option C First Reading from the book of Ruth in 1. The Blessed Virgin Mary, Chosen Daughter of Israel, is found in the Appendix, Option 5, where it has a corresponding Responsorial Psalm from 1 Samuel. In this listing, 1 Sam 2:1, 4–5, 6–7, 8abcd is presented as an option to Responsorial Psalm 113:1–2, 3–4, 5–6, 7–8 appearing first and is identified as Appendix 5. For Option A and Option B Responsorial Psalm 113:1–2, 3–4, 5–6, 7–8 will be used. For Option C, either Responsorial Psalm may be used.

The order for each set of Scripture texts is First Reading, Responsorial Psalm, and Gospel. When there are options, (Option A), (Option B), and (Option C) precede the various notations. Thus, in following the order given above, 1. The Blessed Virgin Mary, Chosen Daughter of Israel, there are three options for the First Reading, two Responsorial Psalms, and no choice for a Gospel. In 2. The Blessed Virgin Mary and the Annunciation of the Lord, there are two options for the First Reading, two options for the Responsorial Psalm, and two options for the Gospel.

Advent Season

CMBVM: Lectionary: 1: The Blessed Virgin Mary, Chosen Daughter of Israel: (Option A) Genesis 12:1–7 or (Option B) 2

Samuel 7:1-5, 8b-11 16 or (Option C) Ruth 2:1-2, 8-11; 4:13-17 [Appendix 5]; Psalm 113:1-2, 3-4, 5-6, 7-8 or 1 Samuel 2:1, 4-5, 6-7, 8abcd [Appendix 5]; Matthew 1-17

CMBVM: Lectionary: 2. The Blessed Virgin Mary and the Annunciation of the Lord: (Option A) Isaiah 7:10-14; 8:10c or (Option B) Isaiah 11:1-5, 10 [Appendix 6]; Psalm 40:7-8a, 8b-9, 10, 11 or Psalm 72:1-2, 7-8, 12-13, 17 [Appendix 6]; (Option A) Luke 1:26-38 or (Option B) Matthew 1:18-23 [Appendix 17]

CMBVM: Lectionary 3. The Visitation of the Blessed Virgin Mary: (Option A) Zephaniah 3:14-18a or (Option B) Song of (Solomon) Songs 2:8-14 or (Option C) Zechariah 9:9-10 [Appendix 8]; Isaiah 12:2-3, 4bcd, 5-6 or Psalm 72:1-2, 7-8, 12-13, 17 [Appendix 8]; Luke 1:39-56

Christmas Season

CMBVM: Lectionary: 4. Holy Mary, Mother of God: Galatians 4:4-7; Psalm 22:4-6, 10-11, 23-24; Luke 2:15b-19

CMBVM: Lectionary: 5: The Blessed Virgin Mary, Mother of the Savior: (Option A) Isaiah 9:1-3, 5-6 or (Option B) Micah 5:1-4a [Appendix 7]; Psalm 96:1-2a, 2b-3, 11-12, 13 or Psalm 2:7-8, 10-11ab [Appendix 7]; Luke 2:1-14

CMBVM: Lectionary 6: The Blessed Virgin Mary and the Epiphany of the Lord: Isaiah 60:1-6; Psalm 72:1-2, 7-8, 10-11, 12-13; Matthew 2:1-12

CMBVM: Lectionary: 7. The Blessed Virgin Mary and the Presentation of the Lord: Malachi 41-4; Psalm 24:7, 8, 9, 10; Luke 2:27-35

CMBVM: Lectionary: 8. Our Lady of Nazareth I: Galatians 4:4-7; Psalm 13:1, 2, 3; (Option A) Luke 2:22, 39-40 or (Option B) Luke 2:41-52

CMBVM: Lectionary: 8. Our Lady of Nazareth II: Colossians 3:12-17; Psalm 84:2-3, 5-6, 9-10; Matthew 2:13-15, 19-23

CMBVM: Lectionary: 9. Our Lady of Cana: Exodus 19:3–8a; Psalm 119:1–2, 10–11, 12 and 14, 15–16; John 2:1–11

Lenten Season

CMBVM: Lectionary: 10. Holy Mary, Disciple of the Lord: Sirach 51:13–18, 20–22; Psalm 19:8–9, 10–11, 15; (Option A) Luke 2:41–52 or (Option B) Matthew 12:46–50

CMBVM: Lectionary: 11. The Blessed Virgin Mary at the Foot of the Cross I: (Option A) Romans 8:31b–39 or (Option B) Colossians 1:21–24 [Appendix 15]; Psalm 18:2–3, 5–6, 7, 19–20 or Psalm 116:12–13, 15–16bc, 17–18 [Appendix 15]; John 19:25–27

CMBVM: Lectionary: 12: The Blessed Virgin Mary at the Food of the Cross II: (Option A) Judith 13:17–20 or (Option B) Genesis 22:1–2, 9–13, 15–18 [Appendix 1] or (Option C) Hebrews 5:7–9 [Appendix 16]; Psalm 145:1–2, 4–6, 8–9 or Psalm 16:5 and 8, 9–10, 11 [Appendix 1] or Psalm 31:2–3b, 3c–4, 5–6, 15–16, 20 [Appendix 16]; John 19:25–27

CMBVM: Lectionary: 13. The Commending of the Blessed Virgin Mary: 2 Maccabees 7:1, 20–29; Psalm 18:2–3, 5–6, 7, 19–20; John 19:25–27

CMBVM: Lectionary: 14. The Blessed Virgin Mary, Mother of Reconciliation: 2 Corinthians 5:17–21; Psalm 103:1–2, 3–4, 8–9, 13–14, 17–18a; John 19:25–27

Easter Season

CMBVM: Lectionary: 15. The Blessed Virgin Mary and the Resurrection of the Lord: Revelation 21:1–5a; Isaiah 61:10a–d and f, 11; 62:2–3; Matthew 28:1–10

CMBVM: Lectionary: 16. Holy Mary, Fountain of Light and Life: Acts 2:14a, 36–40a, 41–42; Psalm 34:2–3, 6–7, 8, 9; (Option A) John 12:44–50 or (Option B) John 3:1–6

CMBVM: Lectionary: 17. Our Lady of the Cenacle: Acts 1:6–14; Psalm 87:1–2, 3 and 5, 6–7; (Option A) Luke 8:19–21 or (Option B) Luke 24:44–53 [Appendix 21]

CMBVM: Lectionary: 18. The Blessed Virgin Mary, Queen of Apostles: Acts 1:12–14; 2:1–4; Psalm 87:1–2, 3 and 5, 6–7; John 19:25–27

Ordinary Time: Section 1

CMBVM: Lectionary: 19. Holy Mary, Mother of the Lord: (Option A) 1 Chronicles 15:3–4, 15–16; 16:1–2 or (Option B) Exodus 3:1–8 [Appendix 3]; Psalm 132:11, 13–14, 17–18 or Psalm 103:1–2, 3–4, 6–7, 8 and 11 [Appendix 3]; Luke 1:39–47

CMBVM: Lectionary: 20. Holy Mary, the New Eve: (Option A) Revelation 21:1–5a or (Option B) Romans 5:12, 17–19 [Appendix 9] or (Option C) Ephesians 1:3–6, 11–12 [Appendix 14]; Isaiah 61:10a–d and f, 11; 62:2–3 or Psalm 40:7–8a, 8b–9, 10, 11 [Appendix 9] or Isaiah 61:10a–d and f, 11; 62:2–3 [Appendix 14]; (Option A) Luke 1:26–38 or (Option B) John 2:1–11

CMBVM: Lectionary: 21. The Holy Name of the Blessed Virgin Mary: Sirach 24:17–21; Luke 1:46–48, 49–50, 53–54; Luke 1:26–38

CMBVM: Lectionary: 22. Holy Mary, Handmaid of the Lord: 1 Samuel 1:24–28; 2:1–2, 4–8; Luke 1:46–48a, 48b–49, 50–51, 52–53, 54–55; Luke 1:26–38

CMBVM: Lectionary: 23. The Blessed Virgin Mary, Temple of the Lord: (Option A) 1 Kings 8:1, 3–7, 9–11 or (Option B) Revelation 21:1–5a; Psalm 84:3, 4, 5 and 10, 11; Luke 1:26–38

CMBVM: Lectionary: 24. The Blessed Virgin Mary, Seat of Wisdom: (Option A) Proverbs 8:22–31 or (Option B) Sirach 24:1–4, 8–12, 18–21; Psalm 147:12–13, 14–15, 19–20; (Option A) Matthew 1:1–12 or (Option B) Luke 2:15b–19 or (Option C) Luke 10:38–42

CMBVM: Lectionary: 25. The Blessed Virgin Mary, Image and Mother of the Church I: Genesis 3:9–15, 20; Judith 13:18bcde, 19; John 19:25–27

CMBVM: Lectionary: 26: The Blessed Virgin Mary, Image and Mother of the Church II: Acts 1:12–14; Psalm 87:1–2, 3 and 5, 6–7; John 2:1–11

CMBVM: Lectionary: 27. The Blessed Virgin Mary, Image and Mother of the Church III: Revelation 21:1–5a; Isaiah 12:2–3, 4bcd, 5–6; Luke 1:26–38

CMBVM: Lectionary: 28. The Immaculate Heart of the Blessed Virgin Mary: Judith 13:17–20; 15:9; Luke 1:46–48a, 48b–49, 50–51, 52–53, 54–55; (Option A) Luke 11:27–28 or (Option B) Luke 2:46–51

CMBVM: Lectionary: 29. The Blessed Virgin Mary, Queen of All Creation: (Option A) Isaiah 9:1–3, 5–6 or (Option B) Zechariah 9:9–10 [Appendix 8] or (Option C) 1 Corinthians 15:20–26 [Appendix 12]; Psalm 45:11–12, 14–15, 16–17, 18 or Psalm 72:1–2, 7–8, 12–13, 17 [Appendix 8] or Psalm 16:5 and 8, 9–10, 11 [Appendix 12]; Luke 1:26–38

Ordinary Time: Section 2

CMBVM: Lectionary: 30. The Blessed Virgin Mary, Mother and Mediatrix of Grace: Esther 8:3–8, 16–17a; Psalm 67:2–3, 4–5, 6–7; John 2:1–11

CMBVM: Lectionary: 31. The Blessed Virgin Mary, Fountain of Salvation I: Ezekiel 47:1–2, 8–9, 12; Isaiah 12:2–3, 4bcd, 5–6; John 19:25–37

CMBVM: Lectionary: 31. The Blessed Virgin Mary, Fountain of Salvation II: Song of (Solomon) Songs 4:6–7, 9, 12–15; Judith 13:18bcde, 19; John 7:37–39a

CMBVM: Lectionary: 32. The Blessed Virgin Mary, Mother and Teacher in the Spirit: (Option A) Proverbs 8:17–21,34–35 or

(Option B) Isaiah 56:1, 6–7; Psalm 15:2–3a, 3bc–4, 5; (Option A) Matthew 12:46–50 or (Option B) John 19:25–27 or (Option C) Mark 3:31–35 [Appendix 19]

CMBVM: Lectionary: 33. The Blessed Virgin Mary, Mother of Good Counsel: (Option A) Isaiah 9:1–3, 5–6 or (Option B) Acts 1:12–14; 2:1–4; Sirach 14:20, 21–22, 23–25, 26–27; John 2:1–11

CMBVM: Lectionary: 34. The Blessed Virgin Mary, Cause of Our Joy: (Option A) Zechariah 2:14–17 or (Option B) Isaiah 61:9–11; Luke 1:46–48, 49–50, 53–54; (Option A) Luke 1:39–47 or (Option B) John 15:9–12

CMBVM: Lectionary: 35. The Blessed Virgin Mary, Pillar of Faith: Judith 13:14, 17–20; Psalm 27:1, 3, 4, 5; Luke 11:27–28

CMBVM: Lectionary: 36. The Blessed Virgin Mary, Mother of Fairest Love: Sirach 24:17–21; Song of (Solomon) Songs 2:10bc and 14ef; 4:8a and 9a, 11cd and 12, 15; Luke 1:26–38

CMBVM: Lectionary: 37. The Blessed Virgin Mary, Mother of Divine Hope: Sirach 24:9–12, 18–21; Luke 1:46–48a, 48b–49, 50–51, 52–53; John 2:1–11

CMBVM: Lectionary: 38. Holy Mary, Mother of Unity: (Option A) Zephaniah 3:14–20 or (Option B) 1 Timothy 2:5–8; Jeremiah 31:10, 11–12ab, 13–14; (Option A) John 11:45–52 or (Option B) John 17:20–26

Ordinary Time: Section 3

CMBVM: Lectionary: 39. Holy Mary, Queen and Mother of Mercy I: Esther C:12, 14–15, 25, 30; Luke 1:46–48a, 48b–49, 50–51, 52–53, 54–55; John 2:1–11

CMBVM: Lectionary: 39. Holy Mary, Queen and Mother of Mercy II: Ephesians 2:4–10; Psalm 103:1–2, 3–4, 6 and 8, 13 and 17; Luke 1:39–55

CMBVM: Lectionary: 40. The Blessed Virgin Mary, Mother of Divine Providence: Isaiah 66:10–14; Psalm 131:1, 2, 3; John 2:1–11

CMBVM: Lectionary: 41. The Blessed Virgin Mary, Mother of Consolation: (Option A) Isaiah 61:1–3, 10–11 or (Option B) 2 Corinthians 1:3–7; Isaiah 12:1, 2–3, 4bcd, 5–6; (Option A) Matthew 5:1–12 or (Option B) John 14:15–21, 25–27

CMBVM: Lectionary: 42. The Blessed Virgin Mary, Help of Christians: (Option A) Revelation 12:1–3, 7–12ab, 17 or (Option B) Genesis 3:1–6, 13–15; Judith 16:13, 14, 15; John 2:1–11

CMBVM: Lectionary: 43. Our Lady of Ransom: Judith 15:8–10; 16:13–14; Luke 1:46–48a, 48b–49, 50–51, 52–53, 54–55; John 19:25–27

CMBVM: Lectionary: 44. The Blessed Virgin Mary, Health of the Sick: Isaiah 53:1–5, 7–10; Psalm 103:1–2, 3–4, 6–7, 8 and 10; Luke 1:39–56

CMBVM: Lectionary: 45. The Blessed Virgin Mary, Queen of Peace: Isaiah 9:1–3, 5–6; Psalm 85:9ab–10, 11–12, 13–14; Luke 1:26–38

CMBVM: Lectionary: 46. The Blessed Virgin Mary, Gate of Heaven: (Option A) Revelation 21:1–5a or (Option B) Genesis 28:10–17 [Appendix 2]; Psalm 122:1–2, 3–4, 8–9 or Psalm 24:1–2, 3–4ab, 5–6 [Appendix 2]; Matthew 25:1–13

CMBVM: Lectionary: Appendix
1. Genesis 22:1–2, 9–13, 15–18 with Psalm 16:5 and 8, 9–10, 11
2. Genesis 28:10–17 with Psalm 24:1–2, 3–4ab, 5–6
3. Exodus 3:1–8 with Psalm 103:1–2, 3–4, 6–7, 8 and 11
4. Numbers 24:15–17a with Psalm 72:1–2, 7–8, 12–13, 17
5. Ruth 2:1–2, 8–11; 4:13–17 with 1 Samuel 2:1, 4–5, 6–7, 8abcd
6. Isaiah 11:1–5, 10 with Psalm 72:1–2, 7–8, 12–13, 17
7. Micah 5:1–4a with Psalm 2:7–8, 10–11ab
8. Zechariah 9:9–10 with Psalm 72:1–2, 7–8, 12–13, 17
9. Romans 5:12, 17–19 with Psalm 40:7–8a, 8b–9, 10, 11
10. Romans 8:28–30 with Psalm 8:4–5, 6–7a, 7b–9

11. Romans 12:9–16a with Psalm 131:1, 2, 3
12. 1 Corinthians 15:20–26 with Psalm 16:5 and 8, 9–10, 11
13. 1 Corinthians 15:54–57 with Psalm 118:14–15, 16–17, 19–21
14. Ephesians 1:3–6, 11–12 with Isaiah 61:10a–d and f, 11; 62:2–3
15. Colossians 1:21–24 with Psalm 116:12–13, 15–16bc, 17–18
16. Hebrews 5:7–9 with Psalm 31:2–3b, 3c–4, 5–6, 15–16, 20
17. Matthew 1:18–23
18. Matthew 13:54–58
19. Mark 3:31–35
20. Mark 6:1–6
21. Luke 24:44–53

Bibliography

"Apostolic Exhortation on the Renewal of Religious Life." In Vatican Council II: The Conciliar and Post Conciliar Documents, edited by Austin Flannery, 680–706. Northport, NY: Costello, 1987.

Behold Your Mother: Woman of Faith. Washington, DC: United States Catholic Conference, 1973.

Book of Blessings. New York: Catholic Book, 1989.

Book of the Gospels. Chicago, IL: Liturgy Training, 2001.

Catechism of the Catholic Church. Washington, DC: United States Catholic Conference, Inc.—Libreria Editrice Vaticana, 1994.

Collection of Masses of the Blessed Virgin Mary: Volume I: Missal. Collegeville, MN: Liturgical, 2012.

Collection of Masses of the Blessed Virgin Mary: Volume II: Lectionary. Collegeville, MN: Liturgical, 2012.

"Constitution on the Sacred Liturgy, The." In Vatican Council II: The Conciliar and Post Conciliar Documents, edited by Austin Flannery, 1–36. Northport, NY: Costello, 1987.

"Directory on Popular Piety and the Liturgy: Principles and Guidelines." In The Liturgy Documents: Volume 4: Supplemental Documents for Parish Worship, Devotions, Formation, and Catechesis, 347–473. Chicago: Liturgy Training, 2013.

"Dogmatic Constitution on the Church." In Vatican Council II: The Conciliar and Post Conciliar Documents, edited by Austin Flannery, 350–426. Northport, NY: Costello, 1987.

Ehrman, Bart D. and Zlatko Plese. The Other Gospels: Accounts of Jesus from Outside the New Testament. New York: Oxford University Press, 2014.

Flannery, Austin, ed. Vatican Council II: The Conciliar and Post Conciliar Documents. Northport, NY: Costello, 1987.

"General Introduction." In Collection of Masses of the Blessed Virgin Mary: Volume I: Missal, xiii–xxv. Collegeville, MN: Liturgical, 2012.

"General Instruction of The Roman Missal, The." In The Roman Missal, 17–87. Collegeville, MN: Liturgical Press, 2011.

Lectionary for Mass: Supplement. Collegeville, MN: Liturgical, 2017.

Lectionary for Mass. Volume I: Sundays, Solemnities, Feast of the Lord and the Saints. New Jersey: Catholic Book, 1998.

Lectionary for Mass: Volume II: Proper of Seasons for Weekdays, Year I, Proper of Saints, Common of Saints. Collegeville, MN: Liturgical, 2002.

Lectionary for Mass: Volume III: Proper of Seasons for Weekdays, Year II, Proper of Saints, Common of Saints. Collegeville, MN: Liturgical, 2002.

Lectionary for Mass: Volume IV: Common of Saints, Ritual Masses, Masses for Various Needs and Occasions, Votive Masses, and Masses for the Dead. Collegeville, MN: Liturgical, 2002.

Liturgy Documents, The: Volume 4: Supplemental Documents for Parish Worship, Devotions, Formation, and Catechesis. Chicago: Liturgy Training, 2013.

"Marialis Cultus: For the Right Ordering and Development of Devotion to the Blessed Virgin Mary." In The Liturgy Documents: Volume 4: Supplemental Documents for Parish Worship, Devotions, Formation, and Catechesis, 483–516. Chicago: Liturgy Training, 2013.

Mayer, Augustin. "Congregation for Divine Worship Decree." In Collection of Masses of the Blessed Virgin Mary: Volume II: Lectionary, xi. Collegeville, MN: Liturgical, 2012.

"Memorial of the Blessed Virgin Mary, Mother of the Church." Washington, DC: United States Conference of Catholic Bishops: Divine Worship (February 11, 2018). www.usccb.org/about/divine-worship/liturgical-calendar/mother-of-the-church.cfm.

O'Day, Gail R., and David Peterson, eds. The Access Bible: New Revised Standard Version with the Apocryphal/Deuterocanonical Books. New York: Oxford University Press, 1999.

"Order for the Blessing of an Image of the Blessed Virgin Mary." In Book of Blessings, 543–50. New York: Catholic Book, 1989.

"Order of Crowning an Image of the Blessed Virgin Mary." Washington, DC: United States Catholic Conference, 1987.

"Order of Mass, The." In The Roman Missal, 511–673. Collegeville, MN: Liturgical Press, 2011.

"Pope Francis Inscribes Mary, Mother of the Church, on Calendar." Newsletter: Committee on Divine Worship LIV (March 2016) 9–10.

"Redemptoris Mater (The Mother of the Redeemer)." Origins 16:43 (1987) 745–66.

Roman Missal, The. Collegeville, MN: Liturgical Press, 2011.

"Universal Norms on the Liturgical Year and the Calendar." In The Roman Missal, 110–35. Collegeville, MN: Liturgical Press, 2011.

"Rosarium Virginis Mariae: On the Most Holy Rosary." In The Liturgy Documents: Volume 4: Supplemental Documents for Parish Worship, Devotions, Formation, and Catechesis, 525–550. Chicago: Liturgy Training, 2013.

Scobey, Annmarie. "Keep Prayer in Mind." U.S. Catholic 83:5 (2018) 43–44.

Solemni Hac Liturgia (Credo of the People of God). http://w2.vatican.va/content/paul-vi/en/motu_proprio/documents/hf_p-vi_motu-proprio_19680630_credo.html.

"Universal Norms on the Liturgical Year and the Calendar." In The Roman Missal, 110–35. Collegeville, MN: Liturgical, 2012.

Vatican Council II: The Conciliar and Post Conciliar Documents. Edited by Austin Flannery. Northport, NY: Costello, 1987.

Weller, Philip T. The Roman Ritual, Volume II. Milwaukee: The Bruce Publishing Co., 1952.

BOOKS BY MARK G. BOYER ON MARIOLOGY

Mary's Day—Saturday: Meditations for Marian Celebrations (Liturgical Press, 1993)
Reflections on the Mysteries of the Rosary (Liturgical Press, 2005)
A Simple Systematic Mariology (Wipf and Stock, 2015)
Rosary Primer: The Prayers, The Mysteries, and The New Testament (Wipf and Stock, 2018)

RECENT BOOKS BY MARK G. BOYER (ALL WIPF AND STOCK UNLESS OTHERWISE NOTED)

Nature Spirituality: Praying with Wind, Water, Earth, Fire
A Spirituality of Ageing
Caroling through Advent and Christmas: Daily Reflections with Familiar Hymns (Liguori)
Weekday Saints: Reflections on Their Scriptures
Human Wholeness: A Spirituality of Relationship
The Liturgical Environment: What the Documents Say (third edition, Liturgical Press)
A Simple Systematic Mariology
Praying Your Way through Luke's Gospel and the Acts of the Apostles
Daybreaks: Daily Reflections for Advent and Christmas (Liguori)
Daybreaks: Daily Reflections for Lent and Easter (Liguori)
An Abecedarian of Animal Spirit Guides: Spiritual Growth through Reflections on Creatures
Overcome with Paschal Joy: Chanting through Lent and Easter—Daily Reflections with Familiar Hymns
Taking Leave of Your Home: Moving in the Peace of Christ
A Spirituality of Mission: Reflections for Holy Week and Easter (Liturgical Press)
An Abecedarian of Sacred Trees: Spiritual Growth through Reflections on Woody Plants
Divine Presence: Elements of Biblical Theophanies
Fruit of the Vine: A Biblical Spirituality of Wine
Names for Jesus: Reflections for Advent and Christmas
Talk to God and Listen to the Casual Reply: Experiencing the Spirituality of John Denver
Christ Our Passover Has Been Sacrificed: A Guide through Paschal Mystery Spirituality—Mystical Theology in The Roman Missal
Rosary Primer: The Prayers, The Mysteries, and the New Testament
From Contemplation to Action: The Spiritual Process of Divine Discernment Using Elijah and Elisha as Models
Love Addict

www.ingramcontent.com/pod-product-compliance
Lightning Source LLC
Chambersburg PA
CBHW051518230426
43668CB00012B/1660